HEURISTIC RESEARCH IN PSYCHOTHERAPY

Heuristic Research in Psychotherapy showcases the power of heuristic enquiry to deepen through discovery, critique, create, and reimagine psychotherapy research.

Building on the interdisciplinary foundation of previous volumes in the Qualitative Research Approaches for Psychotherapy and Allied Disciplines series, this book focuses specifically on heuristic methodology—a form of research grounded in personal experience, reflexivity, and embodied insight. Across 11 chapters, contributors explore phenomena including aesthetics, colonisation, cultural hybridity, motherhood, obsessive-compulsive disorder, and spiritual transformation. Each chapter exemplifies how lived experience and rigorous methodology intersect, offering readers a richly textured and intellectually provocative resource. Edited by Keith Tudor, the volume brings together psychotherapists, researchers, and practitioners across diverse cultural and theoretical contexts. This book challenges medicalised, positivist research models, foregrounding relational, critical, and situated approaches to therapeutic enquiry.

It will be essential reading for postgraduate students, practitioner-researchers, and psychotherapy educators seeking alternatives to conventional methods.

Keith Tudor is Professor of Psychotherapy at Auckland University of Technology (AUT), Aotearoa New Zealand, where he is also a co-lead of the AUT Moana Nui Psychological Therapies Research Group. A qualified social worker and psychotherapist, he is also a certified and a teaching and supervising transactional analyst and a supervisor and trainer of supervisors. Keith has authored or edited over 400 peer-reviewed publications and currently co-edits the Advancing Theory in Therapy series (Routledge) and Qualitative Research Approaches for Psychotherapy and Allied Disciplines series, and edits the Ancestors of the Mind series (Karnac). His work blends scholarly rigour with political and clinical insight, and he is widely recognised as a leading voice in critical psychotherapy research.

‘At a time in contemporary research when we are becoming increasingly concerned with issues of relationality, Keith Tudor’s timely *Heuristic Research in Psychotherapy* makes a valuable contribution to how we think about the nature of personal experience, the experience of others, self-reflection, honesty, discovery, and authentic expression.

The book is significant because it challenges over-categorisation that has resulted from assumptions that heuristic inquiry is predicated on a framework with fixed processes. In this work Tudor draws together a range of perspectives and offers useful insight into differentiations between method, methodology, principles, and stance. *Heuristic Research in Psychotherapy* is a thoughtful, coherent, and astutely edited work. It presents a careful, scholarly understanding of the nature and agency of a researcher’s internal frame of reference.’

Welby Ings, *Professor of Design, Auckland University of Technology*

‘This ground-breaking book addresses a gap in the existing literature by gathering together a body of qualitative heuristic research which illuminates varied and intimate areas of human experience. It therefore further establishes the importance of heuristic enquiry as a research method and methodology and adds to Keith Tudor’s impressive body of work.

Conducting heuristic research can be challenging due to a possible confusion between methodology and method in the literature, but this book begins with a clarification of heuristic concepts and an explanation and expansion of heuristic research methodology. This demonstrates that ‘the concepts that form its methodology have well-established roots’ and should prove invaluable for future researchers in psychotherapy and indeed across all disciplines. The principles that underpin heuristic methodology are further explored and clarified in studies on unintentional racial microaggressions, conversion to Islam, and the impact of time on heuristic research. Further chapters focus on method and then on both methodology and method, exploring diverse areas of human experiencing including a Samoan sense of self, the experience of chronic pain, and abrupt endings. Every study in this book movingly foregrounds the range of human experience and embodies ‘the importance of self-reflection, honesty, and authenticity.

This book focuses not only on the concepts that Moustakas and his colleagues defined, but also on Sela-Smith’s critique and development of heuristic research. Her concepts of resistance and surrender give rise to a rich and engaging account of the researcher’s process in many of the studies presented in this book. These studies illustrate well the interplay between psychotherapeutic practice and psychotherapy research. This focus on the interior life of the researcher in order to reveal something to themselves about themselves mirrors the psychotherapeutic endeavour. Therefore, each of the book’s chapters has implications for clinical practice and should be of interest to anyone in the talking therapies field. This book will be an essential resource for any would-be psychotherapeutic researcher, but it has a wider value for researchers across disciplines who wish to understand the practical application of heuristics.’

Elizabeth Nicholl, *Psychotherapist, United Kingdom*

'The contributions in this volume on *Heuristic Research in Psychotherapy* honour the depth of personal experience as a valid and vital source of knowledge, masterfully showcasing both 'head' and 'heart', cognition and emotion, taha hinengaro and taha wairua. My experience in reading, and re-reading, each chapter mirrored the heuristic approach to research – initial engagement, immersion, incubation, illumination, explication, and creative synthesis – drawing me into my own processes of self-reflection and discovery. The volume's emphasis on reflexivity, relationality, and embodied inquiry resonates with Indigenous worldviews that centre story, connection, and a respect for the rhythms and timing of relational knowledge. I welcome this work as part of a growing movement to enrich and bring diversity to therapeutic practice, research, and supervision.'

Maria Haenga-Collins *(Ngāti Porou, Te Aitanga a Māhaki, Ngāi Tahu), Lecturer, Auckland University of Technology*

Qualitative Approaches for Psychotherapy and Allied Disciplines

Series Editors: Keith Tudor and Jonathan Wyatt

Auckland University of Technology and University of Edinburgh

This series provides both a home and a catalyst for books that explore qualitative methodological approaches to researching psychotherapy and its allied disciplines. Books within the series are theoretically informed, scholarly, reflexive, critical texts that connect readers with their own emerging and/or established research projects. The series is open to both monographs and edited collections, welcoming authors or collections of authors in both the Northern and Southern hemispheres, positioned across a range of disciplinary, theoretical and cultural perspectives. The series seeks to be compelling and challenging, and aims to elucidate and exemplify both established and innovative approaches to undertaking qualitative research.

The series editors invite proposals for texts that are theoretically-informed, scholarly, reflexive and critical, connecting readers with their own emerging or established research projects; that introduce and explore the complexity of each research approach and its ontological, epistemological, and methodological assumptions and underpinnings; and that act as a stimulus, an inspiration, for researchers to think and feel their way into their research endeavours.

Heuristic Research in Psychotherapy
What is Most Personal is Most General
Edited by Keith Tudor

HEURISTIC RESEARCH IN PSYCHOTHERAPY

What is Most Personal is Most General

Edited by Keith Tudor

Routledge
Taylor & Francis Group
LONDON AND NEW YORK

Designed cover image: Getty Images

First published 2026
by Routledge
4 Park Square, Milton Park, Abingdon, Oxon OX14 4RN

and by Routledge
605 Third Avenue, New York, NY 10158

Routledge is an imprint of the Taylor & Francis Group, an informa business

British Library Cataloguing-in-Publication Data
A catalogue record for this book is available from the British Library

ISBN: 9781041166948 (hbk)
ISBN: 9781041162131 (pbk)
ISBN: 9781003685944 (ebk)

DOI: 10.4324/9781003685944

Typeset in Times New Roman
by Newgen Publishing UK

CONTENTS

THE PRINCIPAL AUTHOR

Keith Tudor is Professor of Psychotherapy at Auckland University of Technology (AUT), Aotearoa New Zealand, where he is also a Co-Lead of the Moana Nui Psychological Therapies Research Group. He is a qualified social worker, and psychotherapist, and a certified and a teaching and supervising transactional analyst. He is the author and editor of publications on mental health; psychotherapy, specifically person-centred psychology and transactional analysis; and the interplay of therapy with politics and culture. He is the winner of the International Transactional Analysis Association's Eric Berne Memorial Award – in 2020, with Graeme Summers, for their work on co-creativity, and in 2025 'for his work on revitalising and advancing the critical and social edge of transactional analysis, and critiquing transactional analysis from within and without' – and also in 2025 the American Psychological Association's Carl Rogers Award for outstanding contributions to the theory and practice of humanistic psychology. He has undertaken and written about heuristic research, and co-edited a volume on *Heuristic Enquires* across disciplines (Routledge, 2025).

LIST OF CONTRIBUTORS

Georgina Cardo is a psychotherapist and academic. She lectures in counselling and psychotherapy at the University of Salford, UK, supervises both academics and psychotherapists, and researches identity, liminality, Islamic psychology, and tazkiyat-un-nafs.

Dana Chue is a Chinese Singaporean psychotherapist working in private practice in Aotearoa New Zealand. She has a personal interest in death, meaning, philosophy, and the migrant experience. Dana values working with vulnerable and marginalised communities. Her clinical experience includes a one-year practicum at Kohuora Auckland South Corrections Facility, two years at Lifeline Aotearoa, and five years with Papa Taumata Higher Ground Drug Rehabilitation Trust.

Sian Haydon is a psychotherapist based in Tāmaki Makaurau, Aotearoa (Auckland, New Zealand). Originally Sian completed a Bachelor of Design and worked in creative fields. Her research interests include aesthetics, artistic process, and therapeutic practice. The intersection of these areas as a path to self-awareness and professional development was the focus of her master's research and current writing.

Julia Ioane is of Pasifika descent, a Professor in Clinical and Pacific Psychology at Massey University (Albany campus, Aotearoa New Zealand), and a clinical psychologist serving communities in Justice.

Chris Lorigan is a psychotherapist based in Auckland, New Zealand. He has been in private practice since completing his master's at Auckland University of Technology, and has developed a strong interest in the treatment of obsessive–compulsive disorder and trauma. His work is psychodynamically underpinned, and his process is characterised by a humanist and relational approach that aims to foster clients' self-worth and self-acceptance.

Tzach Maya-Chipman is an integrative-relational psychotherapist, a trauma specialist, and a supervisor in private practice in Auckland, Aotearoa New Zealand. He is a scholar and researcher of chronic pain and chronic illness, with a focus on their lived experience. He integrates heuristic enquiry, chaos theory, psychoanalysis, and the arts in his work to explore the understanding and transformation of embodied suffering.

Malik McCann is a registered psychotherapist currently working in private practice. She is Aotearoa New Zealand born and of Niuean, Samoan Chinese, and Irish descent. She is a member of the Tangata Moana Psychotherapy Collective and the Aotearoa New Zealand Association of Psychotherapists. Through her own journey of decolonisation and re-indigenisation she has a personal interest in exploring unconscious and normative aspects of culturalisation in the colonial environment and how these dynamics may be enacted in therapeutic relationships and training spaces. She has co-written articles alongside Keith Tudor for *Ata: Journal of Psychotherapy Aotearoa New Zealand*, and the *International Journal of Applied Psychoanalytic Studies* on this topic. She is currently undertaking a PhD, exploring unspoken cross-cultural tensions as they exist in training environments through talanoa through the University of Auckland.

Luke Oram is a psychotherapist (registered with the Psychotherapists Board of Aotearoa New Zealand) based in Auckland, New Zealand. His clinical experience involves working in public health settings and prison populations as well as leading men's groups for over ten years. Also a musician and writer, he likes to think of therapy as an act of story and metaphor. He is particularly interested in archetypal psychology, dreamwork, and spirituality.

Karlene Schwencke (née Mamea) is a registered psychotherapist based in Auckland, New Zealand of Samoan descent (*Lefaga, Siumu, Fa'atoia, Aleipata*). She is a member of the Association of Psychotherapists Aotearoa New Zealand and the Tagata Moana Psychotherapy Collective. Her professional background includes work in correctional environments and the field of substance addiction.

Alana West is a psychotherapist at Breakthrough Psychotherapy in Auckland, New Zealand. She holds a Master of Psychotherapy from Auckland University of Technology and is registered with the Psychotherapists Board of Aotearoa New Zealand. Drawing on psychodynamic and psychoanalytic traditions, she works primarily with sexual trauma. Her 2023 research explored motherhood during psychotherapy training.

SERIES PREFACE

Keith Tudor and Jonathan Wyatt

Welcome to *Heuristic Research in Psychotherapy*, which is part of our new series with Routledge, 'Qualitative Research Approaches for Psychotherapy and Allied Disciplines.'

The series arose out of our experience of editing a book on qualitative research in psychotherapy (published in 2023 and now part of this series), which we both enjoyed and which led to both a second volume and the series itself which comprises monographs and edited books exploring approaches to qualitative research both in psychotherapy and across professions allied with it, i.e., counselling, clinical and counselling psychology, social work, and nursing.

The authors of this volume, with Keith as lead, offers, I (Jonathan) may say, a thorough, expansive, current and critical take on heuristic enquiry. It is a comprehensive and enlightening volume in which Keith and his colleagues discuss heuristic enquiry both as a methodology and a method, and give readers exemplars of this research approach (concerning cultural identity, chronic pain, abrupt endings, and more).

As this volume goes to press, we have another three volumes in production which will also appear this year (2026), and others in various stages of proposal, gestation, and twinkling, including a third volume on qualitative research approaches for psychotherapy. In the meantime, we very much hope that you will enjoy this volume.

INTRODUCTION

Keith Tudor

I am delighted to introduce this volume on heuristic research in psychotherapy and equally delighted that it's appearing in the series of books I edit with Professor Jonathan Wyatt on 'Qualitative Approaches in Research for Psychotherapy and Allied Disciplines' (published by Routledge). It is the first specialist volume to be published in the series, i.e., one that focuses on a specific research method, methodology, approach, or area – though it will shortly be joined by volumes on creative-relational inquiry in psychotherapy research (edited by Fiona Murray and Jonathan Wyatt) and hermeneutic research in psychotherapy (edited by Kerry Thomas-Anttila and myself) – and my first acknowledgement and thanks go to Jonathan for his support for me in curating this volume, and for his enthusiasm for it – tēnā koe e hoa | thank you, my friend.

Heurism and me

I have been interested in heuristics and, specifically, qualitative heuristic research in psychotherapy (and, more broadly, the 'psy' disciplines and professions) since I first came across the work of Clark Moustakas when, in the early 1990s, I was immersing myself in the work of Carl Rogers. Both Moustakas and Rogers were involved in the development of humanistic psychology in the early 1960s. Rogers influenced Moustakas's thinking about the nature of human science (Rogers, 1969, 1985); and, in many ways, Moustakas's work on heuristic research (Douglass & Moustakas, 1985; Moustakas, 1990) can be considered the research wing of the humanistic psychology movement. Also, given the focus in heuristics on self-enquiry as well as reflective depictions of others, psychotherapy itself, as well as the supervision of its practitioners, is, arguably, a heuristic practice – see Beck (1979), Moustakas (1990), O'Hara (1986), Stevens (2006), and Merry (2004), respectively.

When I came to engage in my doctoral studies (in February 2007), I took the opportunity to enrol in a doctorate by public (i.e., published) works. This involved me nominating three of my publications – from which I chose a book, *Mental Health Promotion: Paradigms and Practice* (Tudor, 1996), a chapter on ego states (Tudor, 2003), and an article on psychological health (Tudor, 2007, 2008) – and writing a 30,000 word context statement to describe and defend a thesis that a) tied these works together, and b) advanced the field. This I did, using heuristics,

DOI: 10.4324/9781003685944-1

and I successfully defended my thesis – 'that the client develops an organismic integrating functioning as a result of a therapeutic method of co-creative empathic transacting' (Tudor, 2017, p. 145) – in June 2010 (Tudor, 2010; see also Tudor, 2017).

It was an interesting and intensive process, both demanding and revealing, but/and one that gave me a deep appreciation and respect for the process of and the philosophy underpinning this form of heuristic research. (I note 'this form' as I am aware that there is a tradition of *quantitative* heuristic research [see Najafi et al., 2025].)

As a result of my experience and continued reading, and, in 2009, my appointment to an academic position, I have had and created opportunities to supervise students undertaking heuristic research, and, to date, have had the pleasure and privilege of seeing 26 master's students complete their dissertations and two doctoral students complete their theses using this method and methodology on subjects as varied as abrupt endings; aesthetic inquiry; ambivalence; attention-deficit hyperactive disorder; the boarding school self; chronic pain; conversion to Islam; aspects of culture (six); exercise and psychotherapy; the false self; grief; haunting; humour; being an immigrant psychotherapist; Māori identity (two); motherhood and psychotherapy training (two); online video-calling equine-facilitated therapy; parental suicide-loss; reimaging the father; shame; and unintentional racial microaggressions.

As an experienced and enthusiastic writer and editor, I have also encouraged these and other students to publish – which they have done (Alleyne & Tudor, 2022; Cardo & Tudor, 2024, 2025; Cousins et al., 2025; Grennell-Hawke & Tudor, 2018; Harrison & Tudor, 2020; McCann & Tudor, 2022, 2024; Oram & Tudor, 2025; Sherwood, 2021). As you, the reader, will see, this volume represents both my own further work on heuristic research, especially with regard to its methodology, and my continued encouragement of students' work.

At the same time, and more so since 2010, I have come to realise that there are some inconsistencies in Moustakas's own work; some confusion between and conflation of terms used in heuristics, which has led to some misunderstandings, especially about method and methodology; and, finally, some prejudices against this form of research. In the context of encouraging a colleague to enrol on a doctorate, and telling them of my experience of using heuristics, I remember them saying (with a spit in their delivery): 'Oh, I didn't realise that you could do a doctorate based on *that*'! I've also had students admitting that they initially chose to base their master's dissertations on heuristics on the basis that they thought it would be easy – and later realising and acknowledging that this wasn't so! (I also know students who have avoided heuristics because they considered it too hard, and/or too revealing.)

In response to this, I have continued to read about heuristics and to re-read Moustakas's (1990) original work. As a result, I have not only published a paper from my original research (Tudor, 2017), but have also gone on to write a chapter on *doing* heuristic research (Tudor, 2022) which focuses on both methodology and method, as well as a chapter that takes a more critical view of heuristics (Tudor, 2023) including its language, its relation with methodology, and its individualism. Most recently, I engaged with another colleague at my university (Auckland University of Technology) in a different discipline, that of art and design, to edit an interdisciplinary book on *Heuristic Enquiry* (Ings & Tudor, 2025) which encompasses contributions from te ao Māori (the Māori world); care theory; documentary film; Persian illuminative thinking; psychotherapy; and visual arts enquiry.

In undertaking these projects, I have become more interested in exploring and explicating heuristic methodology and method and so, when Jonathan and I were discussing our proposal for a series of books on qualitative research in psychotherapy, I knew that I wanted to bring together work on heuristic research in psychotherapy and, in doing so, to provide greater clarity about methodology and method in heuristic research, and it is this that has informed the rationale for the content and structure of this volume. In a chapter in another publication (Tudor, 2023), I presented my view that there are three strands of thinking about methodology in qualitative heuristic research: the first, that heuristic research does not prescribe a methodology; the second, that heuristic research is based on a specific methodology; and the third, that heuristics is both a methodology and method (strands which are briefly summarised in Chapter 1). While the various chapters in this book elaborate these different strands, they share a common emphasis on discovery – as McLeod (2003) acknowledges, heuristics is 'a powerful discovery-oriented approach to research' (p. 97).

The book

In my experience of writing and editing books, the best laid schemes, to quote Robert Burns (1785/1998) 'Gang aft agley' (Go oft[en] awry), and this has been no less so for this book – interestingly, given the subject of book, possibly more so. In the end, with several goings, comings, and goings, it was clear that the final cut of chapters would – and does – represent a focus on the methodology and method of heuristic enquiry in qualitative research in psychotherapy, and hence the structure of the book.

Part I comprises four chapters which, in various ways, explicate the methodology of this form of heuristic enquiry, which, together, I hope both elaborates and gives greater depth and breadth to the original theory – with regard to the key concepts of heuristic methodology (Chapters 1 and 2), and specifically of Sela-Smith's (2002) concepts of resistance and surrender (Chapter 3); and of the implicit concept of time (Chapter 4).

Part II comprises three chapters which focus on the method of this form of heuristic enquiry, illustrating or illuminating and explicating it in relation to gestation and birth (Chapter 5); unintentional racial microaggressions (Chapter 6); and the Samoan self (Chapter 7).

Part III comprises chapters that, in different ways, encompass both heuristic methodology and method as they report and reflect on their research into personal experiences of obsessive-compulsive disorder (Chapter 8); chronic pain (Chapter 9); aesthetics (Chapter 10); and, finally (lastly and appropriately enough), abrupt endings (Chapter 11). While all the chapters in Part III are interesting in their own right, I do want to highlight the fact that Chapter 9 includes a critique of Moustakas's (1990) definition of incubation, which I think has significant implications for other lived or living experiences and identities, such as being a mother (Ho, 2025; Humphris, 2024), or having a psychiatric diagnosis (Blann, 2025; Lorrigan, 2019; Ozertugrul, 2015, 2017; Wiorkowski, 2015).

All the chapters, though most especially those in Parts II and III also share a profound commitment to reflecting on and reflexing the authors' personal experience (looking inwards), while also making their discoveries about these accessible and applicable to others (looking outwards), and hence the subtitle of the book, which is inspired by Rogers' (1961/1967) statement: '*What is most personal is most general*' (p. 26).

As I am directly involved in all but three of the chapters in this book, I have deliberately kept this summary short, preferring you, the reader, to experience the main text(s). The one thing I would say about the book as a whole, as I see it, is that it represents what I consider to be central principles of qualitative heuristic enquiry, i.e., the centrality of personal experience, including that of others; the importance of self-reflection, honesty, and authenticity; the epistemology of discovery; and the commitment to the freedom of expression. I hope that you find these principles represented in these pages.

In academia, the publication of books is sometimes underrated – in favour of peer-reviewed articles, for a critique of which, see Harley (2019) and Tudor (2021). So, for those who are interested, and in the spirit in which my rights as an editor and author have been asserted (see p. iv), I wish to assert that the material that forms the basis for nine of the eleven chapters has been peer-reviewed (each by two colleagues); that each chapter has been further peer-reviewed by me as the editor, one of which was additionally peer-reviewed by Dr Susan Shaw, and another two rejected; and, finally, that the whole book has been peer-reviewed by Professor Jonathan Wyatt, and also, in effect, by the colleagues who have endorsed it. I note all this to make the point (as it seems that it continues to need to be made) that the chapters in this book are as thoroughly peer-reviewed as are many articles that appear in peer-reviewed journals.

Acknowledgements

Notwithstanding my point about academia (by which I stand), I want to begin my acknowledgements by thanking:

- The Faculty of Health & Environmental Sciences at Auckland University of Technology, Auckland, Aotearoa New Zealand, for its financial support for the copy-editing of this book.

Following this, I acknowledge:

- Professor Jonathan Wyatt for, as noted earlier, his support for this book. It's a genuine pleasure to work with Jonathan as a colleague and co-editor both of books (two to date) and of the series in which this book sits, not least as it's an easy working relationship, for which I am very grateful – tēnā koe anō e hoa | thanks again, my friend.
- All the contributors – Dr Georgina Cardo, Dana Chue, Sian Haydon, Alana West (nèe Humphris), Folasāitu Professor Julia Ioane, Chris Lorigan, Tzach Maya-Chipman, Malik McCann, Luke Oram, and Karlene Schwencke – both for their original work (eight dissertations and a thesis) and their work in synthesising elements of those into the chapters that appear in this book – tēnā koutou katoa | thanks to you all.
- My colleagues who have kindly endorsed the book – Dr Maria Haenga-Collins (Ngāti Porou, Te Aitanga a Māhaki, Ngāi Tahu), Professor Welby Ings, and Dr Elizabeth Nicholl – kei te mihi nui ki a koutou | my sincere thanks to you all.
- Angie Strachan, copy-editor extraordinaire, without whom I could not do what or as much as I do – mihi aroha ki a koe | sincere thanks to you.
- The team at Routledge, including Eleanor Taylor, Adam Woods, Helen Chomyszyn, and Tom Bedford for their interest, support, and expertise – tēnā koutou katoa.
- My family, specifically Louise, my colleague, partner, and wife, supporter and best critic with whom I have enquired into life, heuristically, for some 35 years – tēnā koe, hoa Rangatira | thank you, my chiefly friend.

References

Alleyne, B., & Tudor, K. (2022). A therapist's experience of grief: An heuristic enquiry. In K. Tudor & E. Green (Eds.), *Psyche and academia: Papers from 21 years of the Auckland University of Technology*

Psychotherapy Master's programmes (pp. 144–153). Tuwhera Open Access Publishing. https://doi.org/10.24135/TOAB.10

Beck, G. (1979). *Heuristic psychotherapy* [Unpublished paper]. Merrill-Parker Institute.

Blann, C. A. (2025). *What is my living experience of attention-deficit hyperactive disorder? A heuristic inquiry* [Master's dissertation, Auckland University of Technology]. Tuwhera Open Access Theses & Dissertations. https **[to come]**

Burns, R. (1998). *To a mouse*. Poetry Foundation. www.poetryfoundation.org/poems/43816/to-a-mouse-56d222ab36e33 (Original work published 1785)

Cardo, G., & Tudor, K. (2024). A comparison between the concepts of heuristic enquiry and tazkiyat-un-nafs. *European Journal for Qualitative Research in Psychotherapy*, 14. https://doi.org/10.24377/EJQRP.article3100

Cardo, G., & Tudor, K. (2026). *Being 'Alaq': A heuristic enquiry into the liminal experiences of converts to Islam who are psychotherapists* [Manuscript under review].

Cousins, G., Humphris, A., Kingi, A., Oram, L., & Tudor, K. (2025). Heuristic research in a time-limited context. In W. Ings & K. Tudor (Eds.), *Heuristic enquiries: Research across disciplines and professions* (pp. 162–180). Routledge.

Douglass, B., & Moustakas, C. (1985). Heuristic inquiry: The internal search to know. *Journal of Humanistic Psychology*, *25*(3), 39–55. https://doi.org/10.1177/0022167885253004

Grennell-Hawke, N., & Tudor, K. (2018). Being Māori and Pākehā: Methodology and method in exploring cultural hybridity. *The Qualitative Report*, *23*(7), 1530–1546. https://nsuworks.nova.edu/tqr/vol23/iss7/3

Harley, B. (2019). Confronting the crisis of confidence in management studies: Why senior scholars need to stop setting a bad example. *Academy of Management Learning & Education*, *18*(2), 286–297. https://doi.org/10.5465/amle.2018.0107

Harrison, D., & Tudor, K. (2020). Working (it) out: An heuristic enquiry into psychotherapy and exercise. *Advances in Mind-Body Medicine*, *34*(2), 14–23.

Ho, K. W. (2025) *Why does being a therapist not make me a better mother? A heuristic self-search inquiry into the duality of the mother/child psychotherapist*. [Master's dissertation, Auckland University of Technology]. Tuwhera Open Access Research Outputs. http://hdl.handle.net/10292/20748

Humphris, A. (2024). *Motherhood and psychotherapy training: A heuristic self-search inquiry into a trainee's experience* [Master's dissertation, Auckland University of Technology]. Tuwhera Open Access Research Outputs. http://hdl.handle.net/10292/17878

Ings, W., & Tudor, K. (2025). *Heuristic enquiries: Research across disciplines and professions*. Routledge.

Lorrigan, C. McCann, M., & Tudor, K. (2022). Unintentional racial microaggressions and the social unconscious. *International Journal of Applied Psychoanalytic Studies*, *19*(2), 202–216. https://doi.org/10.1002/aps.1753

McCann, M., & Tudor, K. (2024). The enigma of unintentional racial microaggressions: Implications for the profession of psychotherapy. *Ata: Journal of Psychotherapy Aotearoa New Zealand*, *27*(1), 31–56. https://doi.org/10.24135/ajpanz.2024.03

McLeod, J. (2003). *Doing counselling research* (2nd ed.). Sage.

Merry, T. (2004). Supervision as heuristic inquiry. In K. Tudor & M. Worrall (Eds.), *Freedom to practise: Person-centred approaches to supervision* (pp. 189–199). PCCS Books.

Moustakas, C. (1990). *Heuristic research: Design, methodology and applications*. Sage.

Najafi, H., Tudor, K., & Ings, W. (2025). A review of the evolution of heuristic inquiry. In W. Ings & K. Tudor (Eds.), *Heuristic enquiries: Research across disciplines and professions* (pp. 9–22). Routledge.

O'Hara, M. (1986). Heuristic inquiry as psychotherapy: The client-centered approach. *Person-Centered Review*, *1*(2), 172–184.

Oram, L., & Tudor, K. (2025). Remaking the imago paterna: A heuristic enquiry. *Jung Journal: Culture & Society*, *19*(4), 90–109. https://doi.org/10.1080/19342039.2025.2562680

Ozertugrul, E. (2015). *Heuristic self-search inquiry into one experience of obsessive-compulsive disorder* [Doctoral dissertation, Walden University]. Walden University ProQuest Dissertations Publishing. www.proquest.com/openview/65a1606168471908ad8768f3bea63612/1

Ozertugrul, E. (2017). Heuristic self-search inquiry into one experience of obsessive–compulsive disorder. *Journal of Humanistic Psychology, 57*(3), 215–236. https://doi.org/10.1177/0022167815592503

Rogers, C. R. (1967). 'This is me'. In C. R. Rogers, *On becoming a person: A therapist's view of psychotherapy* (pp. 3–27). Constable. (Original work published 1961)

Rogers, C. R. (1969). *Freedom to learn.* Charles E. Merrill.

Rogers, C. R. (1985). Towards a more human science of the person. *Journal of Humanistic Psychology, 25*(4), 7–24. https://doi.org/10.1177/0022167885254002

Sela-Smith, S. (2002). Heuristic research: A review and critique of Moustakas's method. *Journal of Humanistic Psychology, 42*(3), 53–88. https://doi.org/10.1177/0022167802423004

Sherwood, V. (2021). *Haunted: The death mother archetype*. Chiron Publications.

Stevens, C. (2006). A heuristic–dialogical model for reflective psychotherapy practice. In D. Loewenthal & D. Winter (Eds.), *What is psychotherapeutic research?* (pp. 171–181). Karnac.

Tudor, K. (1996). *Mental health promotion: Paradigms and practice*. Routledge.

Tudor, K. (2003). The neopsyche: The integrating adult ego state. In C. Sills & H. Hargaden (Eds.), *Ego states* (pp. 201–231). Worth Reading.

Tudor, K. (2007). Geestelijk gezond; autonoom én homonoom [Psychological health: Autonomy and homonomy]. *Tijdshrift Cliëntgerichte Psychotherapie, 45*(1), 5–18. www.tpep.nl/artikel/1800

Tudor, K. (2008). Psychological health: Autonomy and homonomy. In B. Levitt (Ed.), *Reflections on human potential: Bridging the person-centered approach and positive psychology* (pp. 161–174). PCCS Books.

Tudor, K. (2010). *The fight for health: A heuristic enquiry into psychological well-being* [Unpublished context statement for a PhD in Mental Health Promotion by Public (Published) Works]. School of Health and Social Sciences, Middlesex University, London, UK.

Tudor, K. (2017). The fight for health: An heuristic enquiry. In K. Tudor, *Conscience and critic: The selected works of Keith Tudor* (pp. 143–168). Routledge.

Tudor, K. (2021). Introduction. In K. Tudor, *20/20 vision, 2020.* Tuwhera Open Access Books. https://doi.org/10.24135/TOAB.6

Tudor, K. (2022). Supporting critical self-enquiry: Doing heuristic research. In S. Bager-Charleson & A. McBeath (Eds.), *Supporting research in counselling and psychotherapy* (pp. 57–79). Springer.

Tudor, K. (2023). Critical heuristics: From 'I who feels' to 'We who care – and act'. In K. Tudor & J. Wyatt (Eds.), *Reflexive research for reflective practice: Qualitative research methodologies for psychotherapy* (pp. 115–132). Routledge.

Wiorkowski, F. (2015). The experiences of students with autism spectrum disorders in college: A heuristic exploration. *The Qualitative Report, 20*(6), 847–863. www.nova.edu/ssss/QR/QR20/6/wiorkowski8.pdf

PART I
Methodology

1

EXPLICATING AND EXPANDING HEURISTIC RESEARCH METHODOLOGY

Keith Tudor and Luke Oram

In the literature on heuristic research, there is some confusion between method and methodology, especially with regard to the use and development of certain concepts in Moustakas's original work (Douglass & Moustakas, 1985; Moustakas, 1990). This chapter offers a clarification of the concepts of heuristic research, i.e., the foundation of its methodology, not least with the aim of contributing to an understanding and development of that methodology.

Moustakas's concepts of heuristic enquiry and their evolution

In his early sketch of heuristic enquiry, Douglass and Moustakas (1985) outline 12 conceptual steps, organised within a three-part model:

> (1) *Immersion* (exploration of the question, problem, or theme)
> Indwelling
> Internal frame of reference
> Self-search
> (2) *Acquisition* (collection of data)
> Tacit knowing
> Intuition
> Inference
> Self-dialogue
> Self-disclosure
> Signitive-symbolic representation
> (3) *Realization* (synthesis)
> Intentionality
> Verification
> Dissemination.
>
> (pp. 45–46)

Later, in his own formative treatise on heuristic enquiry, Moustakas (1990) further refined and consolidated his concepts to seven, i.e., identifying with the focus of inquiry, self-dialogue, tacit knowing, intuition, indwelling, focusing, and the internal frame of reference. As shown in

DOI: 10.4324/9781003685944-3

Table 1.1, Moustakas (1990) refers to a number of other heuristic concepts in passing, but tends to categorise them under these seven main processes. It should be noted that while Douglass and Moustakas (1985) took the view that, as a framework of human science, heuristics does not prescribe a methodology, they do describe these steps as 'critical concepts' (p. 45), thereby providing something of a basis for a heuristic methodology. However – and, in our view, unfortunately – some of these concepts, for instance, verification, refer to a method rather than methodology, a confusion or conflation which has led to a certain lack of clarity in heuristic research between method(s), process(es), concepts, principles, methodology, and philosophy.

Others have expanded on Moustakas's work, most noticeably Sandy Sela-Smith in her unpublished dissertation (2001) and her critique of Moustakas's method published a year later (Sela-Smith, 2002). Synthesising Moustakas's heurism with Wilber's (1996) integral theory, Sela-Smith (2002) reconceptualises Moustakas's original processes, articulating them as: identification with the focus of inquiry, inward reach for tacit awareness, surrender to the question, self-dialogue, self-search, and transformation (see Table 1.1). Where Moustakas made room for other participants in heuristic enquiry, Sela-Smith repurposes the methodology as one that could be undertaken with the researcher as the sole – and, in any case, the principal – participant, naming her revision heuristic self-search inquiry (HSSI). In her explication of HSSI, Sela-Smith (2002) identifies an ambivalence in Moustakas's original work, a resistance to the researcher's 'experiencing-self' (p. 83) – that is to say, according to Sela-Smith, Moustakas's

TABLE 1.1 Heuristic concepts referred to by Moustakas and Sela-Smith.

Concept	*Authors*			
	Douglass and Moustakas (1985)	*Moustakas (1990)*	*Sela-Smith (2001)*	*Sela-Smith (2002)*
Identifying with the focus of inquiry		x	x	x
Self-dialogue	x	x	x	x
Tacit knowing	x	x	x	x
Intuition	x	x	x	x
Indwelling	x	x	x	x
Focusing	x	x	x	x
Internal frame of reference	x	x	x	x
Validation	x	x	x	x
Self-search	x	x	x	x
Inference	x	x		
Self-disclosure	x	x	x	x
Intersubjectivity	x	x		
Signitive-symbolic representation	x			
Differentiation	x			
Intentionality	x			
Verification	x	x	x	
Dissemination	x			
Feelings (acknowledging)	x	x	x	x
Transformation		x	x	x
Resistance			x	x
Surrender			x	x
Inward reach			x	x

shift from the '*I-who-feels*' to the researcher's '*observation of the self responding to feeling*' (p. 83). Thus, resistance became an additional concept in Sela-Smith's expansion of heuristic enquiry, marking a shift away from empirical observation and foregrounding a surrender to the researcher-participant's feelings (see also Chapter 3 in this volume). This focus on feelings in heuristic enquiry has been echoed by Ferendo (2004) and Meents (2006), for a comparative overview of which, see Ozertugrul (2017a). In her inquiry into intuition, Meents (2006) extends Sela-Smith's focus on feelings as integral to HSSI by suggesting that it be solidified into a definitive, separate, and necessary concept in the methodology of and for heuristic enquiry.

Another important concept discussed by Moustakas (although not recognised as a heuristic concept *per se*) and elaborated on by others is validation. Acknowledging that the validation of heuristic research departs from traditional qualitative approaches, Moustakas (1990) suggests that it could be achieved subjectively (if not a little solipsistically):

> The question of validity is one of meaning: Does the ultimate depiction of the experience derived from one's own rigorous, exhaustive self-searching and from the explications of others present comprehensively, vividly, and accurately the meanings and essences of the experience? This judgment is made by the primary researcher, who is the only person in the investigation who has undergone the heuristic inquiry from the beginning.
>
> (p. 32)

Moustakas also emphasises validation as an iterative process via a rigorous and repeated return to raw data, alongside participant feedback. In his summary of heuristic elaborators, particularly in relation to the development of HSSI, Ozertugrul (2017a) sums up the evolution of validation in the method:

1. For Sela-Smith (2002), validation is achieved through felt sense of experience and the trustworthiness of the researcher.
2. Ferendo (2004) emphasises a return to Wilber's (1996) quadrants as a benchmark for validation.
3. Meents (2006) advocates for communal validation via participant as well as academic boards, supervisors, and the researcher's wider community (see also Tudor, 2010).

Although not promoted as a fundamental concept by any of these researchers, the consistent presence of validation and/or verification in writings on heuristic enquiry suggests that it is / they are important. We also think that they are important but consider that validation refers to certain *methods* of validation, and that the related *methodological* concept is validity.

Table 1.1 shows a comparative overview of the concepts referred to by Moustakas and Sela-Smith in their development of heuristic enquiry.

Table 1.1 clearly shows that, in the works of these key contributors to heuristic methodology, some concepts are more ubiquitous than others:

- The first seven are present in all these works (apart from 'Identifying with the focus of inquiry' which does not appear in Douglass and Moustakas [1985]).
- Validation is also present in all these works (and verification in Moustakas's writing), but, as we have argued above, it is a *method* – and so, here, we clarify and promote *validity* as the methodological concept (see Table 1.3 below).

- Some of what we might consider a second set of seven concepts – i.e., self-search, self-disclosure, feelings, transformation, resistance, surrender, and inward reach – appear in Douglass and Moustakas (1985) and Moustakas (1990), and are more developed in Sela-Smith's (2001, 2002) development of HSSI. Regarding the last of these concepts, we note that Sela-Smith (2002) actually writes '*reach inward*' (p. 69, original emphasis).
- Dissemination, which only appears in Douglass and Moustakas's (1985) work, is also a *method*; in our view, the *methodological* equivalent is better conceptualised as *generalisability*.
- Of the remaining concepts:
  - Inference is only referred to briefly in Douglass and Moustakas (1985), who define it as being used 'to interpolate in heuristic research, to link or connect fragments of awareness, to establish new connections of meanings' (pp. 49–50). Inference gets a passing mention in Moustakas (1990): 'In intuition, from the subsidiary or observable factors one utilizes internal capacity to make inferences' (p. 19). In heuristic writing that follows (see Table 1.3.), inference is given similar treatment, usually expressed within descriptions of intuition rather than as a standalone concept.
  - Although intersubjectivity is not named by Douglass and Moustakas (1985) as one of their 'critical concepts' (p. 45), they do include it as another concept and discuss it in some detail, acknowledging that it derives from existentialism and refers to 'a communal flow from the depths of one self to another self, and to the qualities of purity and loving integrity in interactions with others' (pp. 50–51). Interestingly, for those of us who argue for engagement with others and the world, including the discipline and profession of psychotherapy, Douglass and Moustakas (1985) go on to state that: 'In acquiring data during heuristic investigation, one's ability to encounter other people and the world is no less important than the facility for plumbing one's own self experientially' (p. 51).
  - Signitive-symbolic representation is referred to in Douglass and Moustakas (1985), defined as 'those things that we know without need of explication, definition, or interpretation' (p. 51), and identified as growing out of the tacit dimension. However, as a concept in the heuristic literature, it quickly fades into extinction and is not mentioned in subsequent works, with the exception of Mouqué (2005) who lists Douglass and Moustakas's (1985) original concept list as an appendix.
  - Regarding differentiation, Douglass and Moustakas (1985) associate it with focusing, arguing that both are important for 'assessing the quality and direction of the emergent data… [and] for guiding the researcher toward that which is most significant' (p. 51). However, the concept of differentiation appears insufficiently differentiated from focusing in the literature and, therefore, is not included in our list of concepts in Table 1.3 below.
  - Intentionality is one of the concepts in Douglass and Moustakas's (1985) third and final phase of realisation, regarding which they argue that it is 'pertinent in realization through synthesis. In moving from the specific to the general, from the individual to the universal, from appearance to essence, the theme, questions, or problem being explored is recognized as having a life of its own' (p. 52). Nonetheless, it doesn't appear either in Moustakas's subsequent work or in Sela-Smith's work.

Heuristics and methodology

In 2021, Tudor conducted some further research into the methodologies underpinning heuristic enquiries (1999–2021) (Tudor, 2022). In this small-scale research, he found two studies that did not discuss methodology (Atkins & Loewenthal, 2004; Shantall, 1999); one in which the methodology was unclear (Kumar, 2017); and a number of authors who named heuristics as a methodology, but didn't elaborate on it, i.e., Djuraskovic and Arthur (2010), Wiorkowski (2015), and Yeh (2018). In writing this chapter we expanded and updated that survey, searching on 'heuristic enquiry/inquiry' AND 'methodology' AND 'psychotherapy', the results of which are summarised in Table 1.2.

In a previous publication, Tudor (2023) acknowledges a certain confusion and complexity with regard to the philosophical basis of heuristic research, and discerns three strands:

1. Heuristic research does not prescribe a methodology: This strand or perspective derives from the work of Douglass and Moustakas (1985). As they put it: 'As a conceptual framework of human science, heuristics offers an attitude with which to approach research, *but does not prescribe a methodology*' (p. 42, our emphasis), and is represented in the variety of methodologies listed in Table 1.1. Similar – and akin – to the idea that the person-centred

TABLE 1.2 Named methodologies in heuristic enquiries in the field of psychotherapy (2003–2024).

Methodology	*Heuristic enquiries in psychotherapy*
Experiential, autobiographical, narrative	Sela-Smith (2001)
Heuristic hermeneutic, transpersonal psychology	Ferendo (2004)
Heuristic(s)	Mouqué (2005), Casterline (2006), Nuttall (2006), Howie and Brooks (2008), Tudor (2010), Scott (2013), Daniel (2016), Hammond (2016), Mamea (2016), Nicholes (2016), Franklin (2017), Schorr-kon (2017), Sultan (2017), Bell (2018), Grennell-Hawke and Tudor (2018), Loh (2018), Lorigan (2019), Kennedy and Moore (2020), Stewart and Thomas (2020), Williams (2020), Brett (2021), Ciurlionis (2021), Longley (2021), Lu (2021), McCall (2021), Fung (2022), Hill (2022), Hunt (2022), McCann (2022), Cousins (2023), Johnson and Johnson (2023), Oram (2023), Osborne (2023), Campion (2024), Dyson-Horton (2024), Liu (2024), Nguyen (2024), Sharma and Kivell (2024), Wan (2024)
Phenomenological, phenomenology	Casterline (2006), Howie and Brooks (2008), Tudor (2010), Grennell (2014), Haertl (2014), Schulz (2015), Nicholes (2016), Alleyne (2017), Ciurlionis (2021), Hill (2022)
Heuristic self-search inquiry	Ferendo (2004), Meents (2006), Brown-Haysom (2018), Huxtable and Solomon (2020), Huxtable (2020), Fung (2022), McCann (2022), O'Rourke (2022), Humphris (2023), Maya-Chipman (2023)
Kaupapa (Māori) research theory	Grennell (2014), Grennell-Hawke and Tudor (2018)
Constructionism	Schulz (2015)
Holistic	Ozertugrul (2015, 2017b)
Imaginal psychology	Sherwood (2019)
Humanism, humanistic	Osborne (2023)
Interpretivist	Osborne (2023)
Interpretative phenomenological analysis	Daniel (2016)
Art-based heuristic enquiry	Coles (2014), Gregory (2022)
Autoethnography	Liu (2024), Nguyen (2024)

approach to psychology is an approach to life, a psychological posture, or way of being (Wood, 1996), this perspective gives the researcher a freedom to roam, including, as Tudor (2023) suggests, across culture(s). At the same time, it demands that the researcher know their attitudes and, thus, their underlying philosophy and methodology and their constituent concepts (see Table 1.3).

2. Heuristic research is based on a specific methodology: Although Douglass and Moustakas argue that heuristics does not *prescribe* a methodology, they do suggest that, given that, in heuristic research, the object of discovery is human experience, that 'this orientation makes palpable a theoretical marriage of existential philosophy and perceptual psychology' (p. 42). This is represented in Table 1.2 by those enquiries whose methodologies are experiential, autobiographical, and narrative; phenomenological; imaginal; humanistic; interpretive; artistic; and autoethnographical – and (although not represented in Table 1.2), other enquires based in and on existentialism and post-existentialism (Loewenthal, 2011, 2017). There are debates within heuristic research as to whether it is more experiential or phenomenological (see Douglass & Moustakas, 1985; Sela-Smith, 2002; Tudor, 2023), and the implications of this for research practice, for instance whether it's necessary to have personal experience of the subject under investigation (see Kumar & Casey, 2020; Shantall, 1999; Sultan, 2019). Whichever position the researcher takes, it is generally considered good practice that the researcher knows the philosophical and methodological ground on which they stand. Moustakas's own work was influenced by Maslow (1956, 1966, 1971) on self-actualising persons; Jourard (1968, 1971) on self-disclosure; Polanyi (1962, 1964, 1966, 1969) on indwelling and personal knowledge, and the tacit dimension of knowledge; Buber (1958, 1961, 1965) on dialogue and mutuality; Bridgman (1950) on delineations of subjective and objective truth; Gendlin (1962) on the analysis of the meaning of experience; and Rogers (1969, 1985) on human science – so there's plenty of historical material, as well as more since then, to guide the heuristic researcher in search of methodolog(y/ies).
3. Heuristics is both a methodology and a method: For those researchers (and institutions) who (and which) prefer a clear distinction between method and methodology, this perspective may appear confused and confusing. At the same time, it is philosophically consistent and congruent with the view that heuristics is an approach (as implied in point 1 above) grounded in humanism and experientialism. This is represented in Table 1.2 by those enquiries (the vast majority) that are in some way heuristic (i.e., heuristic, heuristic hermeneutic, and based on heuristic self-search inquiry). However, as may be seen from Table 1.2, other heuristic researchers have widened the philosophical and intellectual base of heuristics to include transpersonal psychology, kaupapa (Māori) research theory, constructionism, holism, and imaginal psychology.

Heuristic concepts

On the basis of this research and the identification of those authors who clearly draw on some methodology to underpin their heuristic enquiry, we then conducted further research to identify on which *heuristic* – and, more broadly, humanistic and phenomenological – concepts they based their research (see Table 1.3).

Note that we excluded from Table 1.3 some research which mentioned heuristics as methodology but which did not mention any specific concepts underlying that methodology, i.e., Scott (2013), Daniel (2016), Bell (2018), Wan (2024), and Johnson and Johnson (2023). We also excluded Mouqué's (2005) research in which heuristic concepts appear only as an appendix in an article outlining heuristic steps rather than being integrated throughout.

From this research, it is clear that the most common concepts mentioned in heuristic research studies are: intuition and tacit knowing, closely followed by self-dialogue, focusing, indwelling, and acknowledging feelings, with, a little behind these, the internal frame of reference (see Table 1.4). While it is unsurprising that, in heuristic research studies, the first seven most common concepts all appear in Moustakas's and Sela-Smith's original writing, i.e., Douglass and Moustakas (1985), Moustakas (1990), and Sela-Smith (2001, 2002), the absence of reference to Moustakas's (1990) concept of identification with the focus of enquiry (which appears in only 50% of studies) is more surprising. This, together with the fact that self-search and self-disclosure, the other two concepts that appear in both Moustakas's and Sela-Smith's work, are present in less than half these studies (46% and 44%, respectively), suggests that some heuristic researchers are turning away from the experiential and personal nature of heuristic research. Indeed, ten of the 50 studies (i.e., 20%) do not directly address identification with the focus of enquiry, self-search, or self-disclosure.

The next ranked concepts in the studies are: validity (our word, as explained earlier), which also appears in both Moustakas's and Sela-Smith's work; and resistance and surrender, which appears only in Sela-Smith's work. Finally, it is clear from this research that four of what we referred to earlier as a second set of seven heuristic concepts, i.e., (acknowledging) feelings, resistance, surrender, and transformation, which were more developed by Sela-Smith in her work, appear more significant than the other three, i.e., self-disclosure, self-search, and inward reach.

Finally, this research supports the points we made earlier (p. 12 above), which we wrote before undertaking the research, regarding intersubjectivity, inference, intentionality, and signitive-symbolic representation: that, as far as heuristic research methodology is concerned, they are (and always were) outliers. However, of the four, given Douglass and Moustakas's (1985) point about the importance of being able to encounter other people and the world, and our own positionality as researchers (see Cousins et al., 2025; Tudor, 2010, 2018), we suggest that more work could – and should – be done on intersubjectivity, regarding which, one could do worse than return to Buber's (1965) work, which influenced Douglass and Moustakas (1985).

Ka mua, ka muri – Walking backwards to the future

This Māori whakataukī (or proverb) speaks to the importance of looking to the past in order to inform the future, which in many ways has informed the methodology of this chapter, including, we would say:

- having a strong identification with the focus of this particular enquiry, including acknowledging the origin of ideas and theory; and
- having a drive to provide a certain validity regarding a number of heuristic concepts and their generalisability…

TABLE 1.3 Humanistic, experiential, and phenomenological concepts underpinning heuristic research (2003–2024).

Authors	*Concepts*																			
	Identifying with the focus of inquiry	*Self-dialogue*	*Tacit knowing*	*Intuition*	*Indwelling*	*Focusing*	*Internal frame of reference*	*Validity (validation, verification)*	*Self-search*	*Inference*	*Self-disclosure*	*Intersubjectivity*	*Signitive-symbolic representation*	*Intentionality*	*Acknowledging feelings*	*Transformation*	*Resistance*	*Surrender*	*Inward reach*	*Generalisability*
Ferendo (2004)	x	x	x	x	x	x	x	x	x		x	x			x	x	x	x	x	x
Casterline (2006)	x	x	x	x	x	x	x		x						x				x	x
Meents (2006)	x	x	x	x	x	x	x	x	x		x	x			x	x	x	x	x	x
Nuttall (2006)		x	x	x		x	x	x												
Howie and Brooks (2008)			x	x	x			x	x							x			x	
Tudor (2010)	x			x		x	x			x					x		x			x
Coles (2014)		x	x	x	x	x	x	x						x						x
Grennell (2014)			x	x	x	x		x	x		x				x	x	x	x		
Haertl (2014)	x	x	x	x	x	x	x	x		x						x				x
Ozertugrul (2015)	x	x	x	x	x	x	x	x	x	x	x	x			x	x	x	x		x
Schulz (2015)		x	x		x		x					x			x					
Hammond (2016)	x	x	x	x	x	x	x	x			x	x			x	x	x	x		
Mamea (2016)		x	x	x					x	x	x	x			x	x	x		x	
Nicholes (2016)	x	x	x	x	x	x	x	x												x
Alleyne (2017)	x	x	x	x	x	x	x	x							x	x	x	x		
Brown-Haysom (2018)	x	x	x	x	x	x	x		x						x	x	x	x	x	x
Franklin (2017)		x	x	x	x	x			x		x				x	x	x	x	x	
Ozertugrul (2017b)	x	x	x	x	x	x	x		x			x			x					
Schorr-kon (2017)	x	x	x	x	x	x	x	x	x		x	x		x	x	x	x	x	x	x
Sultan (2017)	x	x	x	x	x	x	x	x	x			x								
Grennell-Hawke and Tudor (2018)		x	x	x	x	x										x				x
Loh (2018)			x	x		x		x			x	x			x			x		x

Lorigan (2019)	x	x	x	x	x	x	x	x	x		x				x	x		x	x	x
Sherwood (2019)	x	x	x	x	x	x	x	x		x	x				x	x	x	x	x	
Huxtable (2020)		x	x	x	x	x		x	x						x		x	x		
Huxtable and Solomon (2020)		x	x	x	x	x									x			x		
Kennedy and Moore (2020)			x		x	x	x	x		x					x			x		
Stewart and Thomas (2020)			x					x									x		x	
Williams (2020)	x	x	x	x	x	x	x													
Brett (2021)			x	x		x			x		x				x		x			x
Ciurlionis (2021)	x	x	x	x	x	x	x	x							x			x	x	x
Longley (2021)	x	x	x	x	x	x	x	x			x				x	x	x	x	x	x
Lu (2021)	x	x	x	x	x	x	x	x							x		x			x
McCall (2021)		x	x	x	x	x	x	x			x	x			x	x	x	x	x	x
Fung (2022)	x	x	x	x	x	x	x	x	x	x	x				x	x	x	x		x
Gregory (2022)		x	x					x	x						x					
Hill (2022)		x	x	x	x	x					x				x				x	x
Hunt (2022)		x	x	x		x	x										x			
McCann (2022)			x	x	x	x	x		x	x	x	x			x	x	x	x		x
O'Rourke (2022)		x	x	x	x											x		x	x	
Cousins (2023)	x	x	x	x	x	x	x	x						x	x	x	x	x	x	x
Humphris (2023)	x	x	x	x	x	x	x		x		x				x		x	x	x	
Maya-Chipman (2023)	x	x	x	x	x	x	x	x			x				x	x	x	x	x	x
Oram (2023)	x	x	x	x	x	x	x			x	x	x			x		x	x		x
Osborne (2023)	x	x	x	x	x	x	x	x	x	x	x				x	x	x	x	x	x
Campion (2024)																		x		
Dyson-Horton (2024)		x	x	x	x	x	x	x	x		x				x	x				
Liu (2024)		x							x											
Nguyen (2024)		x		x																
Sharma and Kivell (2024)		x	x	x					x								x		x	

TABLE 1.4 Heuristic concepts referred to by Moustakas and Sela-Smith ranked according to their use in 50 heuristic studies (2003–2024).

Rank	*In % of studies*	*Concept*	*Authors*			
			Douglass and Moustakas (1985)	*Moustakas (1990)*	*Sela-Smith (2001)*	*Sela-Smith (2002)*
1	92%	Tacit knowing	x	x	x	x
2	88%	Intuition	x	x	x	x
3	82%	Self-dialogue	x	x	x	x
4	80%	Focusing	x	x	x	x
5	76%	Indwelling	x	x	x	x
6	70%	(Acknowledging) Feelings		x	x	x
7	66%	Internal frame of reference	x	x	x	x
8	58%	Validity (validation, verification)	x	x	x	
9=	54%	Resistance			x	x
9=	54%	Surrender			x	x
11=	50%	Generalisability	x (Dissemination)			
11=	50%	Identifying with the focus of inquiry		x	x	x
13	48%	Transformation		x	x	x
14	46%	Self-search	x	x	x	x
15	44%	Self-disclosure	x	x	x	x
16	42%	Inward reach			x	x
17	26%	Intersubjectivity	x	x		
18	20%	Inference	x	x		
19	6%	Intentionality	x			
20	0%	Signitive-symbolic representation	x			

and, as we wrote, researched, revised, and did more research,

- we engaged in a number of dialogues (though these were interpersonal rather than intrapersonal), principally about the initial and changing focus of the chapter, in between which
- we did a certain amount of indwelling, while also
- holding a concern about the intersubjectivity between as authors, the material, and you the reader(s).

So, having gone back to Moustakas, Douglass, and Sela-Smith, and then come forward in researching the application of their concepts in the past 22 years, and (re-)discovering the relevance of intuition, tacit knowing, indwelling, self-dialogue, focusing, indwelling, acknowledging feelings, the internal frame of reference, validity, resistance, surrender, and transformation, we now return to acknowledge the authors on whom Moustakas, Douglass, and Sela-Smith drew, and, finally, come forward to note more recent work on these concepts (Table 1.5). From this, it is clear that more work needs to be done to develop contemporary heuristic understandings of resistance, surrender, and transformation.

Heuristics offers a potent form of research in personal (intrapsychic), interpersonal (social), and transpersonal domains and, as such, deserves to be taken seriously. The concepts that form its methodology have well-established roots, principally in the Western Enlightenment tradition

TABLE 1.5 Original and more recent work on key concepts in heuristic methodology.

Concept	*Original authors cited by Moustakas and Sela-Smith*	*More recent work*
Intuition	Beveridge (1957), Polanyi (1964, 1966), Copen (1990) (In relation to Wilber's four quadrants) Wilber (1997)	Embodied heuristics (Gigerenzer, 2021), Heuristic intuition (Gigerenzer, 2023)
Tacit knowing	Polanyi (1966, 1969, 1983) (Psychognomic perception) Wemer (1948), Wemer and Kaplan (1963) (The core self) Stern (1985)	Malik (2023), tacit knowledge (Johannessen, 2022; Miton & DeDeo, 2022)
Self-dialogue	Developed from Buber (1958, 1961, 1965); see also Varani (1985)	Samacá Bohórquez (2020), Jarvis (2021)
Focusing	Gendlin (1978); see also Patton (1980)	Ikemi et al. (2023), Ollagnier-Beldame (2025)
Indwelling	Polanyi (1962, 1966)	Kawka (2024)
(Acknowledging) Feelings	Rogers (1961, 1969, 1980) Wilber (1997)	Moussawi and Puri (2022)
Internal frame of reference	Rogers (1951, 1969), Combs et al. (1976); see also Snyder (1983), and Varani (1985)	Karimova and Csapó (2021), Stocker et al. (2021)
Validity (validation, verification)	Bridgman (1950), Polanyi (1969), Moustakas (1975); see also Beck (1979)	Briñol and Petty (2022)
Resistance	Jung (1917/1953), Wilber (1993, 1997, 2000)	
Surrender	Suzuke (1950/1994), Wilber (1995, 2000)	
Transformation	James (1902/1999), Wilber (2000)	

from which it arose, which are represented in Table 1.5, and warrant further study – alongside more recent work and influences, not least from other cultural traditions (some of which are represented elsewhere in this volume). We hope that, by acknowledging this history and by widening perspectives on these concepts, we have contributed to a more rigorous approach to the methodology of heuristic research.

References

Alleyne, B. (2017). *A psychotherapist's experience of grief: A heuristic enquiry* [Master's dissertation, Auckland University of Technology]. Tuwhera Open Access Theses & Dissertations. https://hdl.handle.net/10292/10424

Atkins, D., & Loewenthal, D. (2004). The lived experience of psychotherapists working with older clients: An heuristic study. *British Journal of Guidance & Counselling, 32*(4), 493–509. https://doi.org/10.1080/03069880412331303295

Beck, G. (1979). *Heuristic psychotherapy* [Unpublished paper]. Merrill-Parker Institute.

Bell, S. (2018). A music therapist's self-reflection on her indigenous heritage: A heuristic self-inquiry. *Canadian Journal of Music Therapy, 24*, 58–75.

Beveridge, W. I. B. (1957). *The art of scientific investigation*. Vintage Books.

Brett, E. (2021). *Landings: A settler descendent relationship to land* [Master's dissertation, Auckland University of Technology]. Tuwhera Open Access Theses & Dissertations. https://hdl.handle.net/10292/15109

Bridgman, P. (1950). *Reflections of a physicist*. Philosophical Library.

Briñol, P., & Petty, R. E. (2022). Self-validation theory: An integrative framework for understanding when thoughts become consequential. *Psychological Review, 129*(2), 340–367. https://doi.org/10.1037/rev0000340

Brown-Haysom, N. (2018). *My experience of being present: A heuristic self-search inquiry* [Master's dissertation, Auckland University of Technology]. Tuwhera Open Access Theses & Dissertations. https://hdl.handle.net/10292/12497

Buber, M. (1958). *I and thou.* Scribner.

Buber, M. (1961). *Tales of the Hasidim: The early masters* (O. Marx, Trans.). Schocken.

Buber, M. (1965). *Between man and man.* Macmillan.

Campion, N. (2024). I still haven't found what I'm looking for: Early relational–developmental deficits and the search for repair through the erotic. *Counselling & Psychotherapy Research, 24*(2), 532–544. https://doi-org/10.1002/capr.12686

Casterline, G. (2006). *The experience of the act of praying* [Doctoral dissertation, Loyola University]. ProQuest Dissertations & Theses.

Ciurlionis, C. (2021). *In defence of a manic defence: A therapist's experience of humour in psychotherapy* [Master's dissertation, Auckland University of Technology]. Tuwhera Open Access Theses & Dissertations. https://hdl.handle.net/10292/14499

Coles, A. (2014). 'Being time': An exploration of personal experiences of time and implications for art psychotherapy practice. *International Journal of Art Therapy: Inscape, 19*(2), 71–81. https://doi.org/10.1080/17454832.2013.844184

Combs, A. W., Richards, S. C., & Richards, F. (1976). *Perceptual psychology.* Harper & Row.

Copen, R. (1990). *Intuitive connecting* [Unpublished paper]. The Center for Humanistic Studies.

Cousins, G. (2023). *In search of the boarding school self: A heuristic inquiry* [Master's dissertation, Auckland University of Technology]. Tuwhera Open Access Theses & Dissertations. http://hdl.handle.net/10292/17753

Cousins, G., Humphris, A., Kingi, A., Oram, L., & Tudor, K. (2025). Heuristic research in a time-limited context. In W. Ings & K. Tudor (Eds.), *Heuristic enquiries: Research across disciplines and professions* (pp. 162–180). Routledge.

Daniel, S. (2016). The usefulness of role reversal in one-to-one supervision: A qualitative research project using heuristic enquiry. *Zeitschrift fur Psychodrama und Soziometrie, 15*(1), 235–253.

Djuraskovic, I., & Arthur, N. (2010). Heuristic inquiry: A personal journey of acculturation and identity reconstruction. *The Qualitative Report, 15*(6), 1569–1593. https://doi.org/10.46743/2160-3715/2010.1361

Douglass, B., & Moustakas, C. E. (1985). Heuristic inquiry: The internal search to know. *Journal of Humanistic Psychology, 25*(3), 39–55. https://doi.org/10.1177/0022167885253004

Dyson-Horton, G. (2024). The critical voice: A heuristic enquiry into the experience of hearing a critical inner voice to deepen our understanding of its meaning and purpose. *Existential Analysis: Journal of the Society for Existential Analysis, 35*(1), 34–45.

Ferendo, F. J. (2004). *A heuristic and hermeneutic inquiry: Ken Wilber and personal transformation* [Unpublished doctoral dissertation, Union Institute and University].

Franklin, M. (2017). *'Nature and I', an ecotherapy journey: A heuristic inquiry into nature's role in healing from a psychotherapy perspective* [Master's dissertation, Auckland University of Technology]. Tuwhera Open Access Theses & Dissertations. https://hdl.handle.net/10292/11009

Fung, S. W. T. (2022). A journey of self-discovery through the book 'a monster calls': A heuristic inquiry [Master's dissertation, Auckland University of Technology]. Tuwhera Open Access Theses & Dissertations. https://hdl.handle.net/10292/15275

Gendlin, E. (1962). *Experiencing and the creation of meaning.* Free Press.

Gendlin, E. (1978). *Focusing* (2nd ed.). Bantam.

Gigerenzer, G. (2021). Embodied heuristics. *Frontiers in Psychology, 12*, Article 711289. https://doi.org/10.3389/fpsyg.2021.711289

Gigerenzer, G. (2023). *The intelligence of intuition.* Cambridge University Press.

Gregory, Z. (2022). The page as place: How we enter into images as place. *International Journal of Art Therapy: Inscape, 27*(2), 61–71. https://doi.org/10.1080/17454832.2021.1995453

Grennell, N. (2014). *What is the experience of being both Māori and Pākehā? Negotiating the experience of the hybrid cultural object* [Master's dissertation, Auckland University of Technology]. Tuwhera Open Access Theses & Dissertations. www.openrepository.aut.ac.nz/handle/10292/7710

Grennell-Hawke, N., & Tudor, K. (2018). Being Māori and Pākehā: Methodology and method in exploring cultural hybridity. *The Qualitative Report*, *23*(7), 1530–1546. https://doi.org/10.46743/2160-3715/2018.2934

Haertl, K. (2014). Writing and the development of the self-heuristic inquiry: A unique way of exploring the power of the written word. *Journal of Poetry Therapy*, *27*(2), 55–68. https://doi.org/10.1080/08893675.2014.895488

Hammond, M. (2016). *Therapists' experience of shame: An heuristic study* [Master's dissertation, Auckland University of Technology]. Tuwhera Open Access Theses & Dissertations. https://hdl.handle.net/10292/10186

Hill, J. (2022). *Te whakatere i ngā awa e rua (navigating the two rivers): A heuristic investigation of Māori identity as a student psychotherapist* [Master's dissertation, Auckland University of Technology]. Tuwhera Open Access Theses & Dissertations. https://hdl.handle.net/10292/15268

Howie, L., & Brooks, S. (2008). Therapist as researcher: Using heuristic methodology in a study of spoken language in the therapeutic relationship. *Gestalt Journal of Australia and New Zealand*, *5*(1), 13–31. https://search.informit.org/doi/10.3316/informit.511226553434264

Humphris, A. (2023). *Motherhood and psychotherapy training: A heuristic self-search inquiry into a trainee's experience* [Master's dissertation, Auckland University of Technology]. Tuwhera Open Access Theses & Dissertations. http://hdl.handle.net/10292/17878

Hunt, C. (2022). *The human–canine relationship: A heuristic self-inquiry into canine-assisted psychotherapy* [Master's dissertation, Auckland University of Technology]. Tuwhera Open Access Theses & Dissertations. https://hdl.handle.net/10292/15882

Huxtable, C. (2020). *Breathing and relating: Exploring a therapist's heuristic experience* [Master's dissertation, Auckland University of Technology]. Tuwhera Open Access Theses & Dissertations. https://hdl.handle.net/10292/13157

Huxtable, C., & Solomon, M. (2020). Breathing and relating: Exploring a therapist's heuristic experience. *Body, Movement and Dance in Psychotherapy*, *15*(4), 236–250. https://doi.org/10.1080/17432979.2020.1813808

Ikemi, A., Okamura, S., & Tanaka, H. (2023). The experiencing model: Saying what we mean in the context of focusing and psychotherapy. In E. R. Severson & K. C. Krycka (Eds.), *The psychology and philosophy of Eugene Gendlin* (pp. 44–62). Routledge.

James, W. (1999). *The varieties of religious experience: A study in human nature*. Random House. (Original work published 1902)

Jarvis, J. (2021). The dialogical self theory, underpinning empathetic-reflective-dialogical re-storying. In C. Monereo, C. Weise, & H. Hermans (Eds.), *Dialogicality: Personal, local and planetary dialogue in education, health, citizenship and research* (pp. 162–170). Creative Commons.

Johannessen, J. A. (2022). *The philosophy of tacit knowledge: The tacit side of knowledge management in organizations*. Emerald Publishing.

Johnson, L. N., & Johnson, A. T. (2023). Conflicting cultures, compromising care: A heuristic inquiry of women directors of college counseling centers. *Journal of Diversity in Higher Education*. https://doi.org/10.1037/dhe0000516

Jourard, S. (1968). *Disclosing man to himself*. Van Nostrand.

Jourard, S. (1971). *Self-disclosure: An experimental analysis of the transparent self*. Wiley-Interscience.

Jung, C. G. (1953). *Two essays on analytical psychology (Bollingen Series 20)*. Pantheon Books. (Original work published 1917)

Karimova, K., & Csapó, B. (2021). Cognitive and affective components of verbal self-concepts and internal/external frame of reference within the multidimensional verbal domain. *SAGE Open*, *11*(2). https://doi.org/10.1177/21582440211018683

Kawka, M. (2024). A heuristic inquiry into the phenomenon of creating art from a spiritual viewpoint. *Journal for the Study of Spirituality*, *14*(2), 124–142. https://doi.org/10.1080/20440243.2024.2375212

Kennedy, F., & Moore, G. P. (2020). What is the personal and professional significance for the trainee therapist of learning emotion-focused therapy? *Journal of Humanistic Counseling, 59*(2), 86–105. https://doi.org/10.1002/johc.12132

Kumar, S. (2017). My dissertation healed me: A retrospective analysis through heuristic inquiry. *The Qualitative Report, 22*(11), 3025–3038. https://doi.org/10.46743/2160-3715/2017.3051

Kumar, S., & Casey, A. (2020). Work and intimate partner violence: Powerful role of work in empowerment process for middle-class women who experience intimate partner violence. *Community, Work & Family, 23*(1), 1–18. https://doi.org/10.1080/13668803.2017.1365693

Liu, Y. (2024). *Ghost talk: A creative consideration of Zhiguai ghost narratives to discuss Chinese parental expectations* [Master's dissertation, Auckland University of Technology]. Tuwhera Open Access Theses & Dissertations. http://hdl.handle.net/10292/17926

Loewenthal, D. (2011). Research, ideology, and the evolution of intersubjectivity in a post-existential culture. In D. Loewenthal (Ed.), *Post-existentialism and the psychological therapies: Towards a therapy without foundations* (pp. 157–174). Karnac.

Loewenthal, D. (2017). Editorials on thoughtful practice and research. In D. Loewenthal (Ed.), *Existential psychotherapy and counselling after postmodernism* (pp. 185–193). Routledge.

Loh, J. (2018). *Can a psychotherapy student authentically grow under academic demands: A heuristic inquiry* [Master's dissertation, Auckland University of Technology]. Tuwhera Open Access Theses & Dissertations. https://hdl.handle.net/10292/11620

Longley, H. (2021). *A psychotherapist's experience of self-disclosure, when practising in the digital era: A heuristic self-study* [Master's dissertation, Auckland University of Technology]. Tuwhera Open Access Theses & Dissertations. https://hdl.handle.net/10292/14202

Lorigan, C. (2019). *To speak or not to speak: the experience of disclosing and concealing my obsessive-compulsive disorder – A heuristic enquiry* [Master's dissertation, Auckland University of Technology]. Tuwhera Open Access Theses & Dissertations. https://hdl.handle.net/10292/12490

Lu, M. (2021). *Where is home? A heuristic journey exploring the impact of emigration* [Master's dissertation, Auckland University of Technology]. Tuwhera Open Access Theses & Dissertations. https://hdl.handle.net/10292/15518

Malik, A. (2023). Tacit knowing: What it is and why it matters. *Episteme, 20*(2), 349–366. https://doi.org/10.1017/epi.2021.41

Mamea, K. (2016). *Does Melanie Klein's concept of internal objects relate to Samoan writings on internal structures of the self? A phenomenologically-oriented heuristic enquiry* [Master's dissertation, Auckland University of Technology]. Tuwhera Open Access Theses & Dissertations. https://hdl.handle.net/10292/10098

Maslow, A. H. (1956). Self-actualizing people: A study of psychological health. In C. Moustakas (Ed.), *The self* (pp. 160–194). Harper & Brothers.

Maslow, A. H. (1966). *The psychology of science*. Harper & Row.

Maslow, A. H. (1971). *The farther reaches of human nature*. Viking.

Maya-Chipman, T. (2023). *Navigating the wilderness – A heuristic self-search inquiry into the lived experience of chronic pain* [Master's dissertation, Auckland University of Technology]. Tuwhera Open Access Theses & Dissertations. http://hdl.handle.net/10292/17183

McCall, J. (2021). *The art of mourning – Exploring the impact of artistic creation upon the psychotherapist* [Master's dissertation, Auckland University of Technology]. Tuwhera Open Access Theses & Dissertations. https://hdl.handle.net/10292/14395

McCann, M. (2022). *Invisible wounds: A heuristic exploration of unintentional racial microaggressions and their relationship to unconscious racialisation* [Master's dissertation, Auckland University of Technology]. Tuwhera Open Access Theses & Dissertations. https://hdl.handle.net/10292/15067

Meents, J. (2006). *Acres of diamonds: A heuristic self-search inquiry into intuition* [Doctoral thesis, University of Calgary]. www.collectionscanada.gc.ca/obj/thesescanada/vol2/002/NR19162.PDF

Miton, H., & DeDeo, S. (2022). The cultural transmission of tacit knowledge. *Journal of the Royal Society Interface, 19*(195), Article 20220238. https://doi.org/10.1098/rsif.2022.0238

Mouqué, T. (2005). What is the meaning of my resistance to psychotherapy? *Psychodynamic Practice, 11*(2), 153–164. https://doi.org/10.1080/14753630500108257

Moussawi, G., & Puri, J. (2022). 'Bad feelings': Reflections on research, disciplines, and critical methodologies. In K. Davis & J. Irvine (Eds.), *Silences, neglected feelings, and blind-spots in research practice* (pp. 75–90). Routledge.

Moustakas, C. (1975). *The touch of loneliness*. Prentice-Hall.

Moustakas, C. (1990). *Heuristic research: Design, methodology, and applications*. Sage Publications.

Nguyen, T. L. T. (2024). *Exploring women's constraints through non-linear storytelling and visual narratives in Vietnamese society* [Master's dissertation, Auckland University of Technology]. Tuwhera Open Access Theses & Dissertations. http://hdl.handle.net/10292/17816

Nicholes, J. (2016). Video-sharing website writing as identity performance: Heuristic inquiry into experiencing personally meaningful music. *International Journal of Education & the Arts*, *17*(15). www.ijea.org/v17n15

Nuttall, J. (2006). Researching psychotherapy integration: A heuristic approach. *Counselling Psychology Quarterly*, *19*(4), 429–444. https://doi.org/10.1080/09515070601090121

Ollagnier-Beldame, M. (2025). Experiencing life and belonging to nature with focusing. *European Journal of Ecopsychology*, *9*, 158–179. https://ecopsychology-journal.eu/v9/EJE_v9_Ollagnier-Beldame.pdf

Oram, L. (2023). *Remaking the Imago Paterna: How psychotherapy helps a son reimagine the father. A heuristic enquiry* [Master's dissertation, Auckland University of Technology]. Tuwhera Open Access Theses & Dissertations. http://hdl.handle.net/10292/17754

O'Rourke, K. (2022). *Hiding and seeking: A heuristic self-inquiry into concealment discovery and peek-a-boo* [Master's dissertation, Auckland University of Technology]. Tuwhera Open Access Theses & Dissertations. https://hdl.handle.net/10292/15765

Osborne, C. (2023). *What is the client experience of online video-calling equine-facilitated therapy? A heuristic study* [Master's dissertation, Auckland University of Technology]. Tuwhera Open Access Theses & Dissertations. http://hdl.handle.net/10292/17016

Ozertugrul, E. (2015). *Heuristic self-search inquiry into one experience of obsessive-compulsive disorder* [Unpublished doctoral dissertation, Walden University].

Ozertugrul, E. (2017a). A comparative analysis: Heuristic self-search inquiry as self-knowledge and knowledge of society. *Journal of Humanistic Psychology*, *57*(3), 237–251. https://doi.org/10.1177/0022167815594966

Ozertugrul, E. (2017b). Heuristic self-search inquiry into one experience of obsessive–compulsive disorder. *Journal of Humanistic Psychology*, *57*(3), 215–236. https://doi.org/10.1177/0022167815592503

Patton, M. (1980). *Qualitative evaluation methods*. Sage.

Polanyi, M. (1962). *Personal knowledge: Towards a post-critical philosophy*. University of Chicago.

Polanyi, M. (1964). *Science, faith and society*. University of Chicago Press.

Polanyi, M. (1966). *The tacit dimension*. Doubleday.

Polanyi, M. (1969). *Knowing and being* (M. Green, Ed.). University of Chicago Press.

Polanyi, M. (1983). *The tacit dimension*. Peter Smith.

Rogers, C. R. (1951). *Client-centered therapy*. Constable.

Rogers, C. R. (1961). *On becoming a person: A therapist's view of psychotherapy*. Constable.

Rogers, C. R. (1969). *Freedom to learn*. Charles E. Merrill.

Rogers, C. R. (1980). *A way of being*. Houghton Mifflin.

Rogers, C. R. (1985). Toward a more human science of the person. *Journal of Humanistic Psychology*, *25*(4), 7–24. https://doi.org/10.1177/0022167885254002

Samacá Bohórquez, Y. (2020). A self-dialogue with the thoughts of Paulo Freire: A critical pedagogy encounter. *HOW*, *27*(1), 125–139. https://doi.org/10.19183/how.27.1.520

Schorr-kon, C. (2017). *Regarding intuition: An heuristic journey into a psychotherapist's experience of intuition* [Master's dissertation, Auckland University of Technology]. Tuwhera Open Access Theses & Dissertations. https://hdl.handle.net/10292/11506

Schulz, C. (2015). Existential psychotherapy with a person who lives with a left ventricular assist device and awaits heart transplantation: A case report. *Journal of Humanistic Psychology*, *55*(4), 429–473. https://doi.org/10.1177/0022167814539192

Scott, A. (2013). An exploration of the experience of Christian counsellors in their work with both Christian and non-Christian clients, with particular reference to aspects of cultural transition. *Counselling & Psychotherapy Research, 13*(4), 272–281. https://doi.org/10.1080/14733145.2012.761257

Sela-Smith, S. (2001). *Heuristic self-search inquiry: Clarification of Moustakas' heuristic research* [Doctoral dissertation, Saybrook Graduate School and Research Center]. ProQuest Dissertations & Theses.

Sela-Smith, S. (2002). Heuristic research: A review and critique of Moustakas's method. *Journal of Humanistic Psychology, 42*(3), 53–88. https://doi.org/10.1177/0022167802423004

Shantall, T. (1999). The experience of meaning in suffering among Holocaust survivors. *Journal of Humanistic Psychology, 39*(3), 96–124. https://doi.org/10.1177/0022167899393009

Sharma, R., & Kivell, N. (2024). A self-heuristic inquiry: Unpacking the use of 'decolonization' in therapy and mental health care with and for racialized communities. *American Journal of Community Psychology, 73*(1/2), 170–182. https://doi.org/10.1002/ajcp.12657

Sherwood, V. (2019). *Haunting Minnie Dean: A heuristic inquiry into baby farming, psychological infanticide and closed stranger adoption* [Master's dissertation, Auckland University of Technology]. Tuwhera Open Access Theses & Dissertations. https://hdl.handle.net/10292/12582

Snyder, J. (1983). *The initial interview in heuristic psychotherapy* [Unpublished manuscript]. The Center for Humanistic Studies.

Stern, D. N. (1985). *The interpersonal world of the infant: A view from psychoanalysis and developmental psychology*. Basic Books.

Stewart, K., & Thomas, V. (2020). A trainee psychotherapist's heuristic exploration of losing a mother to suicide. *British Journal of Guidance & Counselling, 48*(4), 552–562. https://doi.org/10.1080/03069885.2018.1519181

Stocker, J., Abu-Hilal, M., Hermena, E., AlJassmi, M., & Barbato, M. (2021). Internal/external frame of reference model and dimensional comparison theory: A novel exploration of their applicability among Arab high school students. *Educational Psychology, 41*(4), 483–501. https://doi.org/10.1080/01443410.2021.1887455

Sultan, N. (2017). Embodiment and the therapeutic relationship: Findings from a heuristic inquiry. *Journal of Humanistic Counseling, 56*(3), 180–196. https://doi.org/10.1002/johc.12052

Sultan, N. (2019). *Heuristic inquiry: Researching human experience holistically*. Sage.

Suzuke, D. T. (1994). *The Zen koan as a means of attaining enlightenment*. Charles E. Tuttle. (Original work published 1950)

Tudor, K. (2010). *The fight for health: A heuristic enquiry into psychological well-being* [Unpublished context statement]. PhD in Mental Health Promotion by Public (Published) Works, School of Health and Social Sciences, Middlesex University, London, UK.

Tudor, K. (2018). *Psychotherapy: A critical examination*. PCCS Books.

Tudor, K. (2022). Supporting critical self-enquiry: Doing heuristic research. In S. Bager-Charleson & A. McBeath (Eds.), *Supporting research in counselling and psychotherapy* (pp. 57–79). Springer.

Tudor, K. (2023). Critical heuristics: From 'I who feels' to 'We who care – and act'. In K. Tudor & J. Wyatt (Eds.), *Qualitative research approaches for psychotherapy: Reflexivity, methodology, and criticality* (pp. 115–132). Routledge.

Varani, J. (1985). *Psychological dimensions of mystery: A phenomenological heuristic investigation* [Doctoral dissertation, The Union for Experimenting Colleges and Universities]. ProQuest Dissertations & Theses.

Wan, J. (2024). Integration of emotion-focused therapy and prayer in overcoming a dissociative process – A Chinese counsellor's self-as-subject heuristic inquiry. *Person-Centered & Experiential Psychotherapies, 23*(4), 475–494. https://doi.org/10.1080/14779757.2023.2264944

Wemer, H. (1948). *The comparative psychology of mental development*. International University Press.

Wemer, H., & Kaplan, B. (1963). *Symbol formation: An organismic-developmental approach to language and expression of thought*. Wiley.

Wilber, K. (1993). *Grace and grit: Spirituality and healing in the life and death of Treya Killam Wilber*. Shambhala.

Wilber, K. (1995). *Sex, ecology, and spirituality*. Shambhala.

Wilber, K. (1996). *A brief history of everything*. Shambhala.

Wilber, K. (1997). *The eye of spirit*. Shambala.
Wilber, K. (2000). *One taste: Daily reflections on integral spirituality*. Shambhala.
Williams, N. F. (2020). Going 'beyond the surface' in an app-based group: A heuristic inquiry. *Journal of Humanistic Psychology*, 1–24. https://doi.org/10.1177/0022167820974503
Wiorkowski, F. (2015). The experiences of students with autism spectrum disorders in college: A heuristic exploration. *The Qualitative Report, 20*(6), 847–863. https://doi.org/10.46743/2160-3715/2015.2163
Wood, J. K. (1996). The person-centered approach: Towards an understanding of its implications. In R. Hutterer, G. Pawlowsky, P. F. Schmid, & R. Stipsits (Eds.), *Client-centered and experiential psychotherapy: A paradigm in motion* (pp. 163–181). Peter Lang.
Yeh, T.-J. (2018). A heuristic study on the leadership practices of female faculty in higher education. *The International Journal of Organizational Innovation, 11*(2), 245–259. www.ijoi-online.org/attachments/article/85/0888%20Final.pdf

2

EXPLICATING HEURISTIC METHODOLOGY THROUGH ENQUIRY INTO UNINTENTIONAL RACIAL MICROAGGRESSIONS

Keith Tudor and Malik McCann

This chapter explicates heuristic methodology and method in researching and (re)discovering unintentional racial microaggressions. The first part of the chapter outlines and develops heuristic research methodology by means of a discussion and application of its key concepts, as originally identified by Moustakas (Douglass & Moustakas, 1985; Moustakas, 1990), expanded by Sela-Smith, collated by the first author, and illustrated by the second author. The second part of the chapter offers some critical reflections on both the process and the findings, arguing that the former offers an illustration of an extension to heuristic enquiry, and the latter, a contribution to research that has a social impact.

This chapter is based on some original research undertaken by the second author (McCann, 2022) under the supervision of the first author; a shared interest in culture, race, and racism, albeit it from very different cultural backgrounds and experiences (Haenga-Collins & Tudor, 2021; McCann & Tudor, 2022; Pomare et al., 2021; Tudor, 2025); and a commitment to undertaking and fostering research in psychotherapy that makes a difference in society (Tudor, 2023). From that research, in this chapter, we focus on the methodology and method of heuristic research as a way of (re)discovering racial microaggressions. (Chapter 6 reports the findings of the first author's use of heuristic method in her original research enquiry on the subject of unintentional racial microaggressions [McCann, 2022] in terms of the *phases* of such enquiry.) In keeping with the heuristic tradition, we use first person language, mainly of the second author ('I' unless otherwise stated or clarified), and illustrations from a personal journal she kept during the period of the research (2020–2021), as well as the two of us ('we'). We begin with a discussion of heuristic concepts and methodology.

Heuristic concepts and methodology

Heuristics is a wide field of enquiry, encompassing many disciplines including philosophy, law, mathematics, social geography, and psychology (for a recent volume on which, see Ings & Tudor, 2025), but, broadly, as the word – from the Ancient Greek εὑρίσκω (heurískō) 'I find, discover' – suggests, refers to any approach to problem-solving or self-discovery that employs a practical method which is regarded as sufficient for reaching usually an immediate, short-term

DOI: 10.4324/9781003685944-4

goal or approximation. However, even within psychology, there are different approaches to heuristics: one which focuses more on problem-solving, and on cognition and behaviour by way of the examination of various heuristic devices (e.g., Huffman & Tracy, 2018); and the other, which focuses more on self-discovery, and on a holistic and historical view of the lived experience of a person by way of some form of self-reflective journey (e.g., Watford, 2008), which, while often immediate, is rarely short-term.

The heuristic tradition on which this research draws was first developed by Clark Moustakas, appropriately enough through his own heuristic journey with regard to a self-experience, in his case, of loneliness (Moustakas, 1961). Reflecting on this later, he developed heuristic research in the field of psychology (Douglass & Moustakas, 1985; Moustakas, 1967, 1990, 1994, 2000). In this context, heuristics is a qualitative research method and methodology that aims to discover meaning in significant human experience (Douglass & Moustakas, 1985). It involves a process of exploration of self, which may or may not include others as co-participants, which, nonetheless, emphasises the interiority of experience (Sela-Smith, 2002). It is an approach which values 'imagination, intuition, self-reflection and the tacit dimension in the search for knowledge' (Douglass & Moustakas, 1985, p. 39). Unsurprisingly, Moustakas (1990) describes it as a deeply personal investigation involving 'self-search, self-dialogue, and self-discovery' (p. 11), while Sela-Smith (2002) emphasises the researcher's attention as being 'focused inward on [the] feeling responses of the researcher to the outward situation' (p. 59).

Here we describe the methodology of this approach to heuristics by means of a brief discussion of key concepts identified by Moustakas and his colleagues, i.e., identifying with the focus of inquiry, self-dialogue, tacit knowing, intuition, indwelling, focusing, and the internal frame of reference (Douglass & Moustakas, 1985; Moustakas, 1990); and self-experience, inward reach (for tacit awareness and knowledge), surrender, self-dialogue, self-search, and transformation (Sela-Smith, 2002) – and resistance (Sela-Smith, 2001). Since my own heuristic research (Tudor, 2010) and subsequent publications on heurism – Tudor (2010, 2017, 2022, 2023) and Ings and Tudor (2025) – I have had an interest in collating these key concepts as the foundation of a heuristic methodology and, in supervising Malik's master's dissertation, was grateful to have the opportunity to work with her to order these concepts in a way that captured their relationship to each other, as illustrated with reference to her experience of the research enquiry. This collation has already been found useful in framing the consideration of heuristic methodology (Cardo, 2024) and been cited – by Cardo (2024) and Cardo and Tudor (2024).

Identifying with the focus of enquiry

Heuristic inquiry is a process that begins with a question or problem which the researcher seeks to illuminate or answer. The question is one that has been a personal challenge and puzzlement in the search to understand one's self and the world in which one lives (Moustakas, 1990).

The heuristic research question that was the focus of the study on which this chapter is based was 'What meaning may be made regarding unconscious racialisation from making, encountering, and challenging unintentional racial microaggressions?' This was formed in response to a series of interactions that occurred in an ethics class during a psychotherapy training course. The course and its participants are located in the post-colonial society of Aotearoa New Zealand.

I (Malik) was profoundly affected by a statement which, ironically, was made in the context of cautioning about unintentionally perpetuating racism. The speaker claimed to cite a recent study regarding perceptions of brown versus white robots, which found that (as my classmate put it) 'people see brown robots like brown people as more shit'.

This comment appeared to be received innocuously by the group. I knew my classmates to have egalitarian beliefs and felt that the comment was not meant to cause offence. I also sensed an assumption by the group that the statement referred to racist people 'out there'. However, for myself as a brown person, I had no way to distance myself from the implications of the statement and this set off a series of painful emotions and questions. I felt anger, sadness, confusion, and despair, and, alongside this, a deep sense of shame which led me to want to hide my affective reaction. I recognised that this response indicated something of my own unconscious racialisation, an internalised oppression that lived alongside conscious pride in my heritage.

As I reflected on this interaction in the ensuing days, it felt important to share my experience with the group. Although I knew the microaggression wasn't intentional, I felt it would be valuable for my classmates as future therapists to understand how it had been received by myself as one brown person. I also sensed that staying silent would reinforce my shame and self-invalidation. The act of sharing was a way to challenge this shame and I hoped that this would initiate a vulnerable conversation.

I first shared how the comment had impacted me in a group chat in which a few classmates acknowledged and empathised with my experience. This was raised in the next class where, again, I spoke of my experience. This time I also shared my discovery that the study hadn't measured explicit racism but, rather, referred to implicit bias. I reflected that, when the study spoke of 'people', it seemed to imply that no-one was necessarily immune, and that if we wanted to address racism in a meaningful way, rather than assume it lived somewhere 'out there', it was necessary to consider how we might personally manifest these societally conditioned implicit beliefs.

This time I was met with a palpably uncomfortable silence, and the few responses felt deflective and defensive. These included assertions that those in the room did not personally identify with the statement; that I had not chosen the right forum to express my concerns; and that I was misunderstanding the speaker's intentions – indeed, the speaker stated they had only used the word 'shit' to highlight how reprehensible racism was.

I interpreted the defensive responses of the group as due to feeling accused of being racist. Sue (2013) states that fear of recognising oneself as racist can result in debilitating emotion which interferes with the ability to be present, open, and vulnerable, and can lead to defending a righteous position rather than listening with the intention of understanding. Rather than an honest conversation between individuals with understandably varied perspectives and experiences, I felt an 'active ignorance' to my perspective was being enacted by the group (Castillo, 2018).

In response, I was furious, and asked what it meant that the speaker wanted to advocate for brown people, yet did not want to acknowledge the voice of a brown person. I also stated that not personally identifying with the statement was irrelevant as it spoke to unconscious bias, not explicit beliefs. I was met with silence; the tutor ended the discussion; and the class continued as normal.

As I reflected on this experience, I sensed that, alongside the conscious elements of these interactions, unconscious racialised self and other objects had come alive in both myself and the group (Dalal, 2002). I had a strong sense that these interactions represented an enactment of the interplay of unconscious colonial dynamics that commonly occur in moments of interracial conflict and felt compelled to explore them more deeply. As well as being an issue that had personal importance, it was an opportunity to explore this complex social dynamic which is of relevance to psychotherapists working with clients, as well as for us as citizens in a multi-ethnic society in the bicultural nation of Aotearoa New Zealand. A heuristic self-search seemed the ideal framework for exploring this experience through my own perception of what occurred intra-psychically, interpersonally, and intersubjectively, and to discover the intangible elements of the experience. To adopt a research method that focuses only on what could be observed would miss the complexity of this phenomenon. For this particular topic, it felt vital that I capture the essence of my subjectivity within the context of relational and social engagement in order to elucidate the pervasive themes which characterise unconscious racialisation.

The personal nature of heuristic research acknowledges the importance of subjective truth (Bridgman, 1950), and Rogers' (1969, 1985) ideas about the nature of human science, both of which Moustakas (1990) acknowledges as influences on his work.

Self-experience

Drawing on the work of Stern (1985), Sela-Smith (2001) identifies this as a component of heuristic self-search inquiry (HSSI) and a criterion by which she reviewed 28 research studies that claimed to have followed Moustakas's method. She also refers to this in her argument about validity in heuristic research: 'Validity of the self-experience is established implicitly by the similar experiences of others; yet, validity in subjective discovery-research is not possible by comparing to others' experience' (p. 27). Having a framework which honoured self-experience felt validating of my experience, and especially important because, in my position as a mixed 'race' minority woman in a society dominated by Western traditions, this is sometimes questioned. Moreover, in the course of the research (see Chapter 6), the valuing of self-experience felt holding in moments where I found myself consumed by self-doubt.

Internal frame of reference

Heuristic enquiry and processes always relate back to the internal frame of reference. As Moustakas (1990) puts it: 'Whether knowledge derived is attained through tacit, intuitive, or observed phenomena – whether the knowledge is deepened and extended… through indwelling, focusing, self-searching, or dialogue with others – its medium or base is the internal frame of reference' (p. 27). This aspect of Moustakas's theory draws on person-centred psychology (Rogers, 1959, 1969, 1985), and, specifically, Rogers' (1951) development of this particular concept as the basis of understanding the meaning of a person's behaviour, and of the(ir) opportunities for new learning. In this research, this was particularly important to me as the researcher as, while racial microaggressions (unintentional or otherwise) are observable, the experience of making, encountering, and challenging such aggressions is understood, and interpreted subjectively, through each individual's internal frame of reference.

Self-dialogue

This is the vehicle by which the researcher discovers the constituent aspects and qualities of an experience: one's own self-discoveries, awareness, and understanding (Moustakas, 1990). Informed by Buber's (1958, 1961, 1965) explorations of dialogue and mutuality, in his research, Ozertugrul (2017) has developed this as real-time, self-to-self conversations. In this research, I began a dialogue with the phenomenon of racial microaggressions in the immersion phase (see Chapter 6), reflecting on my own experience and its observable manifestations in order 'to engage in a rhythmic flow with it – back and forth, again and again' (Moustakas, 1990, p. 16), thus: from experience to concept, from part to whole, from thoughts to feelings, from societal to individual – and back again. My self-dialogue took place between various self-states, including my self (my conscious ego identity), and my racialised selves (an internalised brown self-state and an internalised white self-state) as well as a deeply invalidating white object.

Self-search

The process of self-dialogue requires honesty; as Moustakas (1990) puts it: 'In self-dialogue, one faces oneself and must be honest with oneself and one's experience relevant to the question or problem' (p. 23). This, in turn, requires a trust in the tendency of persons (and organisms) to actualise, which is based on both Maslow's (1956, 1966, 1971) work on self-actualising persons, and on Rogers' (1963) view of the actualising tendency as a unitary theory of motivation. Sela-Smith's (2002) contribution to heuristic research is her emphasis on this concept and component; as she puts it, simply, 'The search is a self-search' (p. 69).

Self-disclosure

This emphasis on self-search requires self-disclosure, not only and initially to oneself as the researcher, but also to others: supervisors, co-participants, examiners, editors, reviewers, and so on. In his work, Moustakas draws on that of Jourard (1968, 1971), whose work on this concept informed the development of humanistic psychology in the 1960s and 70s. Again, Sela-Smith (2001, 2002) emphasises this, commenting (in her 2002 article) that, together with self-honesty and self-dialogue, it contributes to 'the path of surrender' (p. 75). As I put it elsewhere: 'The vulnerability I feel in my self-disclosure in this research, and the part of myself which projects invalidation (of my perspective in relation to this dynamic), are deeply uncomfortable' (McCann, 2022, p. 33). I was fearful not only of what I might discover about my own racialisation (and racism), but also of the repercussions from authority figures who might respond defensively (as the group had done).

Surrender

Based on her own critique of Moustakas's work (see the following section), Sela-Smith (2002) emphasises this as a component of HSSI, gauging this by an evaluation that 'The research indicates surrender to the question has taken place' (p. 69), which she describes as 'living, waking, sleeping, and dreaming the question… [and like] jumping into the river, a leap into the darkness' (pp. 69–70) (see also Chapter 3). In surrendering, a racialised perspective began to permeate every aspect of my life. I allowed myself to become necessarily consumed by the lens of unconscious racialisation and felt the impact of this surrender as a paranoid hyper-vigilance of the racial and cultural undercurrents of every interaction.

> A car didn't stop for me at the pedestrian crossing today, and I found myself thinking… 'is it because I'm brown?'
>
> My response – Right now I feel like the truth is that it may be, and how will I ever know for sure. How do I come to terms with this?
>
> (M. McCann, journal entry, 12th June 2020).

Resistance

Although Sela-Smith (2002) does not include this in her list of components of heuristic research, it is the basis of her critique of Moustakas's (1990) work and the ambivalence she finds in it between experience and observation; and of her subsequent critique of his earlier work on loneliness (Moustakas, 1961) and his shift from a focus on experience to that of the phenomenon (Sela-Smith, 2001) (see Chapters 1 and 3). It is central to her development of HSSI and hence our inclusion of this concept here. In her original doctoral research, she quotes Nietzsche (1992): 'All psychology so far has got stuck in moral prejudices and fears; it has not dared to descend into the depths... A proper physio-psychology has to contend with unconscious resistance in the heart of the investigator' (Sela-Smith, 2001, p. 22). The other reason for including it is the link to the field and discipline of psychotherapy, which, especially in its psychodynamic form, is interested in resistance (though see also Speierer, 1990).

My surrender into the relational and societal aspects of this question became a distraction (at times), which reflects the resistance that Sela-Smith (2002) describes to feeling unbearable pain which can lead us to 'shift the research from the self's experience of the experience, to focusing on the idea of the experience' (p. 52). She counsels overcoming this ambivalence by recognising and acknowledging one's own resistance...

> If I can find the external enemy I can engage, challenge, and sometimes attack but what it protects me from is recognising that there are two battlefields, and the other resides in myself.
>
> (M. McCann, journal entry, 3rd September 2020)

At times (as I perceived both society and the group to do), I used racism 'out there' as a convenient container to rally against, rather than attending to the discomfort of addressing aspects of my own racialisation. Fighting it 'out there' was perhaps an unconscious reprieve from confronting self-examination. As my journey progressed, I began to understand resistance as a vital aspect of this phenomenon. Even in the process of looking outward, I realised I was learning about (shadow) aspects of my own psyche (McCann, 2022).

Focusing

Douglass and Moustakas (1985) describe this as 'a process of identifying themes and assessing connected feelings... [through which] a "cognitive-bodily" imaginative variation gradually unfolds and moves to refinements of meaning and perception that register as internal shifts and alterations of behavior' (p. 51). In this they were influenced by Gendlin (1978) and his development of focusing as an internally oriented therapeutic practice. Originally trained in philosophy, Gendlin brought a deep understanding of experiencing to person-centred therapy and research (see Levin, 1997); and, together with Rogers, was another key figure in the development of humanistic psychology, from which Moustakas drew, and to the development of which he contributed. The phenomenological moment-to-moment embodied awareness involved in focusing was an essential tool in this self-exploration as I learned to trust in and follow what my feelings and physiology were communicating about my experience(s) from the different parts of myself.

Inward reach

Referring to the researcher's 'intense or passionate concern', Sela-Smith (2002, p. 69) writes about the necessity to 'reach inward for tacit awareness and knowledge' (p. 69). We like this image and sense of stretching for something that lies just beyond our immediate awareness and its focus on the exercising of that in order to gain greater insight. This also speaks to the discipline of the search for personal awareness and knowledge, for instance, through personal psychotherapy. I experienced this inward reach as spontaneous insight (see section on Illumination in Chapter 6) or, to continue the image of stretching, as a muscle released as a result of dwelling patiently at the painful edges of its capacity.

Indwelling

This refers to the heuristic process of 'turning inward to seek a deeper, more extended comprehension of the nature or meaning of a quality or theme of human experience' (Moustakas, 1990, p. 25). Every possible nuance, texture, fact, and meaning is drawn from dwelling inside the peripheral and central factors of the phenomenon: 'It follows clues wherever they appear, dwells inside them, and expands their meanings and associations until a fundamental insight is achieved' (Moustakas, 1990, p. 26). As with tacit knowing, Moustakas's ideas about this concept draw on Polanyi's work on the subject (Polanyi, 1962). Elsewhere, I (Keith) acknowledge the association between indwelling, home, and the sense and act of residing (Tudor, 2022). For me (Malik), indwelling was akin to staying with discomfort at the edges of the known, and being with the discomfort rather than reacting to it, which, in time, allowed new meanings and associations to arise.

Intuition

This refers to 'an internal capacity to make inferences and arrive at a knowledge of underlying structures or dynamics' (Moustakas, 1990, p. 24). Through intuition, a bridge is formed between the implicit knowledge inherent in the tacit and the explicit knowledge which is observable and describable: 'Intuition makes immediate knowledge possible without the intervening steps of logic and reasoning' (Moustakas, 1990, p. 24). Although Moustakas does not refer to him, in linking this to theory, and specifically, both empiricism and phenomenology, we acknowledge the early work of Eric Berne on the nature of intuition (conducted in the late 1940s) and his identification of particular underlying structures and dynamics (Berne, 1977). For me (Malik), intuition felt inherently linked to inward-reach and indwelling, and a sense of holding all the disparate parts together as they became known so that their links could be intuitively metabolised. According to Moustakas (1990), surrendering to one's inner wisdom is required to achieve integration, unity, and wholeness.

Tacit knowledge

Moustakas (Douglass & Moustakas, 1985; Moustakas, 1990) acknowledges the work of Polanyi (1964, 1966, 1969) on the tacit dimension of human knowing, and that this is deeply embedded in the self and not normally available to conscious awareness. Sela-Smith (2002) states that 'The tacit dimension of personal knowledge is that internal place where experience, feeling, and meaning join together to form both a picture of the world and a way to navigate that world' (p. 59). It is a continually growing, multi-level structural foundation on which all other knowledge stands, and, moreover, a dimension of knowledge which is under construction each time a new experience is introduced (Sela-Smith, 2002), a point that links this concept to constructionism and constructivist approaches to therapy (see Tudor & Summers, 2014). In his work on developmental psychological and interpersonal domains of relatedness, Stern (1985) describes an ongoing process by which 'if what is "out there" doesn't match "in here", new evaluations, thoughts, feelings and behaviours must be formed to make new wholes' (p. 260). Applying this to the interpersonal domain that is the researcher and their research provides a developmental and relational perspective on the necessary challenge of processing discoveries and creating something new.

Transformation

In her work developing HSSI, Sela-Smith (2002) makes a strong case for such research being transformative: 'a relentless inward focus can lead to greater self-understanding, self-transformation, and reconstruction of a hindering worldview' (p. 80). While this could be read as a description of psychotherapy, Sela-Smith is not advocating this as an end in itself – though she does consider it to be 'perhaps the dominant part of heuristics research' (p. 82) – but, rather as necessary to experience and 'in such a way that learning [from it] can be passed on to those who hear, read, or see it' (p. 82).

Reflections on methodology

All these processes are – and, in this case, I (Malik) felt they were – essential in order to make meaning of the experience of making, encountering, and challenging unintentional racial microaggressions. This framework allowed me to explore the dynamics of unconscious racialisation which are abstract and not suitable for purely positivistic interpretations. The deeply transformative reconstruction of tacit knowledge was very much my experience in this self-search journey. It was in the realisation of new tacit knowledge that the implicit aspects of my own racialisation were able to be transformed (see McCann & Tudor, 2024).

Having made links between concepts used in heuristic research and some of the theories and theorists from which they derive, in this section, we discuss the methodology of the research, with regard to axiology, ontology, and epistemology, again in the context of and with reference to the specific research on racial microaggressions. We do so also in the context that there are debates within and beyond heuristic research about its philosophical base, which Tudor (2023) summarises as represented by three strands or positions:

1. That heuristic research does not prescribe a methodology (e.g., Douglass & Moustakas, 1985) – a perspective which gives the researcher more freedom to draw on other methodologies as well as more responsibility to articulate them. With regard to the research presented in this chapter, we suggest that this encompasses critical race theory (Delgado & Stefancic, 2001; see also Solorzano et al., 2000), as well as indigenous thinking about research (Denzin et al., 2008; Tecun et al., 2018; Vaioleti, 2006), including decolonising methodologies (Smith, 2021).
2. That heuristic research is based on specific methodology and underlying philosophy – which is usually identified as phenomenology, though Douglass and Moustakas (1985)

argue that the emphasis in heuristics on discovery 'makes palpable a theoretical marriage of existential philosophy and perceptual psychology' (p. 42). This supports the current research with regard to both the experience of racial microaggressions, and the different reactions to and perceptions of the original incident, as well as the subsequent self-search of the second author.

3. That heuristics is both a methodology and a method – a perspective which means that, just as the person-centred approach to therapy represents a way of being (Rogers, 1980), so heuristics can be thought of and used as an approach to research. With regard to the research under discussion, we have represented this in the previous section of the chapter.

Axiology

The axiological aspect of this research concerns values and, specifically, how racism and racial microaggression exist in the social unconscious (McCann & Tudor, 2022), alongside a person's conscious egalitarian values.

While Aotearoa New Zealand is located in the global South, it is Western – and Northern – in its outlook. Similar to other colonised nations, it is Eurocentric, a worldview that explicitly and implicitly normalises European history, systems, values, and achievements as civilised and superior, and denigrates indigenous Māori and Pasifika values and knowledge, thereby justifying European domination. This is and creates a binary perspective which juxtaposes a 'white progressive civilised European identity' against a Black/Brown/Indigenous 'underdeveloped, uncivilised, barbaric "Other" in the colonies' (Ruddick, 2009, p. 217). Thus, as Ellis (2015) argues, for members of the dominant culture, racism becomes embedded as automatic attitudes and behaviours towards those who are viewed as 'minority' cultures, despite the conscious holding of liberal and non- or anti-racist beliefs and values – attitudes and behaviours which are internalised by those who are 'O/othered'. As a woman of mixed heritage, born and raised in Aotearoa New Zealand, my values, worldview, and the context of my life are inherently interwoven with the meaning I (Malik) make of my experience of unintentional racial microaggressions and their connection to unconscious racialisation.

The psychotherapy programme in which the incident that led to this research took place (described above) is a microcosm of this liberal society, with liberal values, but also with unresolved racial tensions. I felt confident that, as a group, we generally held conscious egalitarian values and were fortunate to have the space to consider racial dynamics and socio-cultural context within our training. Because of this I had hoped this was a space where we could have these challenging conversations about 'race'. However, the vignette illustrates the powerful unconscious resistance to exploring this dynamic even in the psychotherapy space where curiosity and internal exploration are benchmarks of the work, and highlights the depth of unconscious racial conditioning, even as we consciously make progress towards addressing racism in Aotearoa New Zealand.

The explicit inclusion of these axiological factors is necessary in order to capture the meaning the second author made of her experience in the course of the research, which was – and is – contextual and subjective, tangible and intangible.

Ontology

The ontological underpinning of the research is that people are cultural and relational beings, and that this essence is both contextual (in terms of how culture and race have been and are constructed), and experiential (in terms of how we experience this, subjectively). While identity categories can be experienced and used as a source of strength, they can also be regressive and restrictive (Layton, 2006). This includes essential views of the person, whether Pasifika or Palagi (non-Pasifika). Internalised negative beliefs, attitudes, and behaviours which exist outside conscious awareness form racist representations that become introjected and organised into a set of object relationships and form 'bad-cultural objects' (Davids, 2011).

For this particular topic, I considered it vital that I capture the essence of my subjectivity within the context of the society in which I live and the relational engagements in my life (including training), in order to elucidate the pervasive themes that lie within the obscure territory of unconscious racialisation.

Epistemology

As this refers to how we know what we know, epistemology encompasses knowledge systems, and, with regard to this research, the centrality of lived experience, and subjectivity.

In her research, Sela-Smith (2002) examines this with reference to Wilber's (1997) four quadrants of knowledge, which are created by the juxtaposition of two axes: one representing a continuum from individuality to collectivity, and the other, one from interiority to exteriority (see Figure 2.1). In her research Sela-Smith (2001, 2002) focuses on the upper left quadrant, i.e., the internal subjective experience of the '*I-who-feels*' (2002, p. 59), as well as what she refers to as the resistance in addressing the knowledge system represented by this quadrant. She argues that feeling is the door, and heuristic enquiry the key to the territory of the upper left quadrant as it is the feeling, reflective self, rather than the thinking-observing self who provides access to the tacit dimension of nonverbal thought.

We differ from Sela-Smith in that we view all the quadrants as equally important and especially so for dealing with a topic such as racism, which is so socially embedded, constructed, and experienced (see also Tudor, 2023). Indeed, in the course of the research reported here, I (Malik) observed and dialogued with these quadrants in my own exploration of the collective we (lower left) and them (lower right), and the objective you (upper right), before returning to the '*I-who-feels*' (Sela-Smith, 2002, p. 57) and my subjective internal response to these perspectives. In this, I found Wilber's (1997) integral philosophy and framework helped hold the 'reality' of my own perception while leaving space for other realities alongside it.

Sela-Smith (2002) does describe the cyclical nature of feeling responses to external experience, which create meaning which, in turn, influences our being in the world and organises our culture, worldview, and paradigms of reality. More recently, in her work on heuristic enquiry, Sultan (2019) offers the image of the labyrinth as a metaphor – and practice – for the journey inward and the journey outward, an image that Throne (2019) views as drawing a parallel between 'whereby the micro is the macro and the heuristic researcher returns again and again to the center of the labyrinth to better understand not only internal self but the external including others and society' (p. 13). This focus of discovery of both the inner and outer is pertinent in the study of unintentional racial microaggressions as a doorway into unconscious racialisation, precisely because of the interactive dynamics between societal, interpersonal, and intrapsychic domains of experience – and relatedness (Stern, 1985). It also speaks to the value of learning about the macrocosm by going deeply into the microcosm, and vice versa, and suggests that what is discovered in the deepest and most intimate details of one person's experience may contribute to understanding of the phenomena as a whole. As Rogers (1961/1967) famously puts it: '*What is most personal is most general*' (p. 26).

Individuality

	Interior – 'I' Intentional Subjective Involving thoughts, emotions, memories, states of mind, perceptions and immediate sensations Researched through heuristic self-search inquiry (Sela-Smith, 2002)	Exterior – you (it) Behavioural Objective Involving the material body (including the brain), and anything tangible in time and space Researched, for instance, through a range of literature reviews	
Interior view	Researched through heuristic enquiry involving co-participants (Moustakas, 1990) Involving shared values, relationships, language, meanings, and cultural identities Cultural Intersubjective Interior – 'we'	Researched through heuristic literature reviews (views and re-views), for example, through '*heuristic engagement*' or '*heuristic comparison*' (Hiles, 2001) Involving networks, including the natural environment; systems, including government; and technology Social Intersubjective Exterior – them (it)	Exterior view

Collectivity

FIGURE 2.1 The four quadrants of Wilber's (1997) knowledge systems applied to heuristic research enquiry (developed from McCann, 2022; Tudor, 2023).

Nevertheless, and notwithstanding an appreciation of the integral nature of life and the study of it, the research reported in this chapter is based on an epistemology, i.e., interpretivism, that values subjectivity and especially lived experience.

About the theory of heuristic research

We consider that this research project highlights the importance of accounting for both Moustakas's (1990) and Sela-Smith's (2002) contributions to heuristic methodology in terms of identified concepts. While we have ordered them here in a way that makes sense with regard to the heurism or discovery of this specific research, we caution other researchers against viewing or following this as an invariant sequence. Heuristics is fundamentally about discovery, and this includes the researcher's discovery about methodology, concepts, and method, as well as the conceptualisation and explication of the experience and/or phenomenology of the research.

Traditionally, heuristic research has emphasised the personal and the internal: the (personal) identification with the focus of enquiry, self-search, the inward gaze, and so on. However, following Tudor's (2023) argument that heuristics can contribute as much to an understanding of the 'we' as the 'I', we consider that this present work contributes to this expansion of heuristic research. As Crone and Huemer (2018) put it: 'It is now broadly accepted that central issues concerning self-consciousness should not be studied by taking into account the individual alone, but also by exploring the role of intersubjectivity and interaction with the social environment' (p. 2). In this sense, we hope that this study of unintentional racial microaggressions, which are so clearly about the interplay of society, the interpersonal, and the self, helps position heuristic research as a method that can discover and uncover the macro (society and the interpersonal) in relation to the micro (the personal and intrapersonal).

References

Berne, E. (1977). *Intuition and ego states* (P. McCormick, Ed.). TA Press.

Bridgman, P. (1950). *Reflections of a physicist*. Philosophical Library.

Buber, M. (1958). *I and thou*. Scribner.

Buber, M. (1961). *Tales of the Hasidim: The early masters* (O. Marx, Trans.). Schocken.

Buber, M. (1965). *The knowledge of man*. Harper & Row.

Cardo, G. (2024). *A heuristic enquiry of being 'Alaq', suspended in liminality as a convert to Islam* [Doctoral thesis, Middlesex University]. Middlesex University Research Repository. https://repository.mdx.ac.uk/item/1ww842

Cardo, G., & Tudor, K. (2024). A comparison between the concepts of heuristic enquiry and tazkiyat-un-nafs. *European Journal for Qualitative Research in Psychotherapy, 14*. www.ejqrp.org/index.php/ejqrp/article/view/298

Castillo, L. G. de. (2018). Unconscious racial prejudice as psychological resistance: A limitation of the implicit bias model. *Critical Philosophy of Race, 6*(2), 262–279. https://doi.org/10.5325/critphilrace.6.2.0262

Crone, K., & Huemer, W. (2018). Self-consciousness and intersubjectivity: Dimensions of the social self. *Phenomenology and the Cognitive Sciences, 17*(2), 225–229. https://doi.org/10.1007/s11097-017-9547-6

Dalal, F. (2002). *Race, colour and the processes of racialization: New perspectives from group analysis, psychoanalysis and sociology*. Brunner-Routledge.

Davids, M. F. (2011). *Internal racism: A psychoanalytic approach to race and difference*. Palgrave Macmillan.

Delgado, R., & Stefancic, J. (2001). *Critical race theory: An introduction*. New York University Press.

Denzin, N. K., Lincoln, Y. S., & Smith, L. T. (Eds.). (2008). *Handbook of critical and indigenous methodologies*. Sage.

Douglass, B. G., & Moustakas, C. (1985). Heuristic inquiry: The internal search to know. *Journal of Humanistic Psychology, 25*(3), 39–55. https://doi.org/10.1177/0022167885253004

Ellis, E. (2015). *Exploring the conscious and unconscious processes of internalised racism in the therapeutic relationship: A thematic analysis* [Master's dissertation, Auckland University of Technology]. Tuwhera Open Access Theses & Dissertations. http://hdl.handle.net/10292/9832

Gendlin, E. (1978). *Focusing*. Bantam House.

Haenga-Collins, M., & Tudor, K. (2021). Racism in New Zealand. *The Journal of Critical Psychology, Counselling and Psychotherapy, 21*(4), 40–58. www.egalitarianpublishing.com/jcpcp.html

Hiles, D. R. (2001, October). *Heuristic inquiry and transpersonal research* [Paper presentation]. Centre for Counselling and Psychotherapy Education Conference, London, UK. www.psy.dmu.ac.uk/drhiles/HIpaper.htm

Huffman, T., & Tracy, S. J. (2018). Making claims that matter: Heuristics for theoretical and social impact in qualitative research. *Qualitative Inquiry, 24*(8), 558–570. https://doi.org/10.1177/1077800417742411

Ings, W., & Tudor, K. (2025). *Heuristic enquiries: Research across disciplines and professions*. Routledge.
Jourard, S. (1968). *Disclosing man to himself*. Van Nostrand.
Jourard, S. (1971). *Self-disclosure: An experimental analysis of the transparent self*. Wiley-Interscience.
Layton, L. (2006). Racial identities, racial enactments, and normative unconscious processes. *The Psychoanalytic Quarterly*, *75*(1), 237–269. https://doi.org/10.1002/j.2167-4086.2006.tb00039.x
Levin, D. M. (Ed.). (1997). *Language beyond postmodernism: Saying and thinking in Gendlin's philosophy*. Northwestern University Press.
Maslow, A. (1956). Self-actualizing people: A study of psychological health. In C. Moustakas (Ed.), *The self* (pp. 160–194). Harper & Brothers.
Maslow, A. (1966). *The psychology of science*. Harper & Row.
Maslow, A. (1971). *The farther reaches of human nature*. Viking.
McCann, M. (2022). *Invisible wounds: A heuristic exploration of unintentional racial microaggressions and their relationship to unconscious racialisation* [Master's dissertation, Auckland University of Technology]. Tuwhera Open Access Theses & Dissertations. http://hdl.handle.net/10292/15067
McCann, M., & Tudor, K. (2022). Unintentional racial microaggressions and the social unconscious. *International Journal of Applied Psychoanalytic Studies*, *19*(2), 202–216. https://doi.org/10.1002/aps.1753
McCann, M., & Tudor, K. (2024). The enigma of unintentional racial microaggressions: Implications for the profession of psychotherapy. *Ata: Journal of Psychotherapy Aotearoa New Zealand*, *27*(1), 31–56. https://doi.org/10.24135/ajpanz.2024.03
Moustakas, C. (1961). *Loneliness*. Prentice-Hall.
Moustakas, C. (1967). Heuristic research. In J. Bugental (Ed.), *Challenges in humanistic psychology* (pp. 100–107). McGraw-Hill.
Moustakas, C. (1990). *Heuristic research: Design, methodology, and applications*. Sage.
Moustakas, C. (1994). *Phenomenological research methods*. Sage.
Moustakas, C. (2000). Heuristic research revisited. In K. J. Schneider, J. F. T. Bugental, & J. F. Pierson (Eds.), *The handbook of humanistic psychology: Leading edges in theory, research, and practice* (pp. 263–274). Sage.
Nietzsche, F. (1992). Beyond good and evil. In F. Nietzsche, *Basic writings of Nietzsche* (W. Kaufmann, Trans. & Ed.). Modern Library.
Ozertugrul, E. (2017). Heuristic self-search inquiry into one experience of obsessive–compulsive disorder. *Journal of Humanistic Psychology*, *57*(3), 215–236. https://doi.org/10.1177/0022167815592503
Polanyi, M. (1962). *Personal knowledge: Towards a post-critical philosophy*. Routledge.
Polanyi, M. (1964). *Science, faith and society*. University of Chicago Press.
Polanyi, M. (1966). *The tacit dimension*. Doubleday.
Polanyi, M. (1969). *Knowing and being* (M. Green, Ed.). University of Chicago Press.
Pomare, P., Ioane, J., & Tudor, K. (2021). Racism in New Zealand psychology, or is Western psychology a good thing? In C. Newnes (Ed.), *Racism in psychology: Challenging theory, practice and institutions* (pp. 110–130). Routledge.
Rogers, C. R. (1951). *Client-centered therapy*. Constable.
Rogers, C. R. (1959). A theory of therapy, personality and interpersonal relationships, as developed in the client-centered framework. In S. Koch (Ed.), *Psychology: A study of science, Vol. 3: Formulation of the person and the social context* (pp. 184–256). McGraw-Hill.
Rogers, C. R. (1963). Toward a science of the person. *Journal of Humanistic Psychology*, *3*(2), 72–92. https://doi.org/10.1177/002216786300300208
Rogers, C. R. (1967). *On becoming a person: A therapist's view of psychotherapy*. Constable. (Original work published 1961)
Rogers, C. R. (1969). *Freedom to learn: A view of what education might become*. C. E. Merrill.
Rogers, C. R. (1980). *A way of being*. Houghton Mifflin.
Rogers, C. R. (1985). Toward a more human science of the person. *Journal of Humanistic Psychology*, *25*(4), 7–24. https://doi.org/10.1177/0022167885254002

Ruddick, S. M. (2009). Society–space. In R. Kitchin & N. Thrift (Eds.), *International encyclopedia of human geography* (pp. 217–226). Elsevier Science.

Sela-Smith, S. (2001). *Heuristic self-search inquiry: Clarification of Moustakas' heuristic research* [Doctoral dissertation, Saybrook Graduate School and Research Center]. ProQuest Dissertations & Theses.

Sela-Smith, S. (2002). Heuristic research: A review and critique of Moustakas's method. *Journal of Humanistic Psychology*, *42*(3), 53–88. https://doi.org/10.1177/0022167802423004

Smith, L. T. (2021). *Decolonizing methodologies: Research and indigenous peoples.* Zed Books.

Solorzano, D., Ceja, M., & Yosso, T. (2000). Critical race theory, racial microaggressions, and campus racial climate: The experiences of African American college students. *Journal of Negro Education*, *69*(1–2), 60–73.

Speierer, G. W. (1990). Toward a specific illness concept of client-centered psychotherapy. In G. Lietaer, J. Rombauts, & R. van Balen (Eds.), *Client-centered and experiential psychotherapy in the nineties* (pp. 337–359). Leuven University Press.

Stern, D. N. (1985). *The interpersonal world of the infant: A view from psychoanalysis and developmental psychology*. Basic Books.

Sue, D. W. (2013). Race talk: The psychology of racial dialogues. *American Psychologist*, *68*(8), 663–672. https://doi.org/10.1037/a0033681

Sultan, N. (2019). *Heuristic inquiry: Researching human experience holistically.* Sage. www.doi.org/10.4135/9781071802632

Tecun (Daniel Hernandez), A., Hafoka, 'Inoke, 'Ulu'ave, L., & 'Ulu'ave-Hafoka, M. (2018). Talanoa: Tongan epistemology and Indigenous research method. *AlterNative: An International Journal of Indigenous Peoples*, *14*(2), 156–163. https://doi.org/10.1177/1177180118767436

Throne, R. (2019). *Autoethnography and heuristic inquiry for doctoral-level researchers: Emerging research and opportunities*. Information Science Reference.

Tudor, K. (2010). *The fight for health: A heuristic enquiry into psychological well-being* [Unpublished context statement]. PhD in Mental Health Promotion by Public (Published) Works. School of Health and Social Sciences, Middlesex University, London, UK.

Tudor, K. (2017). The fight for health: An heuristic enquiry (2010). In K. Tudor, *Conscience and critic: The selected works of Keith Tudor* (pp. 143–168). Routledge.

Tudor, K. (2022). Supporting critical self-enquiry: Doing heuristic research. In S. Bager-Charleson & A. McBeath (Eds.), *Supporting research in counselling and psychotherapy* (pp. 57–79). Springer.

Tudor, K. (2023). Critical heuristics: From 'I who feels' to 'We who care – and act'. In K. Tudor & J. Wyatt, (Eds.), *Qualitative research approaches for psychotherapy: Reflexivity, methodology, and criticality* (pp. 115–132). Routledge.

Tudor, K. (2025). S is for settler: A psychosocial perspective on belonging and unbelonging in Aotearoa New Zealand. In B. Lythberg, C. Woods, & S. Nemec (Eds.), *Settler responsibility for decolonisation: Stories from the field* (pp. 144–162). Routledge.

Tudor, K., & Summers, G. (2014). *Co-creative transactional analysis: Papers, responses, dialogues, and developments*. Karnac Books.

Vaioleti, T. M. (2006). Talanoa research methodology: A developing position on pacific research. *Waikato Journal of Education*, *12*, 21–34. https://hdl.handle.net/10289/6199

Watford, M. L. (2008). Bereavement of spousal suicide: A reflective self-exploration. *Qualitative Inquiry*, *14*(3), 335–359. https://doi.org/10.1177/1077800407309325

Wilber, K. (1997). *The eye of spirit*. Shambala.

3

RESISTANCE AND SURRENDER

Explication and synthesis from a heuristic enquiry into conversion to Islam

Keith Tudor and Georgina Cardo

This chapter examines the concepts of resistance and surrender in the context of heuristic research. Based on Sela-Smith's (2001, 2002) contribution to the heuristic literature, this chapter discusses both resistance and the importance of surrender(ing) to the feelings in an experience in the context of research. These discussions are illustrated from the second author's doctoral thesis, supervised by the first author, whose enquiry was into the lived experience of being 'Alaq', or suspended in liminality, as a convert to Islam. The chapter discusses a number of ways in which the second author experienced resistance during her research journey – and surrendered to it; the origin of those resistances, some of which were external; and concludes with further reflections on the nature of resistance and surrender and the significance of Sela-Smith's critique of Moustakas's (1990) method and methodology.

As heuristic research is predominantly emic, that is, looking at the internal elements of the subject of enquiry and how they function, and is, therefore, personal, we use and retain from the original thesis Georgina's own voice, thus 'I', 'me', and 'my'. Moreover, as heuristic supervision is also personal (see Merry, 2004; Tudor & Ings, 2025), and as Keith has his own experiences of resistance in heuristic enquiry and supervision his voice also appears in the first person, the distinction between which is either named or clear from the context. Any use of the first-person plural 'we' represents our joint voice and views.

The chapter firstly discusses ideas about resistance in the early literature on heuristic research. This is followed by the first part of what we refer to as a case study of Georgina's experience of resistance in her heuristic research enquiry. In the second half of the chapter, we echo this structure with regard to surrender: firstly, discussing the concept of surrender, especially in Sela-Smith's (2002) work, and, secondly, illustrating this with examples of Georgina's experience.

Resistance in heuristic research

In the introduction to her major contribution to the methodology of heuristic enquiry, Sela-Smith (2002) acknowledges Moustakas's 'significant contribution to research in psychology by describing the heuristic research method' (p. 53). She links this contribution – Moustakas (1967, 1990), and Douglass and Moustakas (1985) – as a way of enquiring into what Polanyi

DOI: 10.4324/9781003685944-5

(1983) refers to as tacit knowledge, and into what, in his four quadrants of knowledge systems (see Chapter 2), Wilber (1997) identifies as the upper left quadrant, that is the interior 'I', the intentional, and the subjective. However, she then critiques Moustakas for, as she views it, the shift in the focus of his research 'from the self's *experience* of the experience to focusing on *the idea* of the experience' (p. 53, our emphasis).

Sela-Smith's (2001, 2002) critique is based on her analysis of Moustakas's (1990) book *Heuristic Research: Design, Methodology, and Applications*, in which she considers that the first two chapters represent 'the path of surrender to an internal question that flows from the internal experience of the *I-who-feels*' (Sela-Smith, 2002, p. 75) and 'the language of internal focus, the "I", feeling in the present and alive in the moment, even when the present "I" is remembering a painful past, for it is the feeling that connects the past to the present' (p. 79) – what Sela-Smith refers to as heuristic self-search inquiry (HSSI). However, for Sela-Smith, the third and fourth chapters of Moustakas's (1990) book move away from self-search to focus on 'the phenomena of the objective, observed experience, not the self who feels' (p. 75), the language of which is '"reporting" oriented… a third-person abstraction of the experiencing "I"… an external language, even though it may be the individual doing a self-report' (p. 79). Sela-Smith explains this shift by suggesting that Moustakas, whose original enquiry was into his own feelings of loneliness (Moustakas, 1961, 1975), became resistant to experiencing the unbearable pain of this loneliness and, in effect, shifted from focusing on experiencing to focusing on phenomena and making meaning.

Interestingly, Douglass and Moustakas (1985) draw a distinction between heuristics and phenomenology thus:

> Whereas phenomenology encourages a kind of detachment from the phenomenon being investigated, heuristics emphasizes connectedness and relationship… phenomenology loses the persons in the process of descriptive analysis, in heuristics the research participants remain visible… Phenomenology ends with the essence of experience; heuristics retains the essence of the person *in* experience.
>
> (p. 43, our emphasis)

I (Keith) experienced this in my own doctoral work on positive mental health and its promotion, in a thesis I titled *The Fight for Health* (Tudor, 2010). In my doctoral viva (oral) examination, I was confronted with the view that, in articulating the ways in which I/we (good, right-minded people) could – and had to – fight for the concept of positive mental health/wellbeing, eudaemonia (from Aristotelian philosophy [see Ryan & Deci, 2001]), salutogenesis (Antonovsky, 1987), etc., against the medical establishment and health authorities, I had discounted the significance of my own experience of this fight. Reflecting on this later (Tudor, 2010), I remembered that one of my examiners had noted

> that 'the early trauma of the rejection of his [Tudor's] work in the early 1990s and his subsequent tendency to polarize is not addressed in the text although became apparent as a key issue in the course of the oral examination'. I realised, both during the viva and with the benefit of further indwelling, how much I had forgotten the hurt of this rejection… and had not dwelt on the connection between that and my subsequent fights with regard to this material. Interestingly, the process of rewriting [the context] statement [for the PhD] twice has, to some extent, paralleled this trauma and the fight. Indeed, in his second set of

> comments [the examiner] speculated whether we [the examiners and I] were getting into a fight over the context statement.
>
> (p. 150)

In terms of Wilber's four quadrants, in my initial research – and fight – I had favoured the lower right quadrant of the exterior (them, it), the interobjective, and the social, rather than, as Sela-Smith (2002) puts it, 'the *I-who-feels*' (p. 57).

Of course, there's nothing wrong with focusing on the other and the social; indeed, elsewhere, I have offered a critical reflection on heuristics as a research method and methodology in psychotherapy, including addressing the criticism that heuristics can be too self-referential and, in effect, too focused on the I-who-feels (Tudor, 2023) and, in response, proposed a movement from 'I who feels to we-who-care – and act' (p. 115). Nonetheless, Sela-Smith's critique of Moustakas invites heuristic researchers to think (and act) deeply about and with regard to their research and to find and maintain a philosophical congruence with regard to all aspects of their research project, including:

- Their method and methodology (see Douglass & Moustakas, 1985; Tudor, 2023).
- Their use of language (see Sela-Smith, 2002; Tudor, 2023).
- Their approach to the literature – view and re-view (see Tudor, 2022).
- Whether they involve participants or, more accurately, co-researchers – or not (see Moustakas, 1990; Sela-Smith, 2002; Sultan, 2019; Tudor, 2022).
- How they address questions of validity or verification, generalisability, and dissemination (Douglass & Moustakas, 1985; Moustakas, 1990; Sela-Smith, 2002; Tudor, 2010/2017).
- How they realise the research (see Douglass & Moustakas, 1985).

We note that one of the problems with heuristic research is that some researchers claim to be heuristic when they are clearly not – for instance, in her heuristic inquiry exploring resistance to spiritual emergence, Michelle (2017) only cites Moustakas (1990) minimally (and only with regard to method), doesn't cite Sela-Smith at all, and doesn't discuss resistance or surrender with regard to the research process. Similarly, Sultan (2019), in her book on *Heuristic Inquiry*, while bemoaning the fact that 'the heuristic approach has been essentially "lost" due to lack of precision and detailed description of the underlying processes' (p. 80), doesn't discuss self-search or HSSI, or refer at all to Sela-Smith. A second problem is that some supervisors and institutions claim to support heuristic research but, in practice, do not; as we elaborate in the case study below, some of Georgina's 'resistance' was, in fact, the resistance of others to the implications and applications of heuristic research.

A case study of resistance and surrender – Part I: Resistance

In undertaking a heuristic research enquiry into her conversion to Islam and in reflecting on her process, especially at the stage of writing it up, we (both) identified a number of resistances, which we describe and then link to heuristic methodology and method.

Resistance to isolation as a researcher

The first resistance chronologically (though it only emerged later) was a resistance due to a sense of isolation. As both a researcher and as a convert to Islam researching conversion,

I (Georgina) experienced a sense of resistance and isolation: a threat to my Muslim identity or personhood, and a felt sense of sickness in the positivist, empirical research paradigm which, to me, felt devoid of soul, which, given the subject of the research, was not only ironic, but was also personal as it then felt like a struggle to be seen, to be me, and/or to become.

Fortunately, at some point in the research, I came across a study on the mental health of doctoral researchers (Hazell et al., 2020), which suggests that a substantial minority of doctoral researchers, in particular female students and candidates employing qualitative research methodology, have reported experiences of depression and anxiety during their studies. In a systematic review of 52 studies of the mental health of doctoral students, Hazell et al. (2020) used a meta-synthesis to categorise qualitative themes such as: (1) always feeling alone in the struggle; (2) feeling a death of personhood; (3) feeling that the system is sick; and (4) seeing, being, and becoming. The study thematises 'the PhD as a process of transcendence' (p. 22), reflecting how the struggles involved in completing a PhD can be transformative and self-actualising.

These are all themes that I experienced, especially during an initial incubation, where tacit dimensions of my experience began 'to be seen and heard' through journal reflections and poetry, expressing this inner conflict:

> Why am I so scared to look within?
> I may be silent, but what is this within?
> A painful current pushes faith with what some call sin,
> 'But is it a sin?' says a voice within
> Live life as the former, be done tiresome reformer,
> An internal dogma binds me before I begin.
> Who writes the rules? Who interprets the way?
> Shackled by two cultures, can I not have my say?
> So silent I float, my soul held by my throat, guarding my feelings within.
>
> (Cardo, 2024, p. 125)

The poem, scribed in my research journal, felt like an expression of intuitive feelings and thoughts during a phase of incubation, which connects with Hazell et al.'s (2020) themes of loneliness (theme 1) and loss of personhood (theme 2) which can be seen when I question myself; 'what is this within?' (line 2 in the poem); sickness in the system (theme 3); 'Who writes the rules, who interprets the way?' (line 7); and overall the poem expresses my struggle to feel seen (theme 4), in particular as a convert, but also parallel to being and becoming (theme 4) through the heuristic research process: 'Why am I so scared to look within?' (line 1).

In terms of methodology, this first resistance may be seen as one to self-experience, which, drawing on the work of Stern (1985), Sela-Smith (2002) identifies as a component of HSSI, and to self-disclosure. In terms of method, it may be seen as a certain resistance to incubation which, as Sela-Smith (2002) argues, requires a certain retreat from the intense, concentrated focus on the question.

Resistance to the research topic

The second resistance was to my research topic as I navigated the heuristic enquiry process of *focus of inquiry* (Moustakas, 1990). The focus of inquiry concept or process aligns with the initial engagement phase, where the researcher identifies their topic of study, often emerging from a deeply personal connection or question.

Early in the research journey, what initially called out to me was still unclear, although I recall knowing instinctively that I did not want to focus the inquiry on my reasons for conversion or specific stuckness in practices of Islam or adoption of its guidance, such as wearing the hijab/ khimar (terms used to refer to the traditional Muslim head covering). Nonetheless, within the liminality of my conversion, my stuckness and the consequent questioning triggered my internal resistance, similar to that I noticed in the literature on converts to Islam. For me, resistance means that I feel under attack, misunderstood, judged, and rejected: emotions that cause me to withdraw myself and in this case from the research focus.

As part of my focus of inquiry, I employed a self-dialoguing method recommended by Sultan (2019), based on the Gestalt technique of two-chair work. In the exercise, the client, or in this case the researcher, dialogues with aspects of themselves by physically moving between two chairs, which represent two different parts or aspects of the person. By talking from each chair to the other (part), I noted what thoughts and feelings came to mind in relation to my enquiry and, specifically, the topic. As Sela-Smith (2002) puts it: 'To participate in… heuristic self-inquiry, the researcher must experience self-dialogue' (p. 63). For me, this exercise was a form of self-enquiry which facilitates a discovery of the tacit dimension and what Moustakas (1990) describes as 'the deepest currents of meanings and knowledge which take place within the individual through one's senses, perception, beliefs, and judgements' (p. 17).

> Self-dialogue – Two-chair exercise
> I sit in one chair, with a second chair placed opposite, and begin by asking myself:
>
> > 'How am I feeling about this research on conversion liminality?'
>
> I then move to the second chair and find myself responding with the following thoughts (which I recorded in my research journal):
>
> > 'I carry this heavy concern, it has travelled with me now for a long time and now, it appears angry, also a bit sad, I feel I'm stuck in the middle creating more confusion and doubt. It is like I am in contained space but the walls around me are like paper'.
>
> I move back to the other chair, noticing my emerging feelings of frustration that compel me to direct a question towards the other chair:
>
> > 'Why am I here? … to find reassurance?' 'Will I always have to be here?'
>
> I sit for a while longer, noticing my frustrations turn to tears. I carry this heavy concern; it has travelled with me for a long time. I reflect for a few moments more wondering how I had ended up in a research study in which I feel so resistant and angry and then wrote in my journal:
>
> > 'What do I need to do to get out of this liminality?'
>
> I stand up, intending to end this two-chair exercise, when a final intuitive thought came to me:
>
> > 'Believe and trust in the process'.
>
> (Cardo, 2024, pp. 73–74)

Following the two-chair exercise, I again employed my research journal and made some notes:

> The literature on converts to Islam says they often feel anxious in their liminal state [Haddad, 1991], a state often reported by my convert clients and an experience which led me to

> psychotherapy. Should I then consider employing case study research with convert clients in psychotherapy? This feels more personally meaningful. Or what about if I interview other converts, converts to Islam who are also psychotherapists?
>
> (Cardo, 2024, p. 74)

Reflecting on this in terms of heuristic methodology, Georgina's decision to interview other converts could be interpreted as a resistance to unbearable pain about her own stuckness. In her critique of Moustakas's heuristics, Sela-Smith (2002) is very clear that 'the inclusion of co-participants seems to create a distraction from the internal process' (p. 71), and that such inclusion inevitably shifts the focus from the researcher's experience to 'the *meaning of the experience* being studied' (p. 77). Thus, heuristic researchers need to be mindful of and intentional about why they engage co-participants (see Sela-Smith, 2002; Tudor, 2022).

Resistance to the methodology

Another aspect of Georgina's research was that, at the beginning of the research and before the confirmation of her candidature, she was being encouraged to conduct interviews as part of what was considered to be sound and useful research. As Georgina herself puts it:

> An example of my resistance due to this fear can be seen where I employ co-researchers, trying to 'please others' by conducting interviews (in this case within the positivist research paradigm) rather than getting on with the self-directed, often disorienting, and unpredictable self-search for which heuristic enquiry is known (Throne, 2019).
>
> (Cardo, 2024, p. 123)

At that time, Georgina was not familiar with heuristic research and I (Keith) was brought in to supervise her doctoral research work. However, I suggest that the privileging of interviews (a particular form of data collection) without sufficient grounding in or justification in terms of a specific methodology represents an institutional ignorance of and/or a resistance to methodology. Unfortunately, I see this all too often in heuristic – or so-called heuristic – work which uses (and often follows) Moustakas's (1990) method (stages and phases of heuristic enquiry), without any reference to or articulation of any methodology, heuristic or otherwise, for examples of which, see Shantall (1999), Stuckey (2001), Atkins and Loewenthal (2004), Kumar (2017), and Michelle (2017).

Resistance to incubation

Having immersed myself in the co-researchers' experiences and my responses to those experiences, I (Georgina) was ready to incubate with the data I had gathered to date, a process Moustakas (1990) defines as when 'the researcher retreats from the intense, concentrated focus on the question' (p. 28). Detaching myself from concentration on the research question was challenging. I felt uncertain about where I was heading after the interviews and unsure of what to illuminate. I began to doubt my use of research methods such as the interviews and wondered if I was on the right track or if I had diverted off course towards more of an interpretive phenomenological approach to others' interpretations of the experience being experienced rather than my own. I pondered for a while on where this diversion was taking me. However, according to Moustakas (1990), preoccupation with something else also 'enables the inner tacit dimension of the experience to reach its full possibilities' (p. 28), and so my diversion was not in vain or without benefit.

However, my first attempt to incubate with the research data was filled with restrictions: my daughter was diagnosed with a debilitating illness; its impact on our family and the restrictions that came with the global pandemic of COVID-19 made for a traumatic year. Due to the traumatic nature of what we faced, my own needs and the research were far from my mind.

Kumar and Cavallaro (2018) highlight four emotional demands that heuristic researchers can face: (1) researching sensitive issues; (2) researching prior life trauma; (3) experiencing traumatic life events during research; and (4) having unexpected events arise during the study of sensitive areas of research. During this phase of incubation, I realised that I experienced all four, thus:

1. The research on converts to Islam is a sensitive issue due to the internal and external conflict converts encounter in adopting Islam in contexts in which we are often judged through a lens of war and terror (Bartoszewicz, 2013; Galonnier, 2018).
2. The research is a susceptible topic of study for me as it related to much of my conflict while converting to Islam, including reminding me of many prior traumatic experiences.
3. The unexpected and unprecedented event of the 2019–2020 global pandemic of COVID-19 during my research.
4. The experience of a traumatic life event during the incubation phase when my eldest daughter became seriously ill.

In experiencing all four of these emotional demands, it was no wonder that my resistance increased, and that I felt emotionally and physically stuck. I needed some more time and space to reflect on and attend to my emotional overwhelm before moving to indwell and focus on what Moustakas (1990) describes as 'nuances, textures, and constituents of the phenomenon' (p. 31).

Reflecting on having time for both resistance and surrender, we are reminded of Moustakas's (1990) emphasis that heuristic inquiry is an extremely demanding process, involving disciplined self-commitment and rigorous self-searching, which does not suit a fixed timeframe for research. Sela-Smith (2002) also underscores the importance of allowing sufficient time for the internal processes that facilitate profound understanding. She highlights that heuristic inquiry requires immersing oneself in uncertainty, dwelling in the research question, and accessing tacit knowledge, all of which necessitate a temporal commitment to fully engage with the phenomenon under study. In heuristic research, time is not merely a procedural element but, rather, a catalyst that enables the unfolding of deep insights and understanding (see Cousins et al., 2025). Rushing through the stages of heuristic enquiry can hinder the natural progression of self-discovery and the emergence of meaningful connections. Allowing adequate time for incubation and reflection is essential to honour the integrity of the heuristic process and to achieve authentic and transformative outcomes (see also Chapter 4).

Resistance to surrender

After what turned out to be a year-long initial phase of incubation had passed, along with the COVID-19 pandemic, and at the point that my daughter's illness was under control, I was able to resume my research, but still felt this sense of resistance to reaching inwardly and enquiring about my experience of liminality as a convert to Islam. Instead, at this point, I focused on how the emotional demands of the research illuminated my resistance (as noted above, p. 45–46).

This focusing was also intended to reach and understand the subsidiary level of knowing, which Polanyi (1969) describes as the below-surface knowledge that underpins our explicit understanding. Subsidiary knowing refers to the implicit or tacit knowledge that supports and informs what we are consciously aware of, while focal knowing pertains to the explicit, surface-level understanding – what is visually apparent or distinguishable in an experience.

What I did know and was certain of is that my sense of resistance had now manifested as back and sciatic nerve pain. This physical manifestation of resistance inhibited my ability to walk or sit for extended periods. I sought medical advice for my pain, and a subsequent MRI scan indicated a herniated spinal disc. Now wholly immersed in my own emotional and physical resistance, I began to indwell on this extraordinary co-incidence – or God-incidence – and pondered on the connections between my pain, and the emotional demands I was experiencing in my research.

In heuristic inquiry, indwelling is a central concept (Moustakas, 1990). It refers to the process of deep reflection, internal search, and prolonged engagement with a question, experience, or phenomenon. Indwelling is a way of turning inward, allowing meanings to emerge organically rather than being imposed externally. I considered my back pain as subsidiary knowledge of a deeper inner emotional pain in response to the stress of holding it all together during my research. My resistance also felt protective: a response to help ward off conflict, criticism, and potential rejection of expressing my lived experiences of being a convert to Islam as well as forcing me into a period or respite as I was now in pain which required rest and rehabilitation.

This point about indwelling reminds us of the importance of the process of surrender, of giving up or letting go of resistance. Having discussed the ways in which the second author experienced resistance during her doctoral research, and how we think about this in terms of heuristic methodology and method, we now turn our attention to the explication of surrender in heuristic research, followed by part two of the case study.

Surrender in heuristic research

> Heuristic self-search inquiry is a psychological process wherein the researcher surrenders to the feeling in an experience and does not know what will be learned at the time the inquiry is begun.
>
> (Sela-Smith, 2002, p. 83)

Based on her own critique of Moustakas's work, Sela-Smith (2002) emphasises surrender as a component of HSSI, gauging this by her evaluation that: 'The research indicates surrender to the question has taken place' (p. 69), a process she describes as 'living, waking, sleeping, and dreaming the question… [and like] jumping into the river, a leap into the darkness' (pp. 69–70). Indeed, as both noted and implied above (p. **xx [internal reference]**), it was the absence of surrender in heuristic research that led to Sela-Smith's original critique. Reporting on her review of 28 research documents whose authors claimed to have followed Moustakas's (1990) method, Sela-Smith (2002) found that: 'Most inquiries presented no evidence of the type of free-fall surrender to the process that was described as a jumping into the river, a leap into the darkness. The majority did not report personal, subjective experience' (p. 70). Having studied Moustakas's work as well as these other research documents, Sela-Smith concludes that there are a number of components intrinsic to heuristic enquiry, and specifically her HSSI, one of which is surrender, that is, that 'the research indicates surrender to the question has taken place (living, waking, sleeping, and dreaming the question)' (p. 69).

Although Moustakas (1990) doesn't refer to the concept or practice of surrender, Sela-Smith (2002) states that 'the Moustakas method of heuristics invites the conscious, investigating self to surrender to the feelings in an experience, which carries the researcher to unknown aspects of self and the internal organizational systems not normally known in waking state consciousness' (p. 59). Later, when commenting on Moustakas's (1990) work and, specifically, the application of his method with regard to the phases of enquiry, Sela-Smith actually states that 'Moustakas emphasizes the need to surrender to them, not to formalize them and mechanically follow them' (p. 77). Both these statements from Sela-Smith (2002) may explain why some heuristic researchers think that Moustakas discusses surrender, for example Kumar (2017).

In her presentation of her HSSI, Sela-Smith (2002) refers to surrender, some aspects of which we summarise here and others we apply to the case study in the next part of the chapter.

- In introducing her emphasis on what she refers to as the last or final frontier of research, that is on 'the interiority of our experience' (p. 54), Sela-Smith (2002) argues that this 'requires setting aside the skills of controlled, objective observation and surrendering to embracing subjective experience and leaping into the unknown' (p. 54). Later she refers to the importance of 'surrender[ing] to the feelings of the experiencing "I"' (p. 55).
- One of the sections in her article is headed 'Surrender to the Six Phases of Experience' (p. 63). She clearly states that, 'if any one of these phases is not completed with full integrity, heuristic research is not successfully accomplished' (p. 63). At the same time, she notes that 'although the phases must be completed, the completion of the phases cannot be the focus' (p. 63). This is particularly important in challenging both researchers and their supervisors to recognise that Moustakas's heuristic phases are neither sequential nor invariant. Indeed, I (Keith) have said to some of my students: 'If you're following Moustakas's stages, you're not following Moustakas – or, more importantly, your own process'. This is not to say that Moustakas's heuristic method is not important or useful; but it is to acknowledge:

  a. that they were what Moustakas discovered in reflecting on his own heuristic self-search;
  b. that they are not meant to be followed; and
  c. that each heuristic researcher needs to revisit them in relation to their own research (see, for example, Tudor, 2010/2017, 2022).

  Within this section of her work, Sela-Smith (2002) writes about surrender with regard to different phases, thus:

  - With regard to the initial engagement, the importance of surrendering to the call of this phase.
  - With regard to immersion, that it:

    > requires the whole self to be engaged in the focus of the research by surrendering to it in such a way that the research unfolds, rather than an observing self attempting to control and direct the process to ensure that it moves in the right direction.
    >
    > (p. 56)

    - That some researchers may resist this phase for fear of losing focus, detaching, walking away from the question, or not completing. Nevertheless, Sela-Smith notes that it is precisely 'the surrender to this process that allows this [incubation] to happen' (p. 67).
- Elsewhere in the article Sela-Smith (2002) recommends 'surrender to the listening' (p. 64), though it is not clear whether this is to oneself or others, so, we consider that it applies to both, i.e., oneself, supervisors, any co-researchers, colleagues, loved ones, etc.; and suggests that 'without surrender to one's nonprojected feelings, the tacit level will not be reached and brought into consciousness' (p. 81).
- The importance of surrender to the validity of heuristic research, arguing that:

> the validity of the research is established by surrendering to the process that is pushing itself into the consciousness of the researcher, allowing the process to unfold and then noticing results in expansion of self-awareness, deepening of self-understanding, and of self-transformation that others can experience in the 'story'.
>
> (p. 79)

- Finally, she links resistance and surrender:

> Resistance on the part of the researcher-as-participant to surrender to the I-who-feels results in research that does not access the Upper Left quadrant, which is needed if there is to be an integration of all of the knowledge regarding what it is to be human.
>
> (p. 85)

Having reviewed the concepts of resistance and surrender in heuristic research and especially through the work of Sela-Smith (2001, 2002), we now illustrate them from Georgina's research process, which, here, we frame as a case study of resistance and surrender.

A case study of resistance and surrender – Part II: Resolving resistance through surrender

My trust in the self-enquiry aspect of heuristic research deepened as I connected with my lived experiences during a phase of incubation. Though the pandemic, illness, and back pain forced me to step back from the research, this period of incubation, which included self-care, allowed me to acknowledge my own needs and re-immerse with my felt sense – *I-who-feels*.

This phase of immersion in self-enquiry coincided with the Islamic month of Ramadan, which requires discipline (or striving), self-examination, and surrender, highlighting parallels between heuristic enquiry and *tazkiyat-un-nafs* (purification of the self). Ramadan, the ninth month of the Islamic calendar, marks the revelation of the Qur'an to the Prophet Muhammad, beginning with the verses of *Surah Alaq* (96). During this time, Muslims who are able observe fasting from dawn until dusk, abstaining from food, water, sexual activity, and entertainment as acts of worship, self-discipline, and spiritual purification.

In 2021, I lacked the strength, willpower, and physical ability to fast during Ramadan. The emotional toll of the earlier phase of incubation, combined with my physical health challenges, led me to abstain from fasting, as permitted for those unable to fulfil religious obligations due to physical or mental impairment. However, this decision was not made lightly – I felt as though I had once again resisted surrender – this time resistance to religious surrender.

Confronting my own resistance triggered deep internal conflict, prompting me to seek guidance from a spiritual supervisor, a *Shaykh of Tazkiyah* (a scholar specialising in the Islamic sciences of self-purification) from whom I had been learning for over a decade. Reaching out to him felt almost like a confessional, and call for support in navigating my struggle with surrender – specifically, in this case, the act of fasting.

The Tides of Conversion
I find myself in a very familiar place, an ambiguous zone.
I am scared to voice it because maybe I am alone?
Maybe it is my reality and no one else's?
This ever-present voice of the ego always chases.
The familiar dark swell of thoughts fills my mind.
Do all tides talk in conflict, or is this just mine?
I end up most days wondering if my convictions are authentic,
or are they just a product of sin, something unrepented?
This dependency of some kind, on wanting recognition,
the swell pulls me down, drowning in my own omission.
Is my conversion a way of pleasing another,
begging for rescue because of an absent other?
I use someone else's rope and cling to hope.
Motionless and heavy, I'm tired of this struggle,
I let the swell take me, and to my surprise those waves begin to cuddle.
Glimmering islands of gifts soon appear,
love and hope begin to come near,
and when these shores of new hope refresh me,
the tide comes back but this time, I stay afloat.
(Cardo, 2024, pp. 126–127)

The poem expressed my quest for truth, clarity, and certainty as I struggled to hold together the fragmented aspects of my self-experience in a flux of conflict between resistance, guilt, and sadness. Out of sheer exhaustion, I 'cling to a rope' of 'love and hope' and feel a sense of ease from the reply I receive from shaykh, in which he acknowledges my struggle and makes a dua (prayer supplication): 'May Allah ease this for you'.

This seeking guidance underscored the shift from *I-who-feels* to *we-who-care – and act* (Tudor, 2023), highlighting the necessity of supervision, guidance, and communal support in overcoming personal resistance to surrender.

Illuminating my guilt and sadness through deep engagement with my experiences in self-dialogue during a phase of immersion, I was moved to integrate a *Tazkiyah*-based method of reflexivity to make sense of what had transpired. This self-examination – assessing potential biases within the experience of the self (in this case, what had been illuminated in incubation in the research) – is known in Tazkiyah as *al-muhasabah* (self-accountability). It is a practice highly encouraged during Ramadan for deepening awareness of the self (*nafs*). When combined with acts of worship such as prayer and *dhikr* (remembrance of God for self-purification), it naturally incorporates *al-muraqabah* – a state of God-conscious self-reflection.

While engaging in al-muhasabah and al-muraqabah during Ramadan, I revisited the poem and noticed my use of sea metaphors to express my liminal experiences of ambiguity. This reflection brought back early childhood memories of conflict during my parents' turbulent marriage and eventual divorce – memories that resurfaced while visiting our former holiday home on the Isle of Anglesey, North Wales, after Ramadan.

During my visit, I walked gently along the vast stretch of sand, my memories ebbing and flowing with the tide, leaving imprints much like the ripples and patterns in the sand. I took photographs that day, capturing the delicate imprints left by the waves – fleeting, yet deeply marked, much like the memories held within me (see Figures 3.1 and 3.2).

Inspired by what had been illuminated through the patterns left by the sea on the sand, my mind pondered an *ayat* (verse/revelation) in the Qur'an that makes meaning of such patterns in the universe: 'By the sky with its marvellous design (Al-Hubuk)' (Qur'an, Surah Adh-Dhariyat, 51:7).

In *tafsir* (interpretation), *al-hubuk* refers to intricately woven patterns in creation – order within seeming chaos. Another verse in the same *surah* (chapter) resonated deeply: 'Surely you are [lost] in conflicting views' (51:8). These *ayat* (revelations) mirrored my troubled memories,

FIGURE 3.1 Ripples and patterns in the sand and water I.

FIGURE 3.2 Ripples and patterns in the sand and water II.

just as the shifting tides had shaped patterns in the sand. Yet, within the same ripples, pools of seawater glimmered, revealing polished pebbles and shells – signs of refinement and renewal. This reflection led me to see my struggles not just as sources of fragmentation but as pathways to meaning and growth.

Looking back at a poem I had written earlier, I saw how my intuition had already hinted at this process: 'Glimmering islands of gifts soon appear, love and hope begin to come near… the tide comes back, but this time I stay afloat' (Cardo, 2024, p. 127).

Building trust through tadabbur (deep contemplation with revelation)

Engaging in *tadabbur* – the deep contemplation of Qur'anic revelation – allowed me to explore further the tacit dimension of my resistance to surrender. Through reflexive methods, I examined how my internal conflicts surfaced in the patterns of nature and how surrender unfolded as an embodied experience. I began to make connections between my conversion, childhood experiences, and the gifts these struggles had revealed. My sense of being seen and heard by Allah deepened, bringing *yaqeen* – certainty amidst liminality. Meaning, insight, and surrender emerged as I acknowledged both the turbulence and unity within my journey.

At last, I arrived at a place of acceptance: I was enough, both as my former self and as a Muslim. My resistance called me to listen, examine, and tend to my inner struggles – not something to fight, but to embrace. Surrender was not passive; it was an active, reflective, and ultimately transformative process.

Surrender, transformation, and the concept of Alaq

The process of surrender as a pathway to transformation aligns closely with Sela-Smith's (2002) concept of '*surrendering to the unknown*' (p. 63) within HSSI. Sela-Smith describes surrender not as passive submission but as an active and intentional engagement with uncertainty, allowing the research process to unfold organically. In heuristic inquiry, the researcher is both subject and participant, navigating layers of self-exploration, resistance, and eventual meaning-making. Surrender becomes a necessary step in moving from intellectual analysis to a deeply embodied knowing.

Sela-Smith (2002) emphasises that heuristic self-search requires the researcher to 'release control' and 'step into the unknown' (p. 63), acknowledging moments of resistance as integral to transformation. This mirrors the Islamic tazkiyah (self-purification) framework, where resistance in self is not viewed as an obstacle (unless it is left unexamined and, if needed, changed) but is an essential part of spiritual and personal development. The Qur'anic concept of tadabbur (deep contemplation) further supports this process by facilitating an introspective engagement with divine wisdom, enabling the researcher to integrate lived experience with revelation.

This transformative process resonates deeply with *Surah Alaq* (Qur'an, 96:1–5), the first revelation received by the Prophet Muhammad (peace be upon him). The chapter begins with the command: 'Read in the name of your Lord who created. Created man from a clinging substance (Alaq). Read, and your Lord is the Most Generous – who taught by the pen – taught man that which he knew not'.

The term Alaq holds profound significance. Linguistically, it refers to something that clings, symbolising human dependence on the Divine. It also represents the embryonic stage of life, signifying growth, transformation, and the unfolding of knowledge. This revelation, marking the beginning of prophetic guidance, underscores the necessity of surrendering to divine wisdom to attain deeper self-awareness and understanding.

In this heuristic inquiry, Alaq became a powerful metaphor for the researcher's exploration of liminal experiences during her conversion to Islam – both as *being Alaq* (existing in a state of transition and dependence) and as *knowing Alaq*, reflecting the Islamic maxim: *To know yourself is to know your Lord.* In this sense, surrendering to the process of inquiry mirrored the act of surrendering to divine knowledge, where self-discovery and spiritual realisation unfolded as intertwined dimensions of transformation.

Conclusion

Despite their centrality to Sela-Smith's (2002) development of heuristic self-search enquiry, the concepts of resistance and surrender are underdeveloped in heuristic research (see Chapter 1). We hope that this chapter has contributed to a greater understanding of them, and stimulates further reflections on and explications of these central concepts to and in this form of research.

References

Antonovsky, A. (1987). The salutogenic perspective: Toward a new view of health and illness. *Advances, 4*(1), 47–55.

Atkins, D., & Loewenthal, D. (2004). The lived experience of psychotherapists working with older clients: An heuristic study. *British Journal of Guidance & Counselling, 32*(4), 493–509. https://doi.org/10.1080/03069880412331303295

Bartoszewicz, M. G. (2013). Controversies of conversions: The potential terrorist threat of European converts to Islam. *Perspectives on Terrorism, 3*(7), 17–29. www.jstor.org/stable/26296937

Cardo, G. (2024). *A heuristic enquiry of the lived experience of being 'Alaq' as a convert to Islam* [Doctoral dissertation, Middlesex University]. Middlesex University Research Repository. https://repository.mdx.ac.uk/item/1ww842

Cousins, G., Humphris, A., Kingi, A., Orams, L., & Tudor, K. (2025). Heuristic research in a time-limited context. In W. Ings & K. Tudor (Eds.), *Heuristic enquiries: Research across disciplines and professions* (pp. 162–180). Routledge.

Douglass, B. G., & Moustakas, C. (1985). Heuristic inquiry: The internal search to know. *Journal of Humanistic Psychology, 25*(3), 39–55. https://doi.org/10.1177/0022167885253004

Galonnier, J. (2018, April 2). *The Islam of converts*. Books & Ideas. https://booksandideas.net/The-Islam-of-Converts.html

Haddad, Y. Y. (Ed.). (1991). *The Muslims of America*. Oxford University Press.

Hazell, C. M., Chapman, L., Valeix, S. F., Roberts, P., Niven, J. E., & Berry, C. (2020). Understanding the mental health of doctoral researchers: A mixed methods systematic review with meta-analysis and meta-synthesis. *Systematic Reviews, 9*, Article 197. https://doi.org/10.1186/s13643-020-01443-1

Kumar, S. (2017). My dissertation healed me: A retrospective analysis through heuristic inquiry. *The Qualitative Report, 22*(11), 3025–3038. https://doi.org/10.46743/2160-3715/2017.3051

Kumar, S., & Cavallaro, L. (2018). Researcher self-care in emotionally demanding research: A proposed conceptual framework. *Qualitative Health Research, 28*(4), 648–658. https://doi.org/10.1177/1049732317746377

Merry, T. (2004). *Learning and being in person-centred counselling*. PCCS Books.

Michelle, K. (2017). *Exploring resistance to spiritual emergence: A heuristic inquiry* [Doctoral dissertation, Sofia University]. ProQuest Dissertations Publishing. www.proquest.com/docview/1936353745/2C945017F751479FPQ/1

Moustakas, C. (1961). *Loneliness*. Prentice-Hall.

Moustakas, C. (1967). Heuristic research. In J. F. T. Bugental (Ed.), *Challenges of humanistic psychology* (pp. 101–107). McGraw-Hill.

Moustakas, C. (1975). *The touch of loneliness*. Prentice-Hall.

Moustakas, C. (1990). *Heuristic research: Design, methodology and applications*. Sage.

Polanyi, M. (1969). *Knowing and being* (M. Greene, Ed.). University of Chicago Press.

Polanyi, M. (1983). *The tacit dimension*. Peter Smith.

Qur'an (Bewley & Bewley, Trans.). (2011). *The noble Qur'an: A new rendering of its meaning in English* (3rd ed.). Ta-Ha Publishers.

Ryan, R. M., & Deci, E. L. (2001). On happiness and human potentials: A review of the research on hedonic and eudaimonic well-being. *Annual Review of Psychology*, *52*(1), 141–166. https://doi.org/10.1146/annurev.psych.52.1.141

Sela-Smith, S. (2001). *Heuristic self-search inquiry: Clarification of Moustakas' heuristic research* [Doctoral dissertation, Saybrook Graduate School and Research Center]. ProQuest Dissertations & Theses.

Sela-Smith, S. (2002). Heuristic research: A review and critique of Moustakas's method. *Journal of Humanistic Psychology*, *42*(3), 53–88. https://doi.org/10.1177/0022167802423004

Shantall, T. (1999). The experience of meaning in suffering among holocaust survivors. *Journal of Humanistic Psychology*, *39*(3), 96–124. https://doi.org/10.1177/0022167899393009

Stern, D. N. (1985). *The interpersonal world of the infant: A view from psychoanalysis and developmental psychology*. Basic Books.

Stuckey, R. L. (2001). *E. Lucy Braun (1889–1971): Ohio's foremost woman botanist; her studies of prairies and their physiographic relationships*. RLS Creations.

Sultan, N. (2019). *Heuristic inquiry: Researching human experience holistically*. Sage.

Throne, R. (2019). *Autoethnography and heuristic inquiry for doctoral-level researchers: Emerging research and opportunities*. Information Science Reference/IGI Global. https://doi.org/10.4018/978-1-5225-9365-2

Tudor, K. (2010). *The fight for health: A heuristic enquiry into psychological well-being* [Unpublished context statement]. PhD in Mental Health Promotion by Public (Published Works). School of Health and Social Sciences, Middlesex University, London, UK.

Tudor, K. (2017). The fight for health: An heuristic enquiry (2010). In K. Tudor, *Conscience and critic: The selected works of Keith Tudor* (pp. 143–168). Routledge. (Original work completed 2010)

Tudor, K. (2022). Supporting critical self-enquiry: Doing heuristic research. In S. Bager-Charleson & A. McBeath (Eds.), *Supporting research in counselling and psychotherapy* (pp. 57–79). Springer.

Tudor, K. (2023). Critical heuristics: From 'I who feels' to 'We who care – and act'. In K. Tudor & J. Wyatt (Eds.), *Qualitative research approaches for psychotherapy: Reflexivity, methodology, and criticality* (pp. 115–132). Routledge.

Tudor, K., & Ings, W. (Eds.). (2025). *Heuristic enquiries: Research across disciplines and professions*. Routledge.

Wilber, K. (1997). *The eye of spirit*. Shambala.

4

IN (MY OWN) TIME

The implicit and inevitable context of time on heuristic research methodology

Luke Oram and Keith Tudor

Introduction

It is said that business maven Robert R. Updegraff was the first to coin the phrase 'time-poor' as recently as 1958 (Updegraff, 1958). Since then, our conception of modern temporality has become even more emaciated: we speak of time poverty, the idea that our days are getting irretrievably shorter and, as J. Taylor Smith (1902) puts it, that we suffer from 'the barrenness of a busy life' (p. 811). From the brutal quantification of the industrial revolution to the boastful hustle of modern productivity culture, our new catch cry seems to rail against the very orbit of the sun – '*There aren't enough hours in the day*'. Yet beneath these laments lies an often-unexamined reality: time isn't just scarce, it's stealthy – an invisible architecture shaping the very contours of our attention, reflection, discovery, and meaning-making.

If time has become a limited resource, drawing and quartering our attention, how can we understand Moustakas's (1990) exhortation to let heuristic enquiry be timeless? In his seminal work on the method and methodology of *Heuristic Inquiry*, he refers to 'endless time', invoking a world of 'timeless immersion', and asserting that 'the heuristic research process is not one that can be hurried or timed by the clock or calendar' (p. 6). His suggestion is that the researcher should endeavour to enter a liminal space in which to encounter their subject, a perspective echoed in Chapman and Whitney's (1971) lyrics: 'I'll be with you in my own time'. However, the problem is, as H. G. Wells (1898) puts it so eloquently, there is no liminal space in a modern chronocracy: we move backwards to remember and forwards to dream; in between, we are ruled by the clock.

In another publication (Ings & Tudor, 2025), we and two colleagues, three of whom were Master's students undertaking heuristic enquiry supervised by Keith, grappled with Moustakas's six heuristic phases, i.e., initial engagement, immersion, incubation, illumination, explication, and creative synthesis, in relation to time (Cousins et al., 2025). Fresh from completing their dissertations, and in the context of these pieces of work (of no more than 10,000 words) having to be proposed, researched, and written within eight months, both Keith and the students (including Luke) reflected on Moustakas's perspective on timelessness, and, considering Moustakas's heuristic phases, experienced and explicated time as both a catalyst

DOI: 10.4324/9781003685944-6

and a constraint. The atemporal process promoted by Moustakas (1990), and emphasised by Sela-Smith (2002), presents research as a revolutionary act: a stepping outside of delineations of clock and calendar, embracing kairos (appropriate time) rather than chronos (clock time), and dialoguing with eternity. Simultaneously, time constrained us, and we had to accede to Taft's (1933) assertion of time scarcity as fundamental to the human condition and observe the ticking of chronological time. At times we had to forego timelessness, choosing Valéry's point of abandonment (McGrath & Comenetz, 2013) or, as McCall (2021) puts it beautifully, settling on a 'satiating point' (p. 61). Ultimately, we realised that in the odyssey of heuristic enquiry, there is a time to wrestle with chronos and a time to embrace earthly limitations. After all, Moustakas's use of the word *phase* suggests both an ongoing journey as well as distinct, boundaried junctures within it.

Heuristic concepts and time

In her heuristic enquiry into abrupt endings, aptly titled *Falling Into the Abyss*, Chue (2021) invokes a conflict between chronos and kairos. In the heuristic process there will always be tension between linear and experiential time, just as our ability to describe a phenomenon will always be constricted by the words we have available to describe it, or the time it takes to tell the story. As Haydon (2024) puts it, heuristic enquiry unearths endless possibilities, but the constraint of time makes full explication of those possibilities paradoxically 'imperative yet entirely unattainable' (p. 24).

It is much the same with this chapter. As shown in Chapter 1, the expansiveness of heurism extends to the description of the process itself. A limited review of Moustakas and his successors unearths 20 possible concepts to be considered within the methodology. Just as a time-conscious view of heuristic phases requires us to know 'when to continue to dwell and when… to leave home' (Tudor, 2022, p. 67), time and editorial constraints require us to be judicious when addressing the concepts. To this end, we limit ourselves to discussion of Moustakas's original seven concepts – identifying with the focus of enquiry, self-dialogue, tacit knowing, intuition, indwelling, focusing, and the internal frame of reference – which are relatively ubiquitous in heuristic literature. To this, we add concepts developed by Sela-Smith (2001, 2002) in her critical development of heuristic enquiry – including self-dialogue, acknowledging feelings, resistance, surrender, and transformation – concepts which have been adopted widely by ensuing authors (see Table 1.4, p. 18). Finally, we address validation which, while not named as a heuristic concept per se, is a salient consideration across the literature.

Moustakas (1990) presents six heuristic phases as fundamental to a thorough enquiry. While there are differing opinions about their sequential linearity, it is widely accepted that each phase must be undertaken in order to complete the journey. When it comes to the concepts however, he seems less rigid, presenting them as tools that support the phases. Reflecting on Moustakas, Sela-Smith (2002) is a little more dogmatic, suggesting that there are certain concepts that are 'key' or 'intrinsic' to heuristic inquiry, including identification with the focus of enquiry, inward reach, surrender, self-dialogue, self-search, and transformation. If heurism's phases provide the route, its concepts are the required navigational tools – and travellers have their own instruments of choice, from star charts to lodestones, inner guides, and compass roses. In this chapter we'll delve into the heuristic toolkit, investigating how selected concepts intersect with the idea of time.

Identifying with the focus of enquiry

In his first concept, Moustakas (1990) promotes a knowledge of the research subject so intimate it feels like mimesis. Before he developed the polio vaccine, the American virologist Jonas Salk (1983) imagined himself as a cancer cell engaged in open combat in the immune system, a technique he called the inverted perspective. Just as the heuristic phase of immersion asks us to live the question, as Rilke (1929/1992) puts it, identifying with the focus of enquiry requires that, like Salk, we *become* the question. Unlike the dispassionate positivist who approaches a phenomenon from an objective distance, this kind of identification asks us to attend to a familiar interior – something personal, experiential, perhaps even obsessive in nature.

Naturally, the focus of such enquiry is likely to be something with which we have identified for some time, or perhaps even something that has always been there. For instance, in the co-authored chapter on time-limits in heuristic research (Cousins et al., 2025) this encompasses: hope (Anna, for three years); being a mother and a trainee psychotherapist (Alana, for five years); the experience of boarding school (Guy, for seven years); mental health and wellbeing (Keith, for over 30 years [see Tudor, 2010, 2017]); and a father–son relationship (Luke, for some 40 years). Moustakas (1990) links the formulation of the research question to time thus:

> Discovering a significant problem or question that will hold the wondering gaze and passionate commitment of the researcher is the essential opening of the heuristic process. The question as such (and the researcher's relationship to it) will determine whether or not an authentic and compelling path has opened, one that will sustain the researcher's curiosity, involvement, and participation, with full energy and resourcefulness *over a lengthy period of time.*
>
> (p. 30, our emphasis)

In making this connection, Moustakas is pointing the researcher towards the future research journey (of some length). In our research, we were reflecting more on the past (of various lengths) in a relatively short period (for the Master's students, of eight months, and for Keith with regard to his doctoral study of three years). We make this point to acknowledge that in the context of time-limited periods of research, study, and completion, there is a benefit of having a focus of enquiry which has some history and, therefore, longevity.

This familiarity with the focus of enquiry doesn't mean that we get simply to retread old familiar ground. While our question may have an authoritative or experiential history behind it, the heuristic process may be the first time we have taken the time to fully inhabit it and interrogate it in an intentional and extended fashion. Paradoxically, this requires us to seek the unknown of our known.

In *Little Gidding*, T. S Eliot (1943) describes this dance between the familiar and the unfamiliar: 'The eyes of a familiar compound ghost | Both intimate and unidentifiable' (p. 23).

Sometimes identification with the focus of enquiry asks us to reside between the intimate and the unidentifiable, to explore the question with an intent to 'arrive where we started and know the place for the first time' (Eliot, 1943, p. 27). As Cousins (in Cousins et al., 2025) puts it, this requires a navigation through temporality, identifying with old memories to examine how they manifest in the present – a kind of internal time travel. Sometimes our identification demands the dissolution of time altogether, residing within; as Loewald (1972/1980) puts it, 'the interrelatedness and the connections between a past, present, and future disintegrate' (p. 141).

Tacit knowing

The substratum of heuristic enquiry, tacit knowing suggests that there is something yet unknown about what we know. Much like the Latin root *tacitus* (silent or wordless), the suggestion is that, if we look long enough at our question, we will find something not yet articulated – something akin to Bollas's (1987) unthought known. Here, Moustakas borrows from Polanyi's (1966) concepts of subsidiary and focal knowledge: subsidiary factors of our experience are those that are immediately visible and conscious, focal factors are the unseen or not yet visible truths below our immediate knowing. We look at our question, constantly adjusting the zoom lens of our perception, shifting from clarity of foreground to sharpness of the farther fields. Polanyi describes this as a dance between vagueness and sharpness of understanding, ultimately a process which recreates experience as a sum of many parts.

It goes without saying that this process begs time. Heuristic enquiry is never satisfied with first impressions. It wants a second impression, then a third, and a fourth. It is an iterative, meditative process that asks us to look 'toward the truth and the truth beneath that as well' (Levine, 1991, p. 19). In heurism, we don't stop at the familiar, we keep dancing past 'the very construct of self, right down to the molecular level of thoughts and feelings we take as self-evident' (p. 30). All of this takes patience – a long, slow exploration of a phenomenon to find 'all its veiled depths to understand' (Wharton, 1880, p. 548). Tacit knowledge is what separates shallow knowing from mastery. It's the invisible layer of wisdom gained over time, usually by doing, observing, reflecting, and absorbing. What often goes unspoken is that tacit knowing is itself a function of time – layered through years of unnoticed experience, returning not on demand but in its own time.

If ever you want a masterclass in tacit knowing, head to the poets and artists, people well versed in finding unseen worlds in everyday life. In *Odas Elementales*, his collection of odes to everyday objects, Pablo Neruda (1994) imagines the humble bed as an existential ferryman: 'We go from one bed to the next | in this journey, | life's journey' (p. 29).

The poet's ability to plumb the hidden depths of experience is exactly what Douglass and Moustakas (1985) mean when they refer to the tacit. They're talking about a realm of knowledge populated by 'subliminal, archetypal, and preconscious perceptions' (p. 48), a place which unearths heurism's 'hunches and vague, formless insights' (p. 49).

It is worth specifying that, in Douglass and Moustakas's articulation, tacit knowing is an active process by which we access the tacit realm, something akin to Sela-Smith's (2001) idea of 'inward reach' (p. 64). This should give us clues as to how the process works or, more specifically, how long it could take. In their original work on heuristic enquiry, Douglass and Moustakas (1985) place the process within the acquisition phase, citing tacit knowing as cyclical 'refinements of meaning and understanding [that] penetrate to the core of the phenomenon until it suddenly yields glimmerings that lead to a unifying picture… moving from clue to clue until the Gestalt is recognized' (p. 50). Borrowing from Boyd and Fales (1983), they suggest that each cycle takes us from discomfort to identification to openness and new information – and while the insights may come suddenly by way of illuminations, the process can be one of protracted excavation.

Tacit knowing is a bit like Persephone's return, a constant cycle of descent, exploration, and reintegration; and, in that sense, it can feel like an endless return. Considering that tacit knowledge is constructed and re-constructed from the moment of birth, Sela-Smith (2001) argues that accessing the tacit dimension is a journey that can take 'moments or even years'

(p. 158). As far as when that journey should be over, Moustakas (1990) doesn't offer a lot of clear direction. He does warn us that when the tacit is curtailed, our possibilities for knowing are limited, but he doesn't suggest that there will be a point at which our knowledge of the subject is complete. One supposes the point is that it never is. Sela-Smith (2002) suggests that there is a moment in which 'there is a breakthrough into conscious awareness of wholes and clustered wholes that form into themes inherent in the question' (p. 67). Perhaps in a time-limited heuristic journey, very real deadlines hem in the tacit knowing that threatens to become an endless odyssey (see Cousins et al., 2025), or maybe Sela-Smith (2002) is proposing the same kind of yedasentience that separates the obsessed researcher from the harried obsessive-compulsive: a subjective feeling of 'That's enough to work with for now'.

Intuition

Intuition is a skill Moustakas (1990) suggests must be consistently exercised in order to guide the researcher to deepen and extend knowledge, to 'look and look again from clue to clue until we surmise the truth' (p. 14). In Moustakas's mind, intuition is a relatively fast process, something that 'makes immediate knowledge possible without the intervening steps of logic and reasoning' (p. 14). In this sense, intuition is the handmaiden of heuristic illuminations, a tool that delivers intuitive awakenings from tacit mysteries (Moustakas, 1990) or, as Polanyi (1969) puts it: 'things that are most surprising and make men see the world in a new way' (p. 118).

Sela-Smith (2002) cautions that intuition should not be equated with shortcuts; in fact, it is the process of surrendering to intuition that makes heuristic enquiry such a lengthy venture (see Chapter 3). She argues that intuition forces the researcher to abandon the security of 'deliberate mental operations and directed effort' (as Moustakas [1990, p. 29] puts it); the enquirer lets intuition take the wheel, rather than allowing the process be hemmed in by 'rigorous planning and controlling the steps' (Sela-Smith, 2002, p. 63). In Sela-Smith's (2001) mind, it is resistance to this kind of unbounded uncertainty that often curtails the integrity of heuristic enquiry. Intuition guides the researcher through the tension of self-understanding which can appear spontaneous, but only within a process that is 'demanding, requires rigorous definition and careful collection of data, as well as a thorough and disciplined analysis' (p. 364). This is a process that 'cannot be directed, ordered, hurried, or timed; it must be allowed to unfold naturally' (p. 364). Meents (2006), whose heuristic self-search inquiry is a beautiful extended meditation on intuition, describes it as an alchemical process of both inspiration and deliberation:

> I experience intuition as not knowing – and then suddenly knowing. It's as if information wasn't there and then it is there. It's as if intuition comes from nothing and suddenly, spontaneously, there is substance. Intuition feels to me like something coming out of nothing. (p. 157)

When it comes to the constraints of time, a counterpoint to this open-ended stance might be found in the work of Nobel laureate Herbert A. Simon (1992), whose theory of bounded rationality argues that human decisions are always constrained by limitations of time as well as emotional and contextual influences. Simon suggests that, when faced with these constraints, our intuition is often influenced by *satisficing*, a neologism that blends 'satisfy' and 'suffice'; in other words, we choose an option that is 'good enough', given our constraints. According to Simon, at some point the need to act overrides the need to have all the information.

Extending this concept to the idea of a heuristic truth, it may be more likely that we often end up employing Simon's *satisficing* in our enquiry. Acknowledging the limitation of time, whether it be an academic deadline or the exhaustion of resources, sometimes we must stop and work with what we've dug up, despite our intuition begging us down another rabbit hole. If heuristic enquiry is working with a lifetime of experience, dipping into a river of tacit knowledge that is always flowing and being reinterpreted, can it ever be more than just a snapshot in time? Perhaps the tension of heuristic enquiry is that on some level, it is an attempt to dam the fluxed river of Heraclitus – a river that is never the same twice. After all, even the act of articulating our experience changes it somewhat, and it will continue to evolve long after we've committed it to paper.

Indwelling

Moustakas's (1990) concept of indwelling channels a meditative deep dive into a vast interior: 'The indwelling process is conscious and deliberate, yet it is not lineal or logical. It follows clues wherever they appear; one dwells inside them and expands their meanings and associations until a fundamental insight is achieved' (p. 15).

In Advaita Vedanta, a school of Hindu philosophy, non-duality teaches that the self and the universe are one. Through deep meditation, the distinctions between the self and the external world blur, leading to an experience where one might feel as though they become the object of their contemplation. As Jung would put it, indwelling is the process of becoming one with the archetype, the entryway into heuristic self-dialogue. Moustakas calls this a 'painstaking, deliberate process', where 'patience and incremental understanding are the guidelines' (p. 15). As with most of his descriptions, these words scream unhurried, steady, sustained, and *lengthy*. Indwelling is a concept intimately linked to Moustakas's immersion phase, in which 'the researcher enters into the material in timeless immersion until it is understood' (p. 51).

But how realistic is this kind of indwelling in this modern age, an epoch defined by information and stimulation overload, a time-poor era where demands on our attention have never been higher? In her dissertation, Grennell (2014) paints an apt picture of indwelling as a near counter-social act. Reflecting on the time demands of this concept while juggling familial responsibilities and a change in employment, she concludes that the heuristic method 'is difficult to adhere to in light of life' (p. 28). Eventually, having to curtail indwelling and immersion to meet a deadline, she wonders if 'disposable time and money are perhaps a prerequisite for this method' (p. 28). Elsewhere, Franklin (2017) decides to honour the process proper:

> I privileged the timing of the heuristic process over externally imposed time frames which meant I did not rush my process to fit into the required academic timeframe. I secured a six-month extension to honour my process, though this incurred significant cost.
>
> (p. 36)

Reflecting on Moustakas's (1990) original assertion that heuristic enquiry cannot be hurried by time or calendar, Sela-Smith (2001) draws a hard line when it comes to the realities of juggling heurism and a busy life. She writes about a PhD student whose original heuristic proposal allocated a three-month timeline, arguing that he couldn't afford to spend a year writing his dissertation. Sela-Smith argues that this student violated the method, concluding that 'heuristic studies cannot be forced to fit a time frame, not even for the researcher's life demands' (p. 82).

Through this lens, it's hard not to think of the criticisms of bell hooks (2000) and others who wonder if higher education is built for the rich. Does heuristic enquiry's privileging of time and space somehow relegate it to the realm of the time-wealthy?

Perhaps the correlation of indwelling and meditation is helpful here, after all, modern Zen teachers have long struggled with how to meditate in a world that doesn't offer us time and space to retreat into a utopian serenity. Meditative poet Stephen Levine (1991) describes a tension that could easily be applied to 21st century heuristic indwelling:

> At certain times in our practice the work might become so difficult, the healing so deep, that we need to sit down with big 'don't know', adjust, look around. Sometimes we need a break before we continue on again… [but] there may be times when meditation recedes into the background noise of the necessities of our life. And we worry we have 'stepped off the path' … The path is the ground beneath your feet. It is the healing to be done. Once you've committed to the heart, there is nowhere else to go. Though the forms may change you are always heading home.
>
> (pp. 233–234)

In the context of time-limited heuristic enquiry, it may be helpful to think of indwelling as a state of mind: a pole star that holds the question in focus throughout the waxing and waning of a busy life. Considering the element of time in her heuristic enquiry, Haydon (2024) equates indwelling with a kind of attitude of resonance. Reframing her journey as a liminal space running parallel to the busy academic life of a training therapist, she imagines indwelling as the way of being proposed by Rogers (1961/1967): an ability to constantly tune in and out of the research question.

Focusing

Borrowing from Gendlin's (1978) eponymous technique, Moustakas (1990) describes heuristic focusing as the process by which the researcher clears a space in which to contact, clarify, elucidate, and explicate the question. According to Moustakas, this process is a sustained mode of inner attention, an intentional pause held long enough to facilitate examination of experience that has so far remained out of conscious reach (Douglass & Moustakas, 1985). Gendlin's (1978) original conception, however, was intentionally economical when it came to time, more rooted in the present moment. In *Focusing*, Gendlin (1978) suggests his six-step process, i.e., clearing a space, felt sense, handle, resonating, asking, and receiving, should take 10–20 minutes for familiar practitioners and 30–40 minutes for beginners. Obviously, Moustakas is co-opting Gendlin's idea as a kind of macro-level exercise running alongside the finite practice, a kind of sustained state of mind that overarches the finite, 'dipping in' to experience.

Gendlin, Moustakas, and Sela-Smith share in the sentiment that this sustained stance of focusing is necessary to facilitate the fullness of discovery. What Gendlin called the 'felt sense' could not be demanded forth; it arrived in its own way and time as the enquirer waited patiently and intently. Moustakas asserts that the wholeness of knowledge was revealed when the researcher turned inward, dwelling persistently in the task of discovery. Sela-Smith advocates committing to the inward reach, embracing whatever arises without turning away – it was this unwavering pilgrimage that fostered discovery and transformation.

For Sela-Smith (2002), focusing requires not only courageous intent, but a relinquishing of control, an agreement with the self to remain in the experience long enough for that which is hidden to reveal itself, including all that is disavowed or distressing. One of her main critiques of Moustakas (1990) is that, when faced with distressing feelings of loneliness, his focus shifted 'from the self's *experience* of the experience to focusing on the *idea* of the experience' (Sela-Smith, 2002, p. 53, our emphasis). She also points out that Moustakas's approach to personal enquiry tends to focus more on intellectual and conceptual understanding rather than on the body's felt sense (a core element of Gendlin's focusing). She argues that, without embracing the embodied experience, the heuristic process may remain surface-level and conceptual rather than transformative. Sela-Smith critiques the way Moustakas emphasises control and structured stages in the research process, noting that this focus could inadvertently limit the true flow of insights, submitting it to the control of chronos rather than kairos. She suggests that heuristic inquiry should include more space for the emotional chaos and surrender that can facilitate deeper revelations.

Perhaps, as Casterline (2006) seems to suggest, focusing is more prayer than processing, a kind of 'thy will be done' spoken to inner body and unconscious. In his poem 'For one who is exhausted', the Irish poet John O'Donohue (2008) evokes this stance as an invitation to enter 'empty time', where the usual compulsions of striving subside. He describes the slowing of thought, the onset of sadness long avoided, and the rising of unwept tears. In this state, one is recalled from false ground to a deeper rhythm of self, urged to notice the overlooked details of life. Through such patient surrender, the individual eventually returns to themselves, with a renewed respect for the heart and an intimacy with the joy found only in 'slow time'.

Internal frame of reference

At the heart of heuristic enquiry is the favouring of subjective experience over observational and analytic understandings. The researcher, positioned as an instrument of knowing, embraces subjectivity as a pathway to meaning rather than a contamination of truth. Moustakas (1990) borrows from Rogers' (1951, 1969) therapeutic concept of the internal frame of reference to make his point:

> To know and understand the nature, meanings, and essences of any human experience, one depends on the internal frame of reference of the person who has had, is having, or will have the experience. Only the experiencing persons – by looking at their own experiences in perceptions, thoughts, feelings, and sense – can validly provide portrayals of the experience.
>
> (Moustakas, 1990, p. 17)

In this way, our internal frame of reference is not concerned with an objective truth as much as it is with the idea of Kierkegaard's 'truth which is true for me' (Bretall, 1946, p. 5).

Nor is our internal frame interested in time, at least not as we know it. The immediacy of Rogers' idea of the frame of reference doesn't tend to separate what 'was' from what 'is'; both are alive together. In the therapeutic setting, the frame of reference invites the client to step into a world in which emotional time dominates. An event from decades ago can feel immediate; a trauma can be more 'now' than the present moment (Stern, 2000; Tudor, 2025). In the internal frame of reference, memory is not a recording device; it's poetic, interpretive, and emotional. The same is true of the heuristic frame of reference; reaching inward towards the tacit, the researcher enters a psychic reality that 'does not follow laws of time' (Hillman, 1983, p. 15). This is a timeless reality that collapses past and future into the present; something like the Dreamtime of Aboriginal culture, or the Celtic Otherworld, where time warps, loops, and recurs.

In Luke's heuristic meditation on his father's imago (Oram, 2023), he imagined his internal frame of reference to be like wandering the hallways of Hillman's (1983) *Memoria*:

> Of course, memory is unreliable, itself just a form of reconstruction. We claim to recall in purity, but in the halls of *Memoria* we also engage in 'remembering-what-never-happened' (Hillman, 1983, p. 50). My Imago Paterna is more commemorative legend than real person, clouded by my own perception and his historical distance. I engage in *mythopoiesis*; remembering as re-creation. An ethical consideration of my father necessitates this distinction. The heuristic journey is one into the self, into a truth I can only call subjective.
>
> (Oram, 2023, p. 3)

In heuristic enquiry, Moustakas (1990) argues that we are constantly slowing the parade of history (Hillman, 1983). When we enter our frame of reference, we don't enter our experience to race into the future or to analyse the past, we dwell in it, letting meaning emerge in its own time to inform our search. The current subjective truth that we find in those moments is a product of time: an amalgam of past experience, future hopes, and present observation.

Self-dialogue

From Socrates' *maieutics* to Jung's encounter with Philemon, an inner archetype summoned via active imagination (Jung, 2009), it has always been thought that our psyches have something important to say to us, if we would just ask. Self-dialogue is an acknowledgement that 'the Self reveals itself, beholding the Self by means of the Self' (Mitchell, 2002, in *Bhagavad Gita*, 6:10–27).

For Moustakas (1990), self-dialogue means speaking directly to the phenomenon in question, and to be questioned by it in return: a kind of oscillation from concept to experience and back, from part to whole and back, from individual to general (or universal) and back (Moustakas, 1990; Sultan, 2019). It is, as Jourard (1971) puts it, 'the act of making yourself manifest' (p. 19). Sela-Smith (2002) adds terms like self-honesty and self-disclosure to this process. As Moustakas puts it, in self-dialogue, 'one faces oneself and must be honest with oneself' (p. 9).

In her heuristic enquiry into aesthetics, Haydon (2024) describes a self-dialogic process as an *object turns to subject relationship*:

> From the start of my research, visions of moulded jelly appeared in my mind. I made a humble drawing with marker pens and notepad and had a long dialogue between the art and myself ('myself' was both the artist and the beholder). This became my standard practice. Almost inevitably during these conversations it became unclear who's role was what, both the art and the artist-beholder shifted between asking questions and answering them. A dual process emerged, clearly defined roles disappeared.
>
> (p. 12)

Luke's own self-dialogue with his internal image of his father seemed to span the historical, social, and collective:

> Dwelling in this thought, I engaged in meditative self-dialogue with this image. I traced the edges of it, holding it up to my mind's eye like a many-sided prism. I was looking at a

> composite built from the strata of personal and collective unconscious. A question formed, applied to each angle: *where did you come from?*
>
> Answers came, scribbled piecemeal in journals. You came from the church, a patriarchal idea borrowed from *Imago Dei*. The head of the house. He who does not spare the rod. The provider. You were created in my men's group, an amalgam of stories about dads we admired, hated, or were destined to overthrow. You come from the television. Chivalrous and resourceful like MacGyver (Winkler & Rich, 1985–1992), with the barrel-chested machismo of David Hasselhoff (Berk et al., 1989–2001), and the mischievous savvy of Maxwell Smart.
>
> (Oram, 2023, p. 23)

When lost in the single-minded heuristic self-dialogue, time can stand still: for a moment, we become at one in an abiding unity with the subject matter. As Moustakas (1990) infers, we learn to inhabit the question in a kind of symbiotic intimacy. There is an identification here, perhaps an over-identification, in which two become one. Self-dialogue becomes Jung's *auseinandersetzung*, the (researcher) 'I' and the (participant) 'I' in mutual conversation, or Sela-Smith's (2002) '*I-who-feels*'. Like any good conversation, the dialogue becomes engrossing, all-encompassing: in a 'unity which abolishes time' (Loewald, 1972/1980, p. 142). Eventually, the conversation takes a turn. The tempo of the dance escalates. Before you know it, you've fallen out of lockstep and into a kind of frenetic shuffle where your routines fail you: you're all left feet, foxtrotting through *terra incognita*, 'becoming one with what one is seeking to know' (Moustakas, 1990, p. 8). Here, time folds in on itself – the researcher engages not only with the present inquiry, but also with the hidden echoes of former selves and anticipations of future transformations. Self-dialogue becomes a recursive act, haunted by a temporal depth often unacknowledged.

Although pivotal to all heuristic phases – Moustakas says that, even in the explication phase, dialogue continues with the data – self-dialogue is most time-consuming during the immersion phase. Moustakas describes it as a kind of constant insanity. It is a conversation that continues in waking, sleeping, and dream states. Its back-and-forth haunts public settings, social contexts, and work meetings. It is both spontaneous and sustained. It is an agreement to live the question (as Rilke, 1929/1992 puts it) for as long as it takes. Many heuristic writers describe self-dialogue as a prolonged, parallel process throughout their enquiry. Meents (2006) literally turned down the volume of her life to make way for self-dialogue, 'doing whatever I needed to do to create the space for me to hear my own inner voice' (p. 97). She paints a picture of a monastic period of time dedicated for dialogue, including reducing her social interactions, apportioning sections of her day to quiet reflection, and avoiding external media. Alleyne (2017) notes being pursued by her own grief, which demanded meaning and associations through an ongoing journal, while Cousins' (2023) dialogue began not only a long-overdue internal conversation with his long-disavowed parts, but also with his parents.

Acknowledging feelings

As one might expect when it comes to a methodology so steeped in subjective experience, feelings are a prominent source of data for Moustakas (1990). Several times in his primer, Moustakas describes heuristic enquiry as the exploration of thoughts, feelings, senses, beliefs, judgements, and values. This is the stuff of the inner world, the wellspring to which concepts such as focusing or self-dialogue intend to lead us. Ferendo (2004) notes that the researcher's use of feelings is the linchpin that separates the heuristic question (what is *my* experience of…?) from a phenomenological one (what is *the* experience of…?). In Ferendo's mind, methodologies such as heuristic self-search inquiry require that 'the researcher works with direct feelings and tacit knowing, instead of being the detached observer' (p. 287).

Moustakas's (1961) original heuristic project revolved around the centrality of a feeling, namely that of loneliness evoked by the illness of his young daughter and his need to make a life-or-death decision about her treatment. He paints an acute picture of just how pervasive his emotions were at the time:

> Lonely self-reflection came at unexpected moments, in the midst of crowds of people, in response to words or phrases in conversation. Many different kinds of situations evoked an inner process of doubt and uncertainty, and a strong feeling of being isolated and alone. Sometimes I awakened in the night, overwhelmed by images and feelings and thoughts.
>
> (Moustakas, 1990, p. 70)

This is a picture of a man in a time of liminal chaos. The Greeks believed that time had many different structures. There was the time of *krisis*, the turning point, a crossroads where urgency clashed with contradiction and confusion. There was *chronos*, the ever-ticking clock demanding decision. Then *kairos*, the felt time, the god of intuition and subconscious subterfuge. Through all of this, Moustakas was chasing *epiphaneia*, a moment of epiphany – a truth made visible. These forces form the nexus of discovery, a concept critical to heuristics, which summons Rogers' (1969) ideas of openness to experience, self-awareness, internal locus of evaluation, and self-process.

But this is where Sela-Smith (2001, 2002) argues that Moustakas made a misstep. In her critique of his method, Sela-Smith (2002) argues that, when faced with his own unbearable pain, Moustakas shifted out of his position as the *I-who-feels*, and into the safety of an observer:

> I speculate that the heuristic question might have been, 'What is *my* experience of feeling lonely?' This question had the potential to take him into the tacit dimension where his globally felt loneliness existed. This is very different from the phenomenological question, 'What is *the* experience of loneliness?'
>
> (Sela-Smith, 2002, p. 74)

Moustakas (1967) himself admits as much. His original question was not so much about the nature of loneliness as it was a struggle to make a life-and-death decision about his daughter. Sela-Smith's critique is still salient. In heuristic enquiry there will always be tension to shift to a position of safety when faced with uncomfortable feelings. However, Sela-Smith considers that, in shifting away from feeling, Moustakas created what she calls an 'amazing contradiction' (p. 74) in his process – a split between experiencing feelings and then abandoning them in order to objectify the phenomenon. Sela-Smith (2002) claims that Moustakas's (1990) original methodology contained two processes. His initial two chapters focused on the self of the researcher, along with internal processes and self-searching for the tacit; the third and fourth chapters see him move outward to other participants and an objective observation of the phenomena.

For Sela-Smith (2002), who adapts Moustakas's methodology into heuristic self-search inquiry, the researcher's ability to acknowledge and experience feelings at all times is imperative for the project's success – without it, the tacit is curtailed and transformation is never achieved: 'There is no controlling the process; in fact, the opposite must take place. It is in this surrender into feeling-the-feelings and experiencing-the-experience that allows the self-as-researcher to enter heuristic self-search inquiry' (p. 83).

Meents (2006) extends Sela-Smith's focus on feelings as integral to heuristic self-search inquiry by arguing that they be codified and considered a necessary concept in heuristic methodology. This, of course, has implications for time. It is an agreement to enter what O'Donohue (2008) calls 'the season of your awkward harvesting, when the pain takes you where you would rather not go' (p. 143). In many ways, describing what we *see* is a relatively economical exercise; staying in the realm of feelings is another matter altogether. Hillman (1983) reminds us that the psyche does not speak its ultimate secret right away. It must be courted, coaxed, and waited for. Committed to the heuristic process, the researcher will eventually make contact with all that is hidden, suppressed, repressed, rejected, and feared in their feeling world. According to Sela-Smith (2002), this kind of sustained, timeless surrender to feelings is essential to the success of the heuristic self-search:

> The researcher must remain internally focused and dwell within the feelings of the tacit dimension, allowing the six phases to unfold naturally by surrendering to the feeling state of the subjective 'I'. Instead of rigorous planning and controlling the steps… the researcher must release control and discover whatever the stage has to offer. If any one of these phases is not completed with full integrity, heuristic research is not successfully accomplished.
>
> (p. 63)

Resistance

With Sela-Smith's critique in mind, it's probably telling that the concept of resistance is absent in both Douglass and Moustakas (1985) and Moustakas's (1990) work. Perhaps in its promotion of unwavering 'full and unqualified interest' (p. 3) Moustakas's (1990) formulation of heuristics assumes there will be none. He does concede that in the process of a heuristic search he (or the researcher) will inevitably 'challenge, confront, or even doubt my understanding of a human concern or issue… [but that] when I persist in a disciplined and devoted way I ultimately deepen my knowledge of the phenomenon' (p. 3). His suggestion seems to be that, if the researcher stays with the process of open reflexivity, resistance can be avoided, and everything will unfold as it should.

Sela-Smith (2001), however, wonders if Moustakas has too much faith in the process – after all, as Jung (1953) says, 'people will do anything, no matter how absurd, to avoid facing their own souls' (pp. 99–100). She notes Moustakas's resistance in the face of painful feelings. Ferendo (2004) also critiques the work of Wilber (1997), whose quadrant system inspired much of Sela-Smith's thinking, stating that Wilber tends to promote witnessing experience over feeling it. In her description of heuristic self-search inquiry, Sela-Smith's (2001) solution is not only to acknowledge resistance, but also to include 'the assumption that the researcher will resist the very search he or she initiates' (p. 191). She considers that resistance is endemic to every heuristic phase. In the initial stages, the researcher may be resistant to selecting the right question – that is, the one that takes them into a disavowed feeling. Within the process, the researcher may resist relinquishing control and surrendering to the journey. In immersion, resistance may lead them to abandon the unearthing of uncomfortable truths. The researcher's desire to speed up the process can also betray a resistance: the very claim of deadlines and temporal reality may be resistance in disguise. Ultimately, Sela-Smith argues, the researcher may get to the end of the journey and resist the transformation that their enquiry demands of them (Sela-Smith, 2001).

In doing so, she is summoning Proteus, the ancient Greek shape-shifting god. According to myth, Proteus was the guardian of knowledge, but he refused to hand it over without a fight. He evaded seekers by turning into fire, serpent, or stone; those who wished to consult him had to bide their time, surprising and binding him during his noonday slumber. There is perhaps no better corollary for the psyche's resistance to self-discovery, the unconscious's protective need to distract, distort, deny, and evade. Like the prophetic knowledge of Proteus, the truth often needs to be earned through persistence – it resists being grasped directly; it must be wrestled with, waited for, endured. As Sela-Smith (2001) puts it:

> The presence of resistance is evidence of the feeling that is being sought. If the researcher does not let go of the commitment to the process in spite of the resistance, and perhaps because of the resistance, in time, in its own time, discovery, understanding, and transformation happens. (p. 192)

According to Sela-Smith, resistance is both a limitation and a parameter of heuristic enquiry – that is to say, when you feel it, you know you're in the right place. She imagines the research question as a sliver deeply embedded in tissue, pushing its way to the surface. The researcher's job is to patiently attend to that point of pain, knowing that like blood, the truth will come out. This means reaching the crossroads of the painful or disavowed and making a decision. Sela-Smith (2001) argues that it was this time of *krisis* that led Moustakas to disconnect, and may tempt others to devalue, deny, or dissociate from their question. In a review of 28 heuristic projects, she found evidence of resistance in all but three which, in her evaluation, had subverted the process. Acknowledging the point of resistance, Sela-Smith argues, is the beginning of a different path. Through courageous and patient self-dialogue with the resistance, the researcher discovers a kind of dharma, a timeless kind of truth – and also a realisation that the truth is not contingent on time. Much like the therapeutic understanding of the word, resistance is a threshold guardian, it defends an insight that can't be forced before its time.

Surrender

The British philosopher Alan Watts once remarked that rowing was one of the clumsiest ways of travelling. Why would you bother pushing a boat across the water when you could just hoist a sail and let nature take its course? At times, Moustakas's (1990) description of heuristic enquiry can border on pragmatic. He mentions 'lifting out' essential meanings, 'actively awakening' and transforming the self. He calls the enquiry 'concentrated, heavy work' (p. 24). While he's also clear about honouring the process as it unfolds (he calls it a 'leashless path'), there's still a sense that, every now and then, he pulls out the oars.

Somewhere amongst this, Sela-Smith (2002) finds resistance, a need (originally) for Moustakas to control and structure the flow of enquiry. In doing this, he heads for the safety of the positivist, describing, defining, explaining, and predicting instead of simply *experiencing* the phenomenon. Sela-Smith argues that full heuristic investigation of a phenomenon requires total surrender to it;

abandoning hypothesis and expectation: 'There is no controlling the process; in fact, the opposite must take place. It is in this surrender into feeling-the-feelings and experiencing-the-experience that allows the self-as-researcher to enter heuristic self-search inquiry' (p. 83).

This is a sentiment that channels the Taoist principle of *wu wei*, or actionless activity. It's not doing nothing as much as it is non-resistance as a state of intense alertness. Like the wisdom underlying the practice of Eastern martial arts, you must yield to overcome – or, as Ferendo (2004) puts it, to cultivate surrender as a paradoxical attitude over action, awareness over activity.

For Sela-Smith (2001), the heuristic enquiry is not something that can be controlled or even steered; the idea is to let the process guide the researcher, whose job is 'letting go and falling into the river or swimming into the unknown current that occurs when one leaps into the unknown self' (p. 77). Only when the enquirer is fully surrendered can resistance be overcome and *terra incognita* breached: 'Each phase is an uncharted territory because the ground is not formed until the inquirer creates both the territory and the path by surrendering to the unknown and then walks the territory to discover what is there' (p. 64).

In her heuristic enquiry into prayer, Casterline (2006) equates this kind of surrender with a trust in the divine. Even under the weight of unbearable pain, Christ surrendered himself to a greater plan – 'not my will, but yours be done' (*English Standard Version Bible*, 2001, Luke 22:42). In the same way, heuristic surrender requires that we remain open to wherever our enquiry takes us, be it pain or revelation – we commit to a journey that 'may be refreshing and peaceful, or it may be disturbing and even jarring' (Moustakas, 1990, p. 13). This is a therapeutic stance promoted by Freud, Jung, Winnicott, and Bollas – that insight comes from staying with and reflecting on emotional experience long enough to transmute it into something helpful. Surrender requires the same kind of catalytic working through of interior material. In her articulation of the heuristic path of healing, Sela-Smith (2001) suggests true surrender takes us through the alliterative path of experiencing, expressing, examining, explicating, and extricating the subject at hand. Considering this process, Sela-Smith wonders if many heuristic researchers discover the point of resistance somewhere between expressing and examining what comes up, which makes sense, given that what is unearthed is often a feeling or experience long disavowed. In her mind, fully surrendering to the journey can take 'moments or even years' – she describes her own 2001 dissertation as the answer to a question seven years in the making. She equates full heuristic surrender with Rinzai Buddhism, where a novice is given a koan, a riddle that makes no rational sense. It's only when the initiate has given up on rational understanding, considering the question without the need to understand it, that enlightenment arrives.

Despite the scaffolding of its phases and concepts, and its toying with linearity and pragmatism, heuristic process is also one of surrender – to coin a phrase often attributed to Fritz Perls, we 'don't push the river – it flows by itself'. As Luke realised in his own dissertation, this means that our quest to know often means surrendering both compass and clock:

> Like Theseus navigating the labyrinth, heurism is an often-exasperating pilgrimage of left turns and circular returns. The seven processes, like Ariadne's thread, keep the explorer close to the heart of the quest. Sela-Smith (2002) suggests we surrender to the six phases, admitting that before we are found we must be lost. This evokes Stephen Levine's (1991) meditative concept of submitting to the great 'don't know', the ground zero at which we abandon preconceived ideas to access tacit knowing.
>
> (Oram, 2023, p. 16)

To surrender is to give ourselves over to the unforced rhythms of discovery. This is a place where illumination cannot be forced or excavated prematurely, where intuition lights only the next step ahead. Deep from the tacit realm, the answer calls in a whisper so faint its proximity is a mystery, and seems to taunt us: 'Lay down easy, stars in my eyes… But if you don't pick up what I choose to find | Oh, I'll be with you in my own time' (Chapman & Whitney, 1971).

Transformation

Transformation is an idea that Sela-Smith (2001) borrows from Ken Wilber in her expansion on Moustakas's original heuristic methodology. Much of Sela-Smith's deepening and critique of heuristic enquiry is inspired by Wilber's four quadrant system of knowledge, first popularised in his 1995 work *Sex, Ecology, and Spirituality*. According to Wilber, the transformation of self is achieved by traversing and interrogating the interior-individual (the *I* of thoughts, emotions, and intentions), the exterior-individual (the *it* of brain, body, and behaviour), the interior-collective (the *we* of culture and shared values), and the exterior-collective (the *its* of system and institution).

In Wilberian terms, Sela-Smith argues that Moustakas's original resistance represented a shift from the interior-individual realm to that of the exterior-individual (a shift from *feeling* the experience to *describing* it) – this shift away from painful inner experience circumvented the opportunity for self-transformation. In his heuristic enquiry into self-transformation, Ferendo (2004) argues that it is only when the researcher can linger in the interior quadrant, experiencing feelings and moving through resistance, that transformation can occur. Investigating 25 heuristic enquiries, Sela-Smith found no evidence of transformation, suggesting that, instead of staying with the experience of the '*I-who-feels*', each researcher headed for the safe ground of phenomenological explication of the experience instead.

Given that the point of heuristic enquiry is to engage with an interior question that demands an answer, it goes without saying that the journey should change us somewhat. Donald Winnicott once said that therapeutic transformation would only begin once the patient began to suffer their symptoms rather than describe them. In the same way, heuristic enquiry seems incomplete if the end result is simply a detailed explication of a phenomenon. To that end, Sela-Smith (2002) argues that one of the key components of heuristic self-search enquiry should be that 'there is evidence that transformation has taken place by way of a "story" that contains the transformation and may transform those who "read" it' (p. 69). Tudor (2023) takes this sense of personal transmutation further, wondering if Sela-Smith (2002) tended to emphasise individual transformation over a more collective stance. Reflecting on Wilber's (1997) bottom left quadrant (the consciousness of the 'we') as well as Rogers' (1961/1967) assertion that 'What is most personal is most general' (p. 26), Tudor suggests that heurism offers more than just a 'self-transformation', but the opportunity to shift from 'I-who-feels' to a 'we-who-care' perspective.

Luke's heuristic project (Oram, 2023) was inspired by his relationship with his father. As Luke reflects:

> A stoic man of English stock, he had always been a staid and largely silent presence to me. As I embarked on my psychotherapy training, a process which asks us to interrogate our psychodynamic DNA, I began to realise how little I knew about him, and how tenuous the thread between us felt. Curiously, the further I pressed into my own self-search, the more

> I felt him draw close to me – as if my own knowing had triggered off a vicarious desire in him to be known.
>
> As I considered the ways in which psychotherapy was helping me reimagine my father, I became overwhelmed with a sense that what was really happening was a call to a rite of passage between the two of us. In this way, the heuristic journey became something much more mythic, something akin to what Stephen Levine (1991) calls 'The great healing'. Levine describes this odyssey as an exploration of a sacred unknown, an investigation of 'the process and the space in which this process is floating… the vibrating boundary between the known and the unknown… the unexplored territory where all growth occurs'.
>
> (p. 56)

There is a quality of liminality to these places, which situate process outside of time and space. Anthropologist Victor Turner (1969) calls these places transitional and transformative. Remarking on Turner's liminal space as a rite of passage, Beels (2007) describes processes of 'being born, of learning, of growing, of entering adulthood, of becoming married, of recovering from an illness, or, finally, of dying' (p. 427). These processes seem extratemporal, rituals which interrupt daily routine, superseding our earthly schedules. They seem outside of time, betraying our very construct of order and importance. This is what lends them their sacredness. Considering the transformational nature of his heuristic process, Luke adds:

> When I think about my heuristic investigation of my father, I think about a kind of initiation, a parallel rite of passage between us. Almost a decade before Moustakas, Van Gennep (1909) was articulating the stages of this transformative journey: from separation to liminality to incorporation. The resemblance is uncanny. Although he doesn't use these phrases, Moustakas's conceptions of identification, immersion and incubation demand a kind of departing from the community, a necessary isolation into a world of single-minded obsession in the topic. We fall into a kind of trance, which threatens to remove us from our daily lives. We become preoccupied with the topic, shuffling through task and tenure in body, while our spirits exist on another plane of existence. At times the work becomes liminal. Heuristic writers speak of time slowing down, perhaps even ceasing to exist for a moment. There were moments in my project where I felt I had taken on a different internal orbit: at times the world whirred around me at double speed; at other times, my mind raced with illuminations that seemed to come faster than I could grab on to them. At times we become extemporal, even in a somatic sense – our mind is in another place, our body on autopilot. We are visitors in a strange, tacit land outside of space and time. This liminal space is reminiscent of the rite of passage, the moment when the child is removed from communitas, taken into the desert and transformed by the quest. This is also the quintessence of heurism – the fact that we don't study the topic from afar, we inhabit it, we live in its world, often departing this one to do so. For a moment, in that desert-place, I had to inhabit my father through self-dialogue, I had to become him in order to understand him. This is the liminal madness of immersion, something schizophrenic, ineffable, and uncertain. For a moment in the rite, the child is neither a child or a man, he is something in between, negotiating with time and generations.

That liminal space – the realm of immersion, of all that is tacit – is not unlike the transformative hero's journey, that of Orpheus, of Jonah, of Jesus. The difference is that it takes place in the 'unconscious realm that we tentatively explore in our own dreams… where the monsters inside of us take on terrifyingly real forms, where our deepest wishes sometimes are fulfilled' (Leeming, 1990, p. 312).

Of course, we all eventually return home. We synthesise and explicate – as Van Gennep (1909) says, we incorporate back into the whole, but we have been transformed in the process. We are different for having left, and we could never have predicted what would return. Both Moustakas and Sela-Smith would argue that this transformation could never have happened within the constraints of ordinary time.

Validation

Foregrounding subjectivity and focusing on inner experience, heuristic enquiry departs even further from traditional approaches to validation in qualitative methods. However, as Amedeo Giorgi (2002) argues, 'knowledge, as a phenomenon in the world, is strictly correlated with subjectivity. Perhaps there are things or events "in-themselves", but there is no "knowledge-in-itself". There is only knowledge for a human subject who apprehends it' (p. 9). He continues:

> the question becomes, when does a human subject apprehend a state of affairs as it really is, and when does a human subject distort a state of affairs by overimposing subjectivity on it, or by not grasping sufficiently because the subject was too little present or inattentive to the state of affairs. The former would be valid knowledge and the latter two would be invalid.
> (p. 9)

Moustakas (1990) would agree, suggesting that the question of validity in heuristics is one of meaning – that is, a comprehensive and vivid explication of the researcher's experience. Douglass and Moustakas (1985) claim that validity in heuristic research is 'inherent, insofar as it pursues the truth, to the extent that it is conducted through authentic self-processes' (p. 44). Taken together, these authors suggest that heuristic research should be considered valid if:

- it is a *true* reflection of the experience 'as it really is'
- it is *subjective* – that is, borne out of personal feelings about and experience of a phenomenon
- it is thoroughly explicated – not resisted or curtailed, but *fully* and presently experienced and explored.

Reflecting on his use of co-participants, Moustakas (1990) also suggests that validity can be achieved through checking one's experience against that of others, but this view is debated. Later heuristic enquirers such as Sela-Smith (2002) insist that co-researchers (if employed) are there as 'valuable reflectors' (p. 76) or to create a 'reaction' (p. 76) in the researcher to support or provoke an inward reach towards illumination of the researcher's tacit knowledge of the experience. Sela-Smith (2002) argues that if co-researchers are employed they can have the opposite effect of validation, and cause the researcher to have a 'dissociated process' (p. 76) and 'distraction from the internal process' (p. 76) (see also Cardo, 2024). Co-researchers are considered more recently by heuristic researchers such as Mihalache (2019) as not there to validate a heuristic enquiry, but there 'as an expansion of it' (p. 141), for, if they were validators of a study, the study would be a phenomenological interpretation such as interpretative phenomenological analysis. Finally and most recently, Tudor (2023) suggests that validation can be sought through the rigorous academic process of the Master's and doctoral research supervision and examination phases from the transfer panel that grants candidature to the final viva voce oral examination (Cardo & Tudor, 2024). Elsewhere, noting the common charge of solipsism levied against heurism, Stewart employed the validation of the collective, complimenting her research with a peer research group, research journals, supervision, and twice weekly therapy (Stewart & Thomas, 2020).

If the ultimate intent of heuristic enquiry is to accept the Delphic injunction to *Know thyself*, then how do we claim that knowledge as valid? At the risk of presenting a circular process, perhaps concepts like transformation become more important. If the researcher has been changed by their quest, if their enquiry has led to new knowledge and insight, surely the process has been successful? If, as Moustakas (1990) says, validity comes through meaning, then a successful heuristic enquiry should deliver a new kind of meaning, cast the research issue, question, or problem posed in a new light. This is why we speak of illuminations and eureka moments – indeed, the word heuristic, born from the Greek word *heuriskein*, means to discover or to find. Souba (2011) suggests that the heuristic process is one of 'languaging the unknown' (p. 53). Thus, in a way, heuristic enquiry becomes valid once we have discovered and named our *terra incognita*, when, as Eliot (1943) puts it: we 'arrive where we started and know the place for the first time' (p. 27).

Validity has implications for time. People like Moustakas and Sela-Smith still advocate for a kind of robustness and rigour to the process, but this applies to the thoroughness of the journey itself. Did the researcher fully surrender to the search, giving it as much time as it needed, or did they prematurely eject or cut corners? Was the clock in charge, or was the leashless path followed? The heuristic enquiry is valid when the researcher can exhibit the patience of Rilke (1929/1992) towards 'all that is unsolved' (p. 24), loving the questions rather than foreclosing on them. Did it take as long as it needed to take?

Conclusion

To engage in heuristic research is to engage in a kind of temporal double vision. On one hand, the enquiry demands a stepping outside of ordinary time – an immersion in *kairos*, a submission to the timeless drift of tacit realms, intuitive whispers, and the recursive rhythm of self-dialogue. On the other, the researcher is inescapably tethered to *chronos*: the clock, the calendar, the creeping insistence of deadlines and life demands. Inasmuch as the researcher is seeking knowledge previously hidden to them, they are also engaging with the hidden context of time. This chapter has explored how time both supports and subverts the heuristic process – how it is at once catalyst and constraint, fertile soil and boundary line.

If Moustakas invites us to 'live the question', then time becomes not a hurdle to overcome but a terrain to navigate with care. We must discern, as Valéry suggests, the point of abandonment – not as failure, but as fidelity to the moment when the question has yielded what it can, for now. Sela-Smith reminds us that this journey is not merely methodological, but mythopoetic: a descent into the self in which resistance, surrender, and transformation form the arc of our passage.

Ultimately, the heuristic journey is not about mastery over time, but about befriending its multiplicity. It is about knowing when to dwell and when to let go, when to seek and when to be still. In this way, heuristic enquiry offers not just insight into a phenomenon, but an invitation into a deeper rhythm of knowing – one that echoes Levine's (1991) 'great don't know' (p. 10) and Eliot's (1943) homecoming: to arrive where we started, and know the place for the first time. So, if the researcher seems to be taking too long, or perhaps not long enough, let us remember: they are keeping and in their own time.

References

Alleyne, B. (2017). *A psychotherapist's experience of grief: A heuristic enquiry* [Master's dissertation, Auckland University of Technology]. Tuwhera Open Access Theses & Dissertations. https://hdl.handle.net/10292/10424

Beels, C. C. (2007). Psychotherapy as a rite of passage. *Family Process*, *46*(4), 421–436. https://doi.org/10.1111/j.1545-5300.2007.00223.x

Bollas, C. (1987). *The shadow of the object: Psychoanalysis of the unthought known*. Columbia University Press.

Boyd, E. M., & Fales, A. W. (1983). Reflective learning: Key to learning from experience. *Journal of Humanistic Psychology*, *23*(2), 99–117. https://doi.org/10.1177/0022167883232011

Bretall, R. (1946). *A Kierkegaard anthology*. Princeton University Press.

Cardo, G. (2024). *A heuristic enquiry of the lived experience of being 'Alaq' as a convert to Islam* [Doctoral thesis, Middlesex University]. Middlesex University Research Repository. https://repository.mdx.ac.uk/item/1ww842

Cardo, G., & Tudor, K. (2024). A comparison between the concepts of heuristic enquiry and tazkiyat-un-nafs. *European Journal for Qualitative Research in Psychotherapy*, *14*, 75–90. https://ejqrp.org/index.php/ejqrp/article/view/298/144

Casterline, G. (2006). *The experience of the act of praying* [Doctoral dissertation, Loyola University]. ProQuest Dissertations & Theses.

Chapman, R., & Whitney, J. (1971). *In my own time* [Record]. Reprise.

Chue, D. (2021). *Falling into the abyss: A heuristic self-inquiry into a psychotherapist's experience of abrupt endings* [Master's dissertation, Auckland University of Technology]. Tuwhera Open Access Theses & Dissertations. https://hdl.handle.net/10292/14790

Cousins, G. (2023). *In search of the boarding school self: A heuristic inquiry* [Master's dissertation, Auckland University of Technology]. Tuwhera Open Access Theses & Dissertations. http://hdl.handle.net/10292/17753

Cousins, G., Humphris, A., Kingi, A., Oram, L., & Tudor, K. (2025). Catalyst and constraint: The question of time in heuristic research. In W. Ings & K. Tudor (Eds.), *Heuristic enquiries: Research across disciplines and professions* (pp. 162–180). Routledge. https://doi.org/10.4324/9781003507758

Douglass, B., & Moustakas, C. E. (1985). Heuristic inquiry: The internal search to know. *Journal of Humanistic Psychology*, *25*(3), 39–55. https://doi.org/10.1177/0022167885253004

Eliot, T. S. (1943). *Four quartets*. Harcourt, Brace and Co.

English Standard Version Bible. (2001). ESV Online. https://esv.literalword.com

Ferendo, F. J. (2004). *A heuristic and hermeneutic inquiry: Ken Wilber and personal transformation* [Unpublished doctoral dissertation, Union Institute and University].

Franklin, M. (2017). *'Nature and I', an ecotherapy journey: A heuristic inquiry into nature's role in healing, from a psychotherapy perspective* [Master's dissertation, Auckland University of Technology]. Tuwhera Open Access Theses & Dissertations. https://hdl.handle.net/10292/11009

Gendlin, E. T. (1978). *Focusing*. Everest House.

Giorgi, A. (2002). The question of validity in qualitative research. *Journal of Phenomenological Psychology*, *33*(1), 1–18. https://doi.org/10.1163/156916202320900392

Grennell, N. (2014). *What is the experience of being both Māori and Pākehā? Negotiating the experience of the hybrid cultural object* [Master's dissertation, Auckland University of Technology]. Tuwhera Open Access Theses & Dissertations. https://hdl.handle.net/10292/7710

Haydon, S. (2024). *Work-in-progress: A trainee psychotherapist's experience with aesthetic inquiry* [Master's dissertation, Auckland University of Technology]. Tuwhera Open Access Research Outputs. http://hdl.handle.net/10292/20043.

Hillman, J. (1983). *Healing fiction*. Spring Publications.

hooks, b. (2000). *Where we stand: Class matters*. Routledge.

Ings, W., & Tudor, K. (2025). *Heuristic enquiries: Research across disciplines and professions*. Routledge. https://doi.org/10.4324/9781003507758

Jourard, S. (1971). *Self-disclosure: An experimental analysis of the transparent self*. Wiley-Interscience.

Jung, C. G. (1953). *Collected works, Vol. 12: Psychology and alchemy*. Pantheon Books.

Jung, C. G. (2009). *The red book: Liber novus* (S. Shamdasani, Ed. & M. Kyburz, J. Peck, & S. Shamdasani, Trans.). W. W. Norton & Company.

Leeming, D. A. (1990). *The world of myth*. Oxford University Press.

Levine, S. (1991). *Guided meditations, explorations and healings*. Anchor Books.

Loewald, H. (1980). The experience of time. In H. Loewald, *Papers on psychoanalysis* (pp. 138–147). Yale University Press. (Original work published 1972)

McCall, J. (2021). *The art of mourning: Exploring the impact of artistic creation upon the psychotherapist* [Master's dissertation, Auckland University of Technology]. Tuwhera Open Access Theses & Dissertations. https://hdl.handle.net/10292/14395

McGrath, H. P., & Comenetz, M. (2013). *Valéry's graveyard: Le Cimetière marin: Translated, described, and peopled*. Peter Lang.

Meents, J. (2006). *Acres of diamonds: A heuristic self-search inquiry into intuition* [Doctoral thesis, University of Calgary]. www.collectionscanada.gc.ca/obj/thesescanada/vol2/002/NR19162.PDF

Mihalache, G. (2019). Heuristic inquiry: Differentiated from descriptive phenomenology and aligned with transpersonal research methods. *The Humanistic Psychologist*, *47*(2), 136–157. https://doi.org/10.1037/hum0000125

Mitchell, S. (2002). *The Bhagavad Gita*. Crown Publications.

Moustakas, C. (1961). *Loneliness*. Prentice-Hall.

Moustakas, C. (1967). Heuristic research. In J. F. T. Bugental (Ed.), *Challenges of humanistic psychology* (pp. 100–107). McGraw-Hill.

Moustakas, C. (1990). *Heuristic research: Design, methodology, and applications*. Sage Publications.

Neruda, P. (1994). *Odes to common things* (K. Krabbenhoft & F. Cook, Trans.). Bulfinch Press.

O'Donohue, J. (2008). *To bless the space between us: A book of blessings*. Harmony/Rodale/Convergent.

Oram, L. (2023). *Remaking the Imago Paterna: How psychotherapy helps a son reimagine the father. A heuristic enquiry* [Master's dissertation, Auckland University of Technology]. Tuwhera Open Access Theses & Dissertations. http://hdl.handle.net/10292/17754

Polanyi, M. (1966). *The tacit dimension*. University of Chicago Press.

Polanyi, M. (1969). *Knowing and being* (M. Grene, Ed.). University of Chicago Press.

Rilke, R. M. (1992). *Letters to a young poet*. New World Library. (Original work published 1929)

Rogers, C. R. (1951). *Client-centered therapy*. Houghton-Mifflin.

Rogers, C. R. (1967). *On becoming a person: A therapist's view of psychotherapy*. Constable. (Original work published 1961)

Rogers, C. R. (1969). *Freedom to learn*. Charles E. Merrill.

Salk, J. (1983). *Anatomy of reality*. Columbia University Press.

Sela-Smith, S. (2001). *Heuristic self-search inquiry: Clarification of Moustakas' heuristic research* [Doctoral dissertation, Saybrook Graduate School and Research Center]. ProQuest Dissertations & Theses.

Sela-Smith, S. (2002). Heuristic research: A review and critique of Moustakas's method. *Journal of Humanistic Psychology*, *42*(3), 53–88. https://doi.org/10.1177/0022167802423004

Simon, H. A. (1992). What is an 'explanation' of behavior? *Psychological Science*, *3*(3), 150–161. https://doi.org/10.1111/j.1467-9280.1992.tb00017.x

Smith, J. T. (1902). Friends of Jesus. *Church Missionary Intelligencer and Record*, *53*, 809–812.

Souba, W. (2011). The language of discovery. *Journal of Biomedical Discovery and Collaboration*, *6*, 53–69. https://doi.org/10.5210/disco.v6i0.3634

Stern, D. (2000). *The present moment in psychotherapy and everyday life*. Norton.

Stewart, K., & Thomas, V. (2020). A trainee psychotherapist's heuristic exploration of losing a mother to suicide. *British Journal of Guidance & Counselling, 48*(4), 552–562. https://doi.org/10.1080/03069885.2018.1519181

Sultan, N. (2019). *Heuristic inquiry: Researching human experience holistically*. Sage.

Taft, J. (1933). *The dynamics of therapy in a controlled relationship.* Macmillan Co.

Tudor, K. (2010). *The fight for health: A heuristic enquiry into psychological well-being* [Unpublished context statement]. PhD in Mental Health Promotion by Public (Published) Works, School of Health and Social Sciences, Middlesex University, London, UK.

Tudor, K. (2017). The fight for health: An heuristic enquiry. In K. Tudor, *Conscience and critic: The selected works of Keith Tudor* (pp. 143–168). Routledge.

Tudor, K. (2022). Supporting critical self-enquiry: Doing heuristic research. In S. Bager-Charleson & A. McBeath (Eds.), *Supporting research in counselling and psychotherapy* (pp. 57–79). Springer.

Tudor, K. (2023). Critical heuristics: From 'I who feels' to 'We who care – and act'. In K. Tudor & J. Wyatt (Eds.), *Qualitative research approaches for psychotherapy: Reflexivity, methodology, and criticality* (pp. 115–132). Routledge.

Tudor, K. (2025). *Transactional analysis proper – and improper: Selected and new papers*. Routledge.

Turner, V. (1969). *The ritual process: Structure and anti-structure*. Aldine de Gruyter.

Updegraff, R. R. (1958). *All the time you need: The greatest gift in the world.* Prentice-Hall.

Van Gennep, A. (1909). *The rites of passage*. University of Chicago Press.

Wells, H. G. (1898). *The time machine*. William Heinemann.

Wharton, E. (1880, April). Patience. *The Atlantic, XLV*, p. 548.

Wilber, K. (1995). *Sex, ecology, and spirituality*. Shambhala.

Wilber, K. (1997). *The eye of spirit*. Shambhala.

PART II
Method

5

GESTATING DISCOVERY

The heuristic journey, from conception to birth and beyond

Alana West[1] *and Keith Tudor*

The process of heuristic research is not unlike the mysterious and transformative journey of gestation and birth. Just as a new life begins with an initial spark of conception, the research process starts with an inspiration or a question – something small, but full of potential. Moustakas (1990) refers to the autobiographical nature of the heuristic process, and that the data lie within the researcher, thus highlighting the importance of the researcher's own awareness and self-discoveries. The heuristic process is, therefore, deeply personal and can be very intimate. In this chapter, based on the first author's heuristic enquiry into the experience(s) both of being a mother and training as a psychotherapist (and hence the first-person voice in the chapter), under the academic supervision of the second author, we explore how the heuristic research process can be understood as a parallel to the natural stages of conception, pregnancy, and childbirth. We conclude with some brief comments on the process of supervision, likening it to a midwifery.

Sela-Smith's (2002) heuristic self-search inquiry (HSSI) encourages the researcher to explore personal experience in a deep and meaningful way and, thereby, to gain insight into phenomena of human experience. It highlights the importance of individual subjectivity rather than objective data, a perspective which was essential in my research of the human experience. HSSI allowed me to capture the experience as it happened, with support of theory. Similar to the stages of pregnancy, this process is iterative, with each phase building on the one before it. The original HSSI dissertation on which this chapter is based (Humphris, 2023) was framed by four of Moustakas's (1990) heuristic phases: initial engagement, immersion, explication, and creative synthesis. Due to university time constraints and my immersion in both motherhood and psychotherapy training while researching and writing the dissertation, there was little or no time for incubation (see Cousins et al., 2024; Maya-Chipman & Tudor, 2026 [Chapter 9 in this volume]), although I experienced illuminations throughout the journey (regarding which, see Tudor, 2022, 2023). It was apparent that this process had parallels to the conception, gestation, labour, and birth phases in the transition to motherhood, otherwise known as matrescense (Raphael, 1975) – and to the journey to becoming a psychotherapist. Although this chapter focuses on the phases, i.e., the *method* of the heuristic research journey, the original research (Humphris, 2023) also drew on Moustakas's (1990) concepts, i.e., identifying with the focus of enquiry, self-dialogue, tacit knowing, intuition, indwelling, focusing, and the internal frame of reference (Moustakas, 1990), and, given the focus

DOI: 10.4324/9781003685944-8

of Sela-Smith's (2002) concepts of self-search, inward reach, resistance, and surrender, all of which contribute to the methodology of heuristic research (see chapters in Part I of this volume). This chapter is illustrated with images from my own pregnancy (see Figures 5.1–5.4).

Initial engagement – Conception

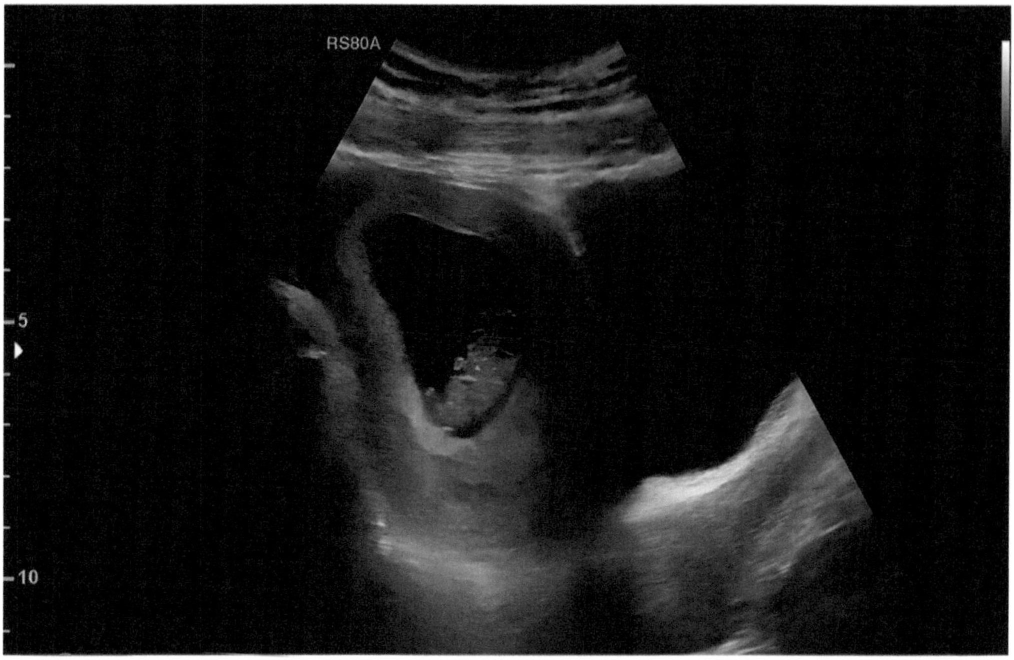

FIGURE 5.1 Conception: 12-week scan. Image source: Alana Humphris (2023).

Conception marks the beginning of life. Similarly, heuristic research begins with an idea: a flicker of curiosity, a compelling question, or a problem that captures the researcher's attention. We suggest that this is the conception phase of the research – which, indeed, is often referred to as the initial conceptualisation. Just as the moment of fertilisation brings together the necessary genetic material to form a new life, the initial question or idea forms the embryo of the research journey. It may be a question that comes from personal experience or a deeper drive to understand a particular phenomenon. Much like the egg and sperm uniting, the researcher's interest and the research subject come together to create something new, something that will grow and develop over time. The researcher is an active participant in the research. The subject of study becomes intertwined with the researcher's own experience, and this convergence sparks the research process into life and development. In many ways, the first stages of heuristic research feel tentative and exploratory, like the first stirrings of life. The researcher senses the potential of what could be, even if the full scope is not yet clear. As I put it (in a journal I kept during the time):

> Beginning this research, I felt lost; after many years of structured academic research, beginning a heuristic inquiry felt unfamiliar and daunting. I found it difficult to look inwards, to experience first and write later.
>
> (A. Humphris, journal entry, 21st April 2023)

The Gestalt therapy technique of the empty chair allowed me to reach inward in a raw and authentic manner. According to Sultan (2019), this technique leads to 'greater understanding of an experience not by thinking about it or by talking about it, but by becoming it' (p. 82). This supports the researcher to reach inward for tacit awareness and knowledge, allowing their intuition to run freely (Moustakas, 1990) – and, metaphorically, parallels conception, as the empty space is filled with new possibilities.

During this phase, I attempted to engage with the topic and document my experiential awareness. Polanyi (1958/2002) explored tacit knowledge, which refers to some knowledge within us that is not easily accessed or articulated. The exploration of this knowledge leads to illumination (Moustakas, 1990). Sela-Smith (2002) observes that tacit knowledge is often embodied, emotional, and plays an important if not requisite role in self-search enquiry. Indwelling is one way of accessing this information by connecting with one's inner world. In my research, the process of accessing tacit knowledge was a challenge as I struggled to find time and space to indwell without distraction. I endeavoured to access the tacit dimension through self-dialogue, which I found difficult to recall. I was, however, sustained by Sela-Smith's (2002) reference to the 'passionate concern that causes the investigator to *reach inward for* tacit knowledge' (p. 69); this helped me maintain motivation throughout the study.

During the period allocated to this work (March–November 2023), not insignificantly nine months, I struggled to submit myself (surrender) to the phases (method) and concepts (methodology) of heuristic research. I observed an avoidance to surveil my authentic experience and struggled to find time without distraction. I put undue pressure on myself to 'discover' and inevitably felt inadequate when I didn't. While I focused my attention on the phenomena, I lost sight of my own existence within it, realising that self-awareness and attention to my experiential process are essential. Sela-Smith (2002) emphasises the concept and practice of surrender, in reference to a process of letting go of preconceived notions, biases, and rigid expectations during the heuristic research journey. Writing about the last frontier of science as exploring the interiority of our experience, Sela-Smith (2002) asserts that:

> Mainstream science, which includes traditional research psychology, has focused on describing, defining, explaining, and predicting the objects of its investigation. However, what I identify as this last frontier requires setting aside the skills of controlled, objective observation and surrendering to embracing subjective experience and leaping into the unknown.
>
> (p. 54)

This is an essential process in order to ensure the authenticity of the study – and parallels the need in pregnancy to surrender as the mother submits herself to and for that process to occur naturally. Both involve letting go of control and allowing authentic experience to come forth. As a solution to this challenge in my research journey, I began recording raw and unedited random thoughts, dreams, and notions in the notes application on my mobile phone. As I subjected my raw, unedited, messy experience to the process, illumination began to spring forth. For me it involved releasing myself from preconceived notions of what the research should be and what constitutes valid knowledge. This allowed me to connect genuinely with myself and interact with the phenomena of my personal experience. This contributed to my ability to be authentic as I explored my genuine human experience rather than superficial or detached observations. Throughout the process, it was important to remember to keep re-surrendering to the phases as

I moved through them and the needs of the study changed. Now, I can simply say that, when I gave myself fully to the process by letting go of the 'not good enough' and a rigid timeline of expectations, I was able to allow the process to happen in a natural and authentic way.

My topic was chosen based on my first-hand experience as a mother in psychotherapy training on which I found little existing research. I wished to document an account of an ever-changing and evolving identity as both a mother and as a training psychotherapist and to identify the unique and interrelated challenges of both. The intention was to illuminate some of the shadowed experiences of mothers engaging in psychotherapy training. As heuristic research values the researcher's subjectivity, I began by describing my world, highlighting some of my own, previous experience of conception and birth:

> When my son was born it felt like a different kind of gravity, the centre of my universe shifted; one part of my awareness always focused on him, even in my sleep. In the first years I lost a sense of self, and I found myself in an ever-changing role of mother, friend, play person, nurse, provider, and protector, driven by one force – attachment… It felt as if I had only just begun to recover from his birth after having my body damaged to save his life and mine. He was now at the age where separating and individuating was a developmental task, just as I began my studies about attachment and developmental stages. He was also moving into the older children's space in his childcare. My awareness and insights into the human experience developed and as I learnt about the importance of 'the mother' in the context of human psychology, I was actively being 'the mother' to a small child.
>
> (A. Humphris, journal entry, 7th May 2023)

Immersion – Gestation

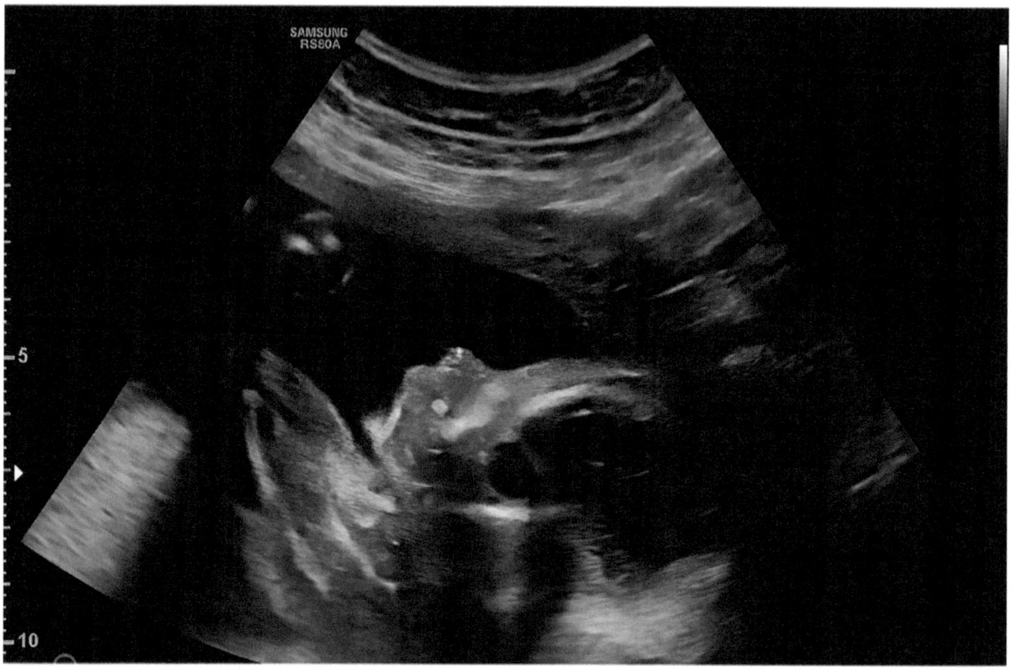

FIGURE 5.2 Foetus: 22-week scan. Image source: Alana Humphris (2023).

In my final research dissertation, I named the chapter relating to this stage 'Gestation – Growing my knowing' to reflect that the researcher may encounter challenges, much like the physical and emotional discomforts of pregnancy. My own periods of gestating my two children were 21 May 2014 – 10 March 2015 and 15 January 2023 – 18 October 2024. During gestation, both biological and intellectual, uncertainty can arise, and the way forward may appear unclear; yet these challenges often serve as catalysts for illumination. They are, in effect, the growing pains that shape the outcome, pushing the researcher to accommodate what is gestating, to adapt, to refine their method(s), and to move closer to a holistic way of being with emerging understanding. The scope of this chapter (in my dissertation) was to outline my engagement with the material, including research about the methodology itself and the topic, in which phase, as Moustakas (1990) puts it: 'virtually anything connected with the question becomes raw material for immersion' (p. 28).

> As I began to engage in heuristic research, I felt overwhelmed by the unknown. It felt like I was looking into an abyss, with no limitations to where I could extend my experience. I have had the experience of being a mother, being told the many ways to parent that others have tried; and of being a training psychotherapist, following a specific modality that has worked for many others. I needed to break out of my repeated experience of 'being told' and 'knowing' what I am doing before I do it (i.e., this dissertation).
>
> (A. Humphris, journal entry, 10th May 2023)

From an experiential perspective, the immersion phase had begun before I began the research. The difference was in actively researching and observing my immersion in the topic in the here-and-now. As I formulated a literature review and reflected on the literature, the topic infiltrated my mind and the minds of those around me. I found conversations with co-workers, friends, and family became implicitly and explicitly related to the topic. Something similar happens in pregnancy, during which the mother enters what Stern (1995) refers to as *The Motherhood Constellation*. When her focus shifts from her other relationships and priorities to that of the unborn child.

Sela-Smith (2002) observes that resistance can arise when the researcher attempts to confront personal experiences during the research process as this can shift the focus from an internal journey of self-exploration to a more external, phenomenological enquiry.

> The incubation and immersion phases felt like I was doing nothing or like I was not doing well enough. My dissertation was like the new baby with needs that I could not yet attune to, and I ended up feeling like I was doing it wrong. I used my personal psychoanalytic psychotherapy as a space to ponder and wonder and realised a resistance to submitting to the process of not knowing in order to come to know something.
>
> (A. Humphris, journal entry, 30th September 2023)

Sela-Smith (2002) emphasises that true heuristic inquiry demands a profound engagement with one's own emotions and experiences. While this is true, such engagement needs external support. For me, supervision supported me to recognise my own resistance early in the research process. In supervision, I explored my resistance and was able to move through it in order to surrender to the process. Interestingly (at least to us), Sela-Smith doesn't refer to supervision as supporting HSSI. I also came to understand that accessing my intuitive clues and hunches required a unique form of attention. Moustakas (1990) suggests recording and then recounting stories. Despite the challenge of scheduling such moments of reflection, I committed to setting aside one day every two weeks for reading and journaling in a state of reverie. Also, throughout this period, I diligently documented my dreams, anticipating that they could offer valuable insights from my unconscious mind. I then recounted these dreams to enhance my understanding and gain deeper insights:

> Throughout the process, as I recognised avoidance, I had to develop creative ways to stretch time which included taking voice recordings while commuting, recording random scribblings and notes, and taking notes in the notes application of my phone.
>
> (A. Humphris, journal entry, 30th September 2023)

As in the first stages of pregnancy where the foetus begins to develop, the heuristic research process is marked by a period of growth, in which the enquiry begins to take shape. The researcher immerses themselves in the subject with deep reflection and enquiry: an exploration of unknowns. Just as an unborn child's development occurs out of sight, at this point the full shape and weight of the research process is not always clear. My self-search enquiry involved engaging heuristic concepts and processes to surrender to the heuristic phases, as Sela-Smith (2002) suggests. It required my own open-ended reflection and data collection. My process was guided by intuition and included reviewing existing literature, self-reflection, reverie, and dreaming: all of which were expanding my potential sources of information and meaning. I reflected on my own feelings, biases, and perspectives, just as in my pregnancies (one before and one after this research) I reflected on the life I nurtured. As a part of my heuristic process, I read Moustakas's work on heuristic research (Douglass & Moustakas, 1985; Moustakas, 1990) and reviewed Sela-Smith's (2002) critique of Moustakas's method and methodology and her adaptation of it as a self-search inquiry, i.e., HSSI. I collated existing heuristic research, along with my own spontaneous reflective writings and dreams for analysis in order to identify themes and concepts. As I delved deeper, the research question and insights evolved, uncovering nuances that shaped the direction of the enquiry, much like how the foetus begins to form distinct features during pregnancy. There is a powerful sense of embodiment in this phase: just as a mother feels the presence of her growing child, the researcher begins to feel a stronger connection to the enquiry. The research becomes a part of the researcher, not just something they study from a distance. This is not a process of simply collecting facts; rather, it is an internal journey of discovery and engagement with the question on a deeper level.

Traditionally, the incubation phase would involve the researcher separating themselves from the research topic and trying not to think about it. In critical consideration of my specific research, I found that I could not objectively separate myself from my research topic as it directly related to aspects of my identity. Incubation as a phase was impossible. Therefore, it became an ongoing parallel process, where I moved in and out of relating consciously to the topic. I realised it required me to separate physically and psychologically from both my home life and university life and intentionally concentrate on something else. I attempted intentional mind wandering (Bar, 2022) regarding which Baird et al. (2012) suggest that the conditions that favour such wandering also enhance creativity *during an incubation period*. For me, this process supported spontaneous self-dialogue and self-searching as information.

Explication – Labour

As labour approaches, the expectant mother must prepare for the intense process of birthing her child. This stage mirrors the final phase of heuristic research, in which the researcher synthesises all the data, reflections, and experiences into a coherent whole. The metaphorical labour involves the tension between theory, practice, analysis, and interpretation.

This required focus and a willingness to confront the unknown as I pulled together the various threads of my data and findings or, more consistent with heurism, discoveries. Just as a mother experiences physical pain and exhaustion during labour, I felt the strain of processing insights from different perspectives, experiences, and data – and integrating them into a unified understanding. I felt a sense of urgency, as we neared the due date, knowing that the moment of birth was drawing near. Alongside my drive to bring the research into the world in a meaningful way, I felt moments of doubt. Moustakas (1990) describes this phase as intending to examine illuminations that have arisen to consciousness and identify deeper themes and meaning. This phase required further reflective self-searching and self-disclosure. It also required recognition and valuing of my unique experience and appreciation of my internal frame of reference. Explication required attendance to and observation of my existing frame of reference in preparation of analyses and development of concise and clear findings (Moustakas, 1990).

Reflecting on these points, I became aware of the repetition of the word 'required' in the previous paragraph, which represents underlying demands in both childbirth and academic research. The mother/researcher does not just fulfil hopes and expectations, but also biological and academic 'requirements'. The process and result(s) are meaningful and impactful not only to/on the mother/researcher, but also to those the outcome (baby/research) will affect throughout its existence.

A broad-minded depiction of the dominant themes was illuminated, bringing together, and making sense of experience(s) both as a mother and as a training psychotherapist. The act of creation in research, like in childbirth, is often messy, painful, and chaotic, but also transformative and profound.

In this stage, again, supervision was a particular grounding support, as I brought together months of research to create an academic output: my dissertation. In doing so, I grappled with the ethical dilemma and implications of self-disclosure as my research was to be published on the university's website and, thereby, accessible to existing and potential clients, and others. For me, it was essential to consider my son's privacy, and to limit the degree to which anything implicating or relating to him was explored in my writing – and, again, in this publication. Winnicott (1964) refers to holding as the emotional and physical support that the caregiver offers to the baby; and Stern and Bruschweiler-Stern (1998) highlight the importance of a support system for new mothers as they journey through motherhood. I consider – and posit – that academic supervision is the principal holding environment for new researchers – and that a heuristic approach to supervision is most helpful for undertaking heuristic research (see Tudor & Ings, 2025). As I put it, in my contribution to a chapter on the subject:

> My supervisor [Keith] would offer tacit knowledge and intuition, holding the uncertainty and the 'not knowing' with openness, interest/enthusiasm, understanding, and curiosity. This, in turn, elicited enthusiasm in me and sparked a light for the dying fire, leaving me feeling like I was on the right track… He also challenged my prescribed way of writing by pointing out when my approach wasn't heuristic, and, by doing this he protected the method.
>
> (in Tudor & Ings, 2025, pp. 195–196)

For me, supervision was an essential part of my heuristic research, not only as a supportive space where I could bring my academic difficulties and search for guidance, but also as a space to process uncontained and raw material and be supported to open to new ideas and emerging understandings. It also provided a mirror to highlight my resistance to the process and an environment to which I – and we – could find different ways forward. Finally, regular and engaged supervision reduced the limitations of heuristic research as I was not limited to my own level of knowledge and bias.

For me (Keith), I conceptualise supervision, whether academic or clinical, as offering wider sight rather than oversight (Tudor & Worrall, 2004), and as a maieutic process, that is, originally, the process of helping a woman to give birth, and, in this context, helping a person to give birth to new ideas (for further discussion of which, see Embleton Tudor & Worrall, 2007).

Creative synthesis – Birth

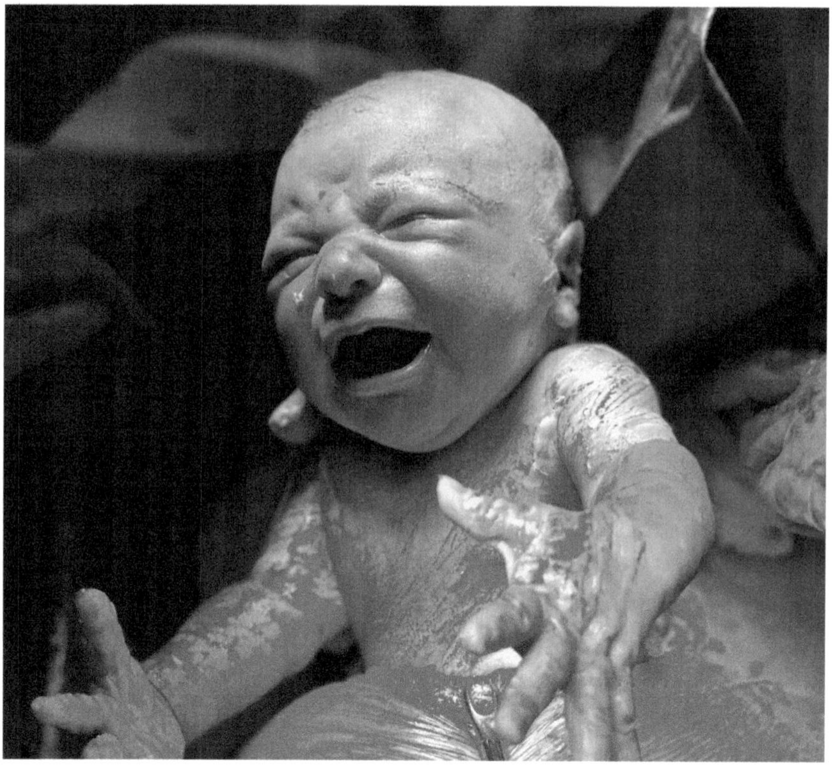

FIGURE 5.3 The birthing. Image source: Alana Humphris (2023).

The final stage of heuristic research mirrors the moment of birth – the revelation of a new understanding, a new contribution to knowledge. The sources for my research were a combination of my own subjective experiences (as referred to here) and references to existing literature (see Humphris, 2023). Illumination is the heuristic phase that expects there will be a lightbulb moment which marks the discovery of new knowledge or ideas. I feared illumination would not arise and it was difficult to surrender to the idea that the research would have viability or be successful without it/them. Tudor (2022) argues that illumination is not a set phase, as it happens throughout rather than at a particular stage of the heuristic research process. This was true in my experience, as illumination occurred throughout several of the research phases as I mined into my experience and deepened my understanding of my experience(s) – and the phenomena.

Developing the creative synthesis was difficult. I had a resistance to sum up my experience due to fearing that it would not be 'good enough' or, as a heuristic researcher, 'not illuminative enough'. I tried to find space for meditation in order to focus and to allow my inhibitions and restrictions to drop, while self-searching in an attempt to access the tacit dimension and intuition and to allow something to emerge (Moustakas, 1990). I spent time ruminating about what I had written and, fortunately, found meaning in my writing. After the intensity of labour, there is the release of tension. Having struggled through the challenges and complexities of the heuristic research process, I could now experience the reward: the birth of the research, a new life, a new understanding of the experience and phenomenon at hand.

Due to the constraints of time and word limits, imposed by the university for this particular master's dissertation, there were limits to the fuller exploration of tacit knowing (Cousins et al., 2024; Tudor, 2022). Traditionally, heuristic research is timeless, as the researcher moves through the phases in their own time and pace. In the original research project, it was essential to schedule specific time each week in order to meet the university requirements. There were also benefits of the time limit in that there was a certain pressure to focus on and recognise my resistance (Sela-Smith, 2002). In this sense, the time and word limits also acted as a catalyst (Cousins et al., 2024). Time-limited heuristic research paralleled the process as an expecting mother, where I had nine months to prepare for the birth which was coming (whether I was ready or not). The time limitations in pregnancy require the mother's submission to a biological process which has already begun and will ultimately end with a birth of some kind. The impending due dates of my births were the catalysts for a real and necessary internal and external growth, and preparation and attention to what was and what was to come. I recall taking time to attend to the growing bump and caressing the protruding lumps of feet and elbows as I mourned the existing versions of myself. The birth: raw and messy, birthing not just a new life but a new me, a me armed with new knowledge, purpose, and meaning.

Reflection and integration – After birth

In the days and weeks following birth, both the mother and the child experience a period of adjustment and reflection. Stern and Bruschweiler-Stern (1998) refer to a psychological birth of the mother as she gains a new identity. We propose that, just as a mother undergoes a recovery phase after childbirth, the researcher too enters a phase of integration and transition. The researcher examines the implications of their findings and considers the next steps, be they in their research journey or in the world outside of their study, for instance, in preparing papers for publication. They reflect on the journey, the challenges they overcame, and the insights they gained. This stage is important for processing the full experience and understanding how the research has changed both the researcher and the world they were investigating. The researcher may revisit their work, revise their conclusions, or simply reflect on how the process of research has altered their understanding of themselves and the subject. Just as a child's first breath signifies their entry into the world, the researcher's first breath once the dissertation has been submitted, then marked, then lodged represent the culmination of their intellectual and emotional journey.

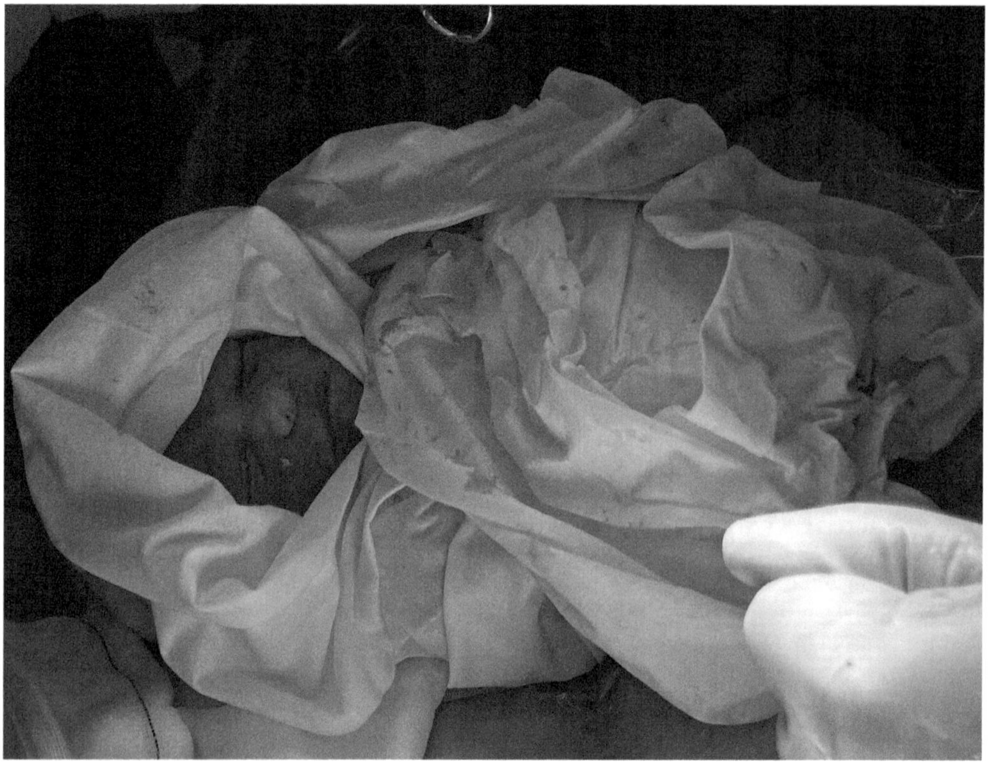

FIGURE 5.4 Child: Placental transfusion. Image source: Alana Humphris (2023).

In my own research this stage continues as I have been able to contribute to a book chapter on time limits in heuristic research (Cousins et al., 2024), and this chapter, and am preparing another publication: all of which are building on the knowledge gained from the original dissertation.

Like conception, pregnancy, and birth, the heuristic research process starts with the spark of inspiration, grows through phases of enquiry and reflection, reaches a moment of creation, and then transitions into a period of integration and new beginnings. Heuristic research is not simply a process of gathering data, but is a journey, one that offers insight into human experience and phenomena, and the potential to be generalised for, as Rogers (1961/1967) puts it, '*What is most personal is most general*' (p. 26, original emphasis). With its emphasis on deep, personal engagement with the experience and phenomenon under study, heuristic research mirrors the personal, intimate, intricate, and complex process of human development, from conception, through gestation, to the moment of birth – and beyond.

Note

1 Nèe Humphris.

References

Baird, B., Smallwood, J., Mrazek, M. D., Kam, J. W. Y., Franklin, M. S., & Schooler, J. W. (2012). Inspired by distraction: Mind wandering facilitates creative incubation. *Psychological Science*, *23*(10), 1117–1122. https://doi.org/10.1177/0956797612446024

Bar, M. (2022). *Mindwandering: How it can improve your mood and boost your creativity*. Bloomsbury Publishing.

Cousins, G., Humphris, A., Kingi, A., Oram, L., & Tudor, K. (2024). Heuristic research in a time-limited context. In W. Ings & K. Tudor (Eds.), *Heuristic enquiries: Research across disciplines and professions* (pp. 162–180). Routledge.

Douglass, B. G., & Moustakas, C. (1985). Heuristic inquiry: The internal search to know. *Journal of Humanistic Psychology*, *25*(3), 39–55. https://doi.org/10.1177/0022167885253004

Embleton Tudor, L., & Worrall, M. (2007). Supervision as maieutic process: The birthing of insight. In K. Tudor & M. Worrall (Eds.), *Freedom to practise II: Developing person-centred approaches to supervision* (pp. 16–25). PCCS Books.

Humphris, A. (2023). *Motherhood and psychotherapy training: A heuristic self-search inquiry into a trainee's experience* [Master's dissertation, Auckland University of Technology]. Tuwhera Open Access Theses & Dissertations. http://hdl.handle.net/10292/17878

Maya-Chipman, T., & Tudor, K. (2026). The burden of chronic pain on heuristic methodology and method. In K. Tudor (Ed.), *Heuristic research in psychotherapy* (pp. xx–xx [to be updated]). Routledge.

Moustakas, C. (1990). *Heuristic research: Design, methodology, and applications*. Sage.

Polanyi, M. (2002). *Personal knowledge: Towards a post-critical philosophy*. Routledge. (Original work published 1958)

Raphael, D. (1975). *Being female: Reproduction, power, and change*. Mouton Publishers.

Rogers, C. R. (1967). 'This is me': The development of my professional thinking and personal philosophy. In C. R. Rogers, *On becoming a person* (pp. 3–27). Constable. (Original work published 1961)

Sela-Smith, S. (2002). Heuristic research: A review and critique of Moustakas's method. *Journal of Humanistic Psychology*, *42*(3), 53–88. https://doi.org/10.1177/0022167802423004

Stern, D. N. (1995). *The motherhood constellation: A unified view of parent–infant psychotherapy*. Taylor & Francis Group.

Stern, D. N., & Bruschweiler-Stern, N. (1998). *The birth of a mother: How the motherhood experience changes you forever*. Basic Books.

Sultan, N. (2019). *Heuristic inquiry: Researching human experience holistically*. Sage.

Tudor, K. (2022). Supporting critical self-enquiry: Doing heuristic research. In S. Bager-Charleson & A. McBeath (Eds.), *Supporting research in counselling and psychotherapy* (pp. 57–79). Springer.

Tudor, K. (2023). Critical heuristics: From 'I who feels' to 'We who care – and act'. In K. Tudor & J. Wyatt (Eds.), *Reflexive research for reflective practice: Qualitative research methodologies for psychotherapy* (pp. 115–132). Routledge.

Tudor, K., & Ings, W. (2025). Discovering heuristic supervision: A collaborative enquiry. In W. Ings & K. Tudor (Eds.), *Heuristic enquiries: Research across disciplines and professions* (pp. 181–201). Routledge.

Tudor, K., & Worrall, M. (2004). Introduction. In K. Tudor & M. Worrall (Eds.), *Freedom to practise: Person-centred approaches to supervision* (pp. 1–8). PCCS Books.

Winnicott, D. W. (1964). *The child, the family, and the outside world*. Da Capo Press.

6

A SELF-SEARCH HEURISTIC ENQUIRY INTO RACIAL MICROAGGRESSIONS

Malik McCann

The self-search heuristic enquiry: The method

> The researcher must remain internally focused and dwell within the feelings of the tacit dimension, allowing the six phases to unfold naturally by surrendering to the feeling state of the subjective 'I'.
>
> (Sela-Smith, 2002, p. 63)

Moustakas (1990) identifies six phases of heuristic enquiry – initial engagement, immersion, incubation, illumination, explication, and creative synthesis – which I use as a structure for this chapter, though I follow what Tudor (2023) argues elsewhere, that, as illumination is a process:

> illuminations do not occur conveniently between the heuristic stages or phases of incubation and explication and so should not be viewed as forming a certain and invariant part of a stage theory but, rather, as illuminative, 'eureka' moments through the research.
>
> (p. 121)

Initial engagement

'The task of the initial engagement is to discover an intense interest, a passionate concern that calls out to the researcher, one that holds important social meanings and personal, compelling implications' (Moustakas, 1990, p. 27). My engagement with this topic began with a profound experience, which opened up an only vaguely known place inside myself which I felt a deep desire to understand as described previously.

Douglass and Moustakas (1985) describe initial engagement as 'a passionate and discerning personal involvement in problem solving, an effort to know the essence of some aspect of life through internal pathways of the self' (p. 39). Moustakas (1990) speaks of the personal

DOI: 10.4324/9781003685944-9

question, as one rooted in tacit knowledge, creating a sense of unease that the researcher seeks to resolve, but which also has a potentially broader significance. This phenomenon of unconscious racialisation is difficult to grasp at its depths from an empirical perspective. It holds great significance as it is part of the invisible framework of society and thus the social unconscious, and therefore cannot easily be addressed. It is a phenomenon which insidiously leaves the imprint of society in the psyche, which is maintained through social discourse over generations. Formulating something which is usually unspoken has been challenging. Discovering the language of racial microaggressions, I found a foundation, an observable starting place. Adding unconscious racialisation to my original question satisfied the depths to which I wished to go in this exploration. I hoped to use the observable manifestations of unintentional racism to explore the intrapsychic processes and outcomes of unconscious racialisation. I include making, encountering, and challenging unintentional racial microaggressions intentionally as a way to remain open to the reality that, at times, I may also be a perpetrator as well as a victim in this dynamic. An intersubjective focus on the dynamics of this issue highlights its relational and cyclical nature in that what gets unconsciously ingested is likely to be unconsciously egested in some form.

Immersion

Loewenthal and Winter (2006) describe immersion into the topic in question to the point where it permeates every aspect of day-to-day life. My immersion involved journaling to capture my own process and my responses to social discourse, research, current affairs, social media threads, and other depictions of racial microaggressions in Aotearoa New Zealand. I was alarmed at how prevalent racial ruptures were and was unsure if this was due to current social issues and/or I was becoming more attuned to what was always there.

During immersion I was drawn to explore the interpersonal aspects of my personal experience in response to the original incident, and to put words to my sense of the underlying interpersonal dynamics. This took the form of a micro-analysis of my perception of these unconscious racial dynamics in the vignette. This analysis was unavoidably influenced by my own self-object and object relations and others' perceptions of these interactions would undoubtedly differ. Yet considered intersubjectively, an interplay between my internal world, and the self-object and object relations of the group occurred which I felt drawn to explore.

I also wanted to place these interactions in their larger context: to understand the relationship between colonisation, racism, and disparity within Aotearoa's historical socio-cultural-political context in which they have manifested, and their relationship to unconscious racialisation. I explored the colonial history and societal developments in 'race' relations in Aotearoa New Zealand as well as the issues we as a society currently face in regard to racism.

I was concerned that I was diverging from the purely inward-focused nature of Sela-Smith's (2002) heuristic self-search inquiry (HSSI); yet, as I went deeper into the process, I felt that the separation of or splitting between psyche and society were reflective of the dynamics of this phenomenon. In this way, I found my exploration of the historical and social context of racism and microaggressions crucial in making meaning of my own unconscious racialisation.

Placing this interaction in its social, interpersonal, and historical context validated the strength of my affective response as reflecting broader societal dynamics. It also helped to highlight that my reaction in these moments was not only about an external perpetrator but that it awakened an internal white object that represented the entirety of my oppressive racialised experiences.

Incubation

Incubation necessitates retreating from the intense, concentrated focus on the question, and detaching from conscious contemplation to allow a resting phase which facilitates a space in which tacit knowing and intuition can surface (Moustakas, 1990). Making and/or having space to clarify and understand on levels outside immediate awareness 'results in discoveries that do not occur through deliberate mental operations and directed effort' (Moustakas, 1990, p. 29). Incubation, particularly moments of freedom from the grip of intense deliberation, often led to illumination.

> I am not in immersion or illumination right now but in a crushing state of inertia and stress. Incubation?
>
> (M. McCann, journal entry, 6th June 2020)

Incubation often happened of its own accord when I reached saturation, a place I would often reach not by choice, but out of necessity. It also happened outside any scheduling I had planned: a protective mechanism which kicked in when my feeling and thinking self was spent.

Illumination

Illumination involves facilitating a receptive state of mind without conscious striving or concentration, a space for synthesis (Moustakas, 1990). For me, it felt magical to experience the way tacit knowing and intuition created these moments of illumination that came when I was absorbed in a task where conscious thought felt suspended: in the shower, walking, swimming in the ocean, driving. These were the seemingly inconsequential moments when new insights would rise from the unconscious. Illumination came in fragments.

Explication

In heuristic research, explication involves fully examining 'what has awakened in consciousness, in order to understand its various layers of meaning' (Moustakas, 1990, p. 31). In doing this, I utilised focusing, indwelling, and self-searching, to allow meanings which were unique and distinctive to my experience and which depended on my internal frame of reference to emerge. In this phase, I conceptualised my own experience within the wider context of social and interpersonal engagement: a zooming in and out and in again from my inner world, to the outer world, and back.

> I feel like Neo in the Matrix [Wachowski & Wachowski, 1999], woken from an illusion. Much like the Matrix, I believe society and the social unconscious to constitute a powerful force which creates an invisible web that suspends us in a system much greater than ourselves, but is also sustained by us as individuals. Like a child adapts unconsciously to their early environment in ways they are unaware, I believe I too have adapted unconsciously to hold (hierarchical) racialised positions which exist in society and echo in my psyche.
>
> (M. McCann, journal entry, 3rd June 2021)

This journal entry captures my sense of explication as involving a growing critical consciousness, as Freire (1968/1994) puts it: 'learning to perceive social, political, and economic contradictions, and to take action against the oppressive elements of reality' (p. 17). Watts et al. (1999) describe critical consciousness as an 'antidote to oppression' (p. 255), due to its ability to provide people with the awareness, motivation, and agency to recognise and address societal inequities. I see this awareness as also necessary in recognising and addressing the imprint of racialisation (for both the oppressed and the oppressor) on my inner self. This involved the painful confrontation of my own disavowed racialisation, a recognition of my own trauma on both sides of this binary equation.

In the original research, I identified five themes which explicated my findings: (1) Internalised racial self-states and their relationship to the '*I-who-feels*'; (2) Awakening to the power of unconscious racialisation and its influence on my psyche; (3) The impact of essentialist racial constructs; (4) Opening to my own disavowed racialisation; and (5) Healing experiences of an interracial intersubjective third.

Creative synthesis

> There is something transpersonal about what emerges that seems to take on a life of its own. It is an amazing time of synchronicity, harmony, connection and integration.
>
> (Sela-Smith, 2002, p. 69)

Creative synthesis occurs when the components, core themes, and learnings about the question can be synthesised and communicated. I identify key learnings through creative expression, which translated into transformation in my tacit knowledge and self-transformation.

> I am finding freedom from the exhaustion of feeling I have to conform, to prove I am something else. This dissertation is shaking off the shackles of an invisible imprisonment in a world of measuring myself between two ideals, the western perspective and the essentialist notions of being Pasifika and finding myself coming up short. A freeing of the desire to have to prove myself to be enough. To realise that 'wrong' or 'right' are arbitrary. I am more complex than any binary constructs which exist outside of myself. I am acceptable to me.
>
> (M. McCann, journal entry, 4th June 2021)

From my internal frame of reference, the narrative of my life experience, I gain a sense of how my particular iteration of racialisation was formed. This also illuminated how it was previously unconscious; it was woven into the fabric of family and my society and hidden in plain sight, as I imagine it is for all of us, regardless of 'race' in Aotearoa New Zealand.

The synthesis of this particular research project has been expressed both creatively and productively: in the original dissertation (McCann, 2022), and published articles that focus on the social unconscious of unintentional racial microaggressions (McCann & Tudor, 2022) and the implications of this material for the psychotherapy profession (McCann & Tudor, 2024), as well as this present work.

The findings

These fall into three areas: findings about the subject of the research itself; those about the research process; and those about the theory of heuristic research (see Chapter 2), in the reporting of which I maintain the personal (first-person) language.

About the subject

Immersion in the heuristic process allowed me to recognise how racialisation is formed and reinforced through social and historical discourses and interpersonal interactions. This heightened my awareness of the undercurrents of racialisation in the social unconscious which sustain disparity and power asymmetry.

As well as unintentional racial microaggressions being an expression of racialised norms, I found them to be an instrument of indoctrination into such norms, thereby perpetuating and reinforcing unconscious racialisation. I conceptualised unintentional microaggressions as observable outcomes of unconscious racialisation.

I propose that the distress and rupture caused in and by unintentional racial microaggressions is due to mutual narcissistic wounding which occurs on either side of such binary interactions and hypothesise that this wounding occurs as a result of mutual exposure to disavowed racialised self-states. Discrete racial and cultural constructs, and the repressive nature of these constructs, influence the formation of disavowed racialised self-states, resulting in racialised 'false selves' which can both identify and counter-identify with socially constructed racial and cultural narratives. For myself, awakening to my own disavowed unconscious racialisation was a form of recognition, and initiated a process of acknowledgement and grieving.

Unintentional racial microaggressions are inevitable, and, at best, can represent opportunities for deeper recognition of differing racial realities and oppressive norms, and for exploration of unconscious racialisation. Rather than promoting blaming and/or defensive responses to such aggression and ruptures, a re-orientation towards learning – 'What can I learn about myself and the other?' and even 'Can we feel the grief of our racialisation together?' – can create a different end to this story. Through the creation of an interracial, intersubjective third, these ruptures can become moments of 'I–Thou' relating – or, indeed, following Schmid (1988), and in the context of uneven relationships involving privilege and oppression, 'Thou–I' relating, in which the racialised other is given priority (see McCann & Tudor, 2022, 2024).

About the research process

The following poem reflects my sense of self-discovery and liberation through this heuristic self-search, of bringing something painful into the light so it could be understood, grieved, and processed.

My voice
She felt them –
Those words,
the feelings a key
to a door that has never been opened,
to a secret universe
where She hides.

Her voice,
a whisper.
Where silence is safety
she wants Her voice,
it's time.

She opens the door
the 'I who feels'
and finds Herself
in a lonely sanctuary, or was it a prison

inside herself?
The journey
a final frontier.

A pioneer
For her own liberation.

My voice.
(M. McCann, 7 July 2020)

This poem illustrates some of what I experienced as the strengths of the heuristic process, including finding its spaciousness liberating. As a person who historically and psychologically has lived by many shoulds, I found this framework (especially the phases of heuristic enquiry) sufficiently holding, while also freeing enough for me to be able to forge my own path(s) within it. That said, there were times when I found the freedom within this process terrifying. The permission I had within this method to follow my intuition, hunches, and curiosity led to an expansive exploration of context, environment, and the in-between: an overwhelming deluge of stimuli to metabolise. At times, trusting the process was a challenge, and my level of self-doubt was overwhelming, particularly in my internal experience of viewing this phenomenon from shifting and varying paranoid-schizoid racialised self-states. This points to the importance of having spaces and places in which to process the trust – and the mistrust and self-doubts.

Observing my experience and noting it (through journaling) was important, especially in those periods of self-doubt and fragmentation, as they were crucial with respect to understanding them as manifestations of the experience(s) and phenomena I was researching. I was also reassured (in supervision) that feeling lost was a common experience in the heuristic journey, which helped me maintain an overall trust in the process. HSSI also offers a freedom from external judgements of right and wrong and knowing that my discoveries, findings, and conclusions primarily need to feel valid to myself (Moustakas, 1990).

I found it challenging to hold the vulnerability that my findings are *my* truth in this moment as opposed to *the* Truth. The vulnerability I felt and still feel in my self-disclosure in this research, and the part of myself which projects invalidation within this topic, are deeply uncomfortable to sit with. Alongside the challenge of self-exposure, an ethical consideration in the heuristic process is of being true to my experience while protecting the identity of others. The comfort of empirical knowledge, the anonymity of participants' experience, the neutrality of the researcher, and the distance from affect extolled by other research methods and methodologies are not afforded in the heuristic process.

References

Douglass, B. G., & Moustakas, C. (1985). Heuristic inquiry: The internal search to know. *Journal of Humanistic Psychology*, *25*(3), 39–55. https://doi.org/10.1177/0022167885253004

Freire, P. (1994). *Pedagogy of the oppressed.* Continuum. (Original work published 1968)

Loewenthal, D., & Winter, D. (2006). *What is psychotherapeutic research?* Karnac.

McCann, M. (2022). *Invisible wounds: A heuristic exploration of unintentional racial microaggressions and their relationship to unconscious racialisation* [Master's dissertation, Auckland University of Technology]. Tuwhera Open Access Theses & Dissertations. http://hdl.handle.net/10292/15067

McCann, M., & Tudor, K. (2022). Unintentional racial microaggressions and the social unconscious. *International Journal of Applied Psychoanalytic Studies*, *19*(2), 202–216. https://doi.org/10.1002/aps.1753

McCann, M., & Tudor, K. (2024). The enigma of unintentional racial microaggressions: Implications for the profession of psychotherapy. *Ata: Journal of Psychotherapy Aotearoa New Zealand*, *27*(1), 31–56. https://doi.org/10.24135/ajpanz.2024.03

Moustakas, C. E. (1990). *Heuristic research: Design, methodology, and applications*. Sage.

Schmid, P. F. (1988). 'Face to face' – The art of encounter. In. B. Thorne & E. Lambers (Eds.), *Person-centred therapy: A European perspective* (pp. 74–90). Sage.

Sela-Smith, S. (2002). Heuristic research: A review and critique of Moustakas's method. *Journal of Humanistic Psychology*, *42*(3), 53–88. https://doi.org/10.1177/0022167802423004

Tudor, K. (2023). Critical heuristics in psychotherapy research: From 'I-who-feels' to 'We-who-care—and act'. In K. Tudor & J. Wyatt (Eds.), *Qualitative research approaches for psychotherapy: Reflexivity, methodology, and criticality* (pp. 115–132). Routledge.

Wachowski, L., & Wachowski, L. (Directors). (1999). *The matrix* [Film]. Warner Bros; Village Roadshow Pictures.

Watts, R. J., Griffith, D. M., & Abdul-Adil, J. (1999). Socio-political development as an antidote for oppression—Theory and action. *American Journal of Community Psychology*, *27*(2), 255–271. https://doi.org/10.1023/A:1022839818873

7

HEURISTIC METHOD AND A SAMOAN SENSE OF SELF

Karlene Schwencke[1] *and Julia Ioane*

Introduction

This chapter presents a way in which the heuristic method in phenomenological analysis was applied to a master's thesis by the first author (the 'I', 'me', and 'my' voice in the chapter), supervised by the second author. The original dissertation examined a Samoan sense of self in terms of object relations theory (Mamea, 2016). This chapter, which focuses on the research method of that original enquiry, firstly outlines what a phenomenological method involves in order to construct meaning; secondly, contextualises the chapter with regard to the worldviews of the authors, which includes a discussion of existing literature regarding the Samoan sense of self; and thirdly, discusses how the heuristic method, as developed by Moustakas (1990), was applied in this research to explore a Samoan sense of identity and self. Finally, this chapter concludes with a reflection and acknowledgement of the first author's journey in (a) using the heuristic methodology within one's perceived Samoan sense of self, (b) recognising how identity shifted along this journey, and (c) pondering on whether the use of a Samoan methodology may have provided a different journey to the one experienced.

Tamasese et al. (2005) refer to the Samoan sense of self as being relational to land, sea, ancestors, and God. The Samoan self cannot be separated from these relationships, and needs to be seen holistically, i.e., including physical, mental, and spiritual elements. The concept of vā is important to discuss here given that the vā is what governs the relationship within the Samoan culture (Mo'a, 2015). Va is fundamental to the identity and existence of Samoan people as the identity of Samoan people is relational (Tamasese et al., 2005). Va can be seen as one's relationship with one's family, village, land, ancestors, and spiritual cosmos (Mo'a, 2015). Within the Samoan culture there are arguably three dimensions of the vā. (The first two are teu le vā (build the relationship) and tausi le vā (nurture the relationships) (Ioane, 2023).) These can be seen synonymously or separately whereby values of the Samoan culture are implemented in tausi le vā. Samoans also believe that whilst a relationship is built and nurtured, part of the process is that at some point there can be disharmony or conflict. This is known as soli le vā, when there has been a violation of the sacred space of the relationship between people, land, ancestors, or any other being. However, while a breakdown is expected, there is also opportunity for the vā to be restored and healed throughout appropriate cultural processes.

DOI: 10.4324/9781003685944-10

Western psychology in general, and psychodynamic psychotherapy in particular, refers to the person and their identity within the structure and occurrences of early infant and child relationships and attitudes, and, according to Mageo (1989), highlights the ego self. We Samoans, however, see ourselves as a collective group underpinned by relatedness and interdependence (Ioane & Tudor, 2017; Mageo, 1989). Both authors of this chapter are Samoan, raised in Aotearoa New Zealand, yet trained clinically (in psychotherapy and psychology, respectively) within a Western worldview. The first author's experiences through psychotherapy training contextualised and informed the purpose of the original research.

Background

Articulations of self through traditional stories contain subtle clues to largely hidden knowledge (Mamea, 2016). Many female characters in Samoan mythology are represented as either creative or destructive figures (Gabbard, 2014), and, indeed, the female characters in the stories I have chosen for the research display both powerfully aggressive and resourceful drives. The research considered a Samoan myth *Sina and the eel*, the novel *Telesā: The Covenant Keeper* (Wendt-Young, 2011), and traditional song *Tatau Samoa*. An example of the vā below as a communal sense of responsibility is central to the construction and existence of a 'self' in Samoan terms.

Sina and the eel describes the origin of the coconut tree in Samoa and is important to a sense of self, giving voice to the idea that aggression, conflict, and destruction can exist whilst maintaining relationships and connection. Sina's relationship to the eel is complex and she deals with the violation of her relational boundary – vā – through her connection to her wider family.

The novel *Telesā: The Covenant Keeper* describes local ancient myths of the *Telesā* (originally *teinesā*) spirit women (Wendt-Young, 2011) and the relationship of these myths to the main characters' sense of themselves. It highlights the struggle between keeping a traditional heritage alive in the face of the modern world. An identity scuffle occurs between Leila's spiritual relationship with the land of Samoa, and her physical relationship to the rest of the world, which highlights the ambivalence Leila carries in relation to her identity in a cultural and spiritual sense, becoming torn between two perspectives and worlds.

The song *Tatau Samoa* describes the journey of how traditional tattooing on male and female bodies arrived in Samoa. According to Wendt (1999), 'the *tatau* and the *malu* (women's *tatau*) are not just beautiful decoration, they are scripts/texts/testimonies to do with relationships, order, form and so on' (p. 5). As an external expression of 'Samoan-ness', the markings in the *tatau* have often been adapted by those wishing to assert their Samoan heritage, different to the rituals and responsibilities of the traditional *malofie* and *malu*. I chose this song for its commentary on symbolism which I believe points to crucial aspects of the Samoan psyche.

The above narratives were used to examine a Samoan articulation of self, and a heuristic method for research was applied to explore a Samoan sense of self for the participant/first author.

Phenomenological analysis for literature review

Douglass and Moustakas (1985) describe the purpose of phenomenological investigation as 'attempts to reveal the actual nature and meaning of an event, perception, or occurrence, just as it appears' (pp. 42–43). Phenomenological research recognises the world as an essential piece in the puzzle of truth, through its focus on the structure of experience. According to Goes and Simon (2017), the primary goal of a phenomenological study is to illuminate the meaning, structure, and essence of a specific occurrence through the eyes of those who have lived experience of it.

Thus, in order to understand my own subjective experience, it was – and is – important for me to look at both the experience of self through analysis as well as my own connectedness to the aforementioned stories. I found heuristic enquiry the best way to do this. The relationship I held and still hold to this research reflects my journey through psychotherapy training, and the visibility of my process that allows both an 'inside out' look through the heuristic method, as well as an 'outside in' view through psychotherapeutic theory.

Heuristic method

> The power of heuristic enquiry lies in its potential for disclosing truth. Through exhaustive self-search dialogues with others, and creative depictions of experience, a comprehensive knowledge is generated, beginning as a series of subjective musings and developing into a systematic and definitive exposition.
>
> (Douglass & Moustakas, 1985, p. 40)

As heuristic research begins with personal reflections, I started the original research with formulations about my own lived experience, keeping in mind internal objects theory, while wondering how my own Samoan-specific sense of self had been created (Mamea, 2016). My intention in the original research project was to interpret the stories and song I chose, using my felt cultural experiences of being a Samoan student researching Kleinian theory (Mamea, 2016). These initially rather vague intentions evolved into more definitive discussions through persistent self-search.

Moustakas (1990) outlines six phases guiding the researcher through this 'self-search', stating these phases are not linear, and that the researcher may move between phases, leaping forward to others and perhaps back again. Initially, I began with the premise that my question required a consideration of the way one phenomenon relates to another. Therefore, in order to deeply understand the question, it was necessary to become immersed in both the Kleinian theory of a landscape populated with internal objects and in traditional Samoan stories. Immersion and incubation may seem opposite to each other as the former requires deep engagement, and the latter a less conscious, more detached position. In actual fact, heuristics is primarily concerned with meanings, not measurements; with essence, not appearance; with quality, not quantity; and with experience, not behaviour (Douglass & Moustakas, 1985). Heuristic investigation focuses inwardly on the felt experience of the researcher, as well as outwardly to the situation, rather than the relationship between parts of the outside situation (Sela-Smith, 2002).

Moustakas (1990) describes 'tacit knowledge' as a structure which interprets experience, and is composed of distinctive views, emotions, beliefs, and values that govern behaviour. Although tacit knowledge is not normally available to conscious awareness (Moustakas, 1990; Polanyi, 1969), Sela-Smith (2002) suggests that consideration is needed as to whether one's tacit knowledge is useful or a hindrance. My own tacit knowledge around my cultural self both led me to this research, and obstructed my approach to it. There were many times in which I felt frozen with deep cultural shame and unworthiness. Rose and Loewenthal (2006) state that the topic of a heuristic method emanates from the researcher's own lived experience and involves the pursuit of others' experience of the phenomenon. My cultural shame had not emerged as forcefully or as clearly as in the three years of intensive personal therapy and psychotherapy training as it did during this research. Tacit knowing, it seems, precedes intuition, guiding me into new directions and sources of meaning.

A fellow student shared a quote she had found along her journey:

> The heuristic researcher is not only intimately and autobiographically related to the question but learns to love the question. It becomes a kind of song into which the researcher breathes life... because the question itself is infused in the researcher's being.
>
> (Moustakas, 1990, p. 43)

When researching the question 'How does Melanie Klein's concept of internal objects relate to Samoan writings on internal structures of the self?' I listened carefully to the movements internal object theory made within me. I wrestled with their meanings, fought against my feelings for the theory, and hoped for a clean, simple battle. I wanted to understand Klein with a Samoan lens, and I wanted Samoan stories to be viewed clearly within Kleinian thinking. A critique of Moustakas's method includes neglect of natural resistance to experiencing unbearable pain, and therefore the focus shifts towards the idea of the experience rather than the self's experience of this process (Sela-Smith, 2002). Therefore, documenting one's experience of the process to expose any resistance was important.

During the research, I kept a journal documenting my experience and reflections in response to reviewing each resource, a process which linked my external and internal experiences, and, as it transpired, indicating a clear tension between my experience, and the relationship to both my cultural and theoretical background as a psychotherapist, and highlighting the influence of this in the research. As Moustakas (1990) acknowledges, the heuristic response is autobiographical, yet also illuminates social significance of my own experience and its relevance.

Rose and Loewenthal (2006) adapt Moustakas's six phases into eight steps, a model I chose to use due to their further development of Moustakas's 'initial engagement' and 'immersion' phases. I also included the explicit inclusion of lived experience in the research process, as this suited my enquiry into the experience or sense of 'self' (see Table 7.1).

TABLE 7.1 The eight steps of the heuristic method (Rose & Loewenthal, 2006).

1. Research focus, i.e., defining a subject area of lived experience for investigation, so, from my experience, what is it that I wish to know more about? Why do I want to know more about this phenomenon? Has this been researched before? How would this add to the body of knowledge in this field?
2. The researcher's 'lived experience': recording in a reflexive journal 'lived experience' of the phenomenon, for thoughts and feelings during investigation so personal experience is transparent.
3. Identifying potential 'participants': asking 'what is your experience of x?' – use this question to stay with their / keep the focus upon the lived experience. Consider who is most likely to have had a lived experience of this.
4. Recruiting participants
5. Data generation
6. Immersion, i.e., examples recognised in day-to-day life. Thoughts and feelings from this recorded in the journal. Re-reading data, looking for commonalities, and grouping them together for presentation of findings.
   a. Phase one of presentation: individual depictions of experience of phenomena
   b. Phase two: composite depiction group presentation of lived experience
   c. Phase three: presenting exemplary portraits, individual stories
7. Incubation, the reverse of immersion phase: switching off from subject.
8. Creative synthesis: drawing upon knowledge gained during investigation to explain for others; may be in the form of a narrative, story, poem, work of art, metaphor, analogy, or tale.

In the rest of this chapter, I describe how I applied these steps in the research.

Step one: Research focus – Defining the subject area

'Heuristic research… is premised on how an individual interprets their experiences' (Moustakas, 1994, quoted by Rose & Loewenthal, 2006, p. 133). Rose and Loewenthal's (2006) extension of Moustakas's (1990) 'initial engagement' phase demands that I ask myself what I would like to know more about and explore why I want to know more about this phenomenon. I also pondered on my experience as a Samoan woman studying and practising psychotherapy. At times I felt alone and misunderstood, unsure of how I fit in the classroom and in the therapy room. Furthermore, I have rarely come into contact with other Samoan students or clients, resulting in a sense of isolation at times. I was further interested in my specific experience as a Samoan – the meaning this might hold, and how my own experience is articulated.

A heuristic enquiry contains a research topic which emanates from the researcher's own lived experience, but also is often in pursuit of others' experience of the phenomenon (Rose & Loewenthal, 2006). In my search to find a reflection of my experience, I was disappointed not to find any specific writing on a Samoan cultural experience of psychotherapeutic theory. According to psychotherapeutic thinking, a sense of self can be understood through the lens of object relations theory. In turn, my curiosity grew around how a Samoan sense of self is currently theorised, and whether both theories can be seen through each/the other's eyes. Perhaps there may be a connection found between the two, maybe more differences will be found.

Step two: The researcher's lived experience

Moustakas (1990) recommends the use of a reflexive journal in which the researcher records 'lived experience' of the phenomenon, including thoughts and feelings during the investigation so that personal experience is transparent. In this step, I had continuing conversations with my peers at university and at work, with family and friends.

I scheduled time with those who held knowledge and experience with Samoan culture and identity, and gathered information from these conversations. These included free flowing discussions around themes of identity, what it meant to them to be Samoan, and what it stirs up in their psyche. This jostled my own emotional experience and interaction with the data – an emerging theme around anger and feeling torn between identities appeared. In ethical terms, such conversations fell within the exceptions to activities requiring ethical approval from the Auckland University of Technology Ethical Committee (AUTEC, 2016).

In noting down themes or persistent thoughts and feelings I noticed during and after these sessions, patterns and ideas began to emerge. This same method of collecting data occurred when absorbing the literature around my topics, and audio and visual material involved in my research. I began to write in my journal with no particular agenda – just noting what has stood out to me to draw any connections to these reflections later on. I drew mind maps of the key words and themes month to month, and noted dreams, recurring thoughts, and emotions. I wanted to capture what was happening around me, what was evoked inside of me, and what emerged unconsciously.

Step three: Identifying potential participants

As the sole participant and an author for the research, the experience of a Samoan sense of self and internal object theory was noted from a first-person perspective. In choosing a participant/

author experience, the research remained subjectively focused. Sela-Smith (2002) writes 'Validity of the self-experience is established by similar experiences of others; yet validity in subjective discovery-research is not possible by comparing to others' experience' (p. 76). The validity of the Samoan self and object relations experience was therefore emphasised for the authors (another resistance that came up in the research).

Step four: Recruiting participants

No other participants were needed for this project. Ozertugrul (2017) states that in heuristic research using the author as the participant, the entire range of the experience is the focus. He states:

> the intent was to explicate the full range of the [obsessive-compulsive disorder] experience that resides within me. The criterion is to explore an individual who has personal experience with the phenomenon… In this heuristic self-search study, I was the researcher/participant, the single individual.
>
> (p. 219)

The full range of a Samoan sense of self entails the markers of representation: the authors' villages of origin, the Samoan community, and their family. These figures remain part of the research as elements of the first author's identity and are discussed in the next section.

Step five: Data generation

> Heuristics permits and even encourages spontaneous creation of methods that will evoke or disclose experiential meanings.
>
> (Douglass & Moustakas, 1985, p. 49)

Rose and Loewenthal (2006) describe the importance of experience in interviews, which are typically conducted in this phase, and in the transcripts which are typically sent to participants. In my adaptation, I analysed the data gathered from my sources (by using the text to answer the question 'What is your experience of a Samoan sense of self?') and from my own experience in order to present a narrative of the process.

In looking at the relationship (if indeed one ever existed) between the concept of internal objects and the research on Samoan texts, key concepts needed to be broken down. For example, terms needed to be translated back and forth from English to Samoan many times to discern their deeper meaning. In looking for keywords I had connected to whilst reading Kleinian theory, as well as the novel, I sought both Samoan and English terms that I believed linked to each other in some way, but also expressed the core meanings of what I saw in the stories. Key words and themes I focused on included '*mauli*' (psyche or soul), '*mafaufau*' (memory and memories), '*loto*' (desire), 'internal object', 'external object', 'spirit', 'mother', 'father', 'internalised', 'externalised', 'projection', and 'introjection'.

Douglass and Moustakas (1985) also describe the importance of tacit knowledge to acquire information in this phase, in which 'the tacit dimension is the forerunner of inference and intuition, guiding the person to untapped aspects of awareness… that elude analysis or explanation' (p. 49). Tacit knowing is acquired through persistent self-dialogue and self-disclosure. It also occurs throughout the immersion phase, through self-search.

Self-disclosure, whereby 'an emphasis on disclosing self sparks disclosure from others' (Douglass & Moustakas, 1985, p. 50), has been useful where conversations have unveiled ideas, opinions, and awareness of my own emotive processes about this project. Upon presenting my project to others, the extent of my fear of the tenderness and sacredness of these stories was revealed. Words such as 'colonisation' and 'painful' stood out to me and reflected my will for a third possibility in a dyadic relationship between these two components of my research and original personal dilemma.

Upon reflection by the second author as a supervisor, the need for two co-supervisors emerged, one of Samoan descent, the other who had expertise in object relations (who was of British descent). There were times when the feedback was contradictory. Both supervisors often reflected on this, acknowledging the tension experienced in the research journey, and the parallel reflected in the different worldviews expressed by the supervisors. However, to manage this, the supervisors prioritised their relationship with one another as colleagues, being respectful of one another. This tension was recognised as an expected outcome of navigating between Western (individual) and Samoan (collective) worldviews.

Tension was also apparent within the Samoan stories, inherent in object relations theory, and the desire for harmony and resolution became an overwhelming theme.

Step six: Immersion

> Immersion carries the sense of total involvement in a research theme or question… vague and formless wanderings are characteristic in the beginning, but a growing sense of meaning and direction emerges.
>
> (Moustakas, 1990, p. 47)

For me, the immersion phase started in June 2015 when I began to deepen my understanding of psychoanalytic theory, in particular Melanie Klein's conception of object relations theory, through familiarising myself with writings by Klein and others' interpretations of her work, for example, Segal (1988) and Hinshelwood (1991, 2012). A journal entry highlighted my early reactions to the immersion:

> In my confusion around the material [reading Melanie Klein's *Envy, Gratitude and Other Works*], it feels difficult to access my feelings about it.
>
> (K. Mamea, journal entry, 22nd July 2015)

As I became further immersed in Kleinian theory, I recorded a dream which highlights my own unconscious integration of an infant's innate destructive impulses, becoming deflected outward and creating persecutory objects (Klein, 1975).

> [I] noticed dreams of natural disasters in the past three weeks; an earthquake, tornado, tsunami, as well as toileting dreams and urgent sensations to go to the bathroom. Perhaps the 'evacuation' describes the anxiety of the process of dissertation research, getting rid of the bad.
>
> (K. Mamea, journal entry, 11th August 2015)

As my immersion continued to deepen, further unconscious material emerged in dreams, thoughts, sensations, and emotions. However, immersion in the data came to a halt during November and December as a result of other academic pressures combined with a desire to soothe myself by doing what felt easy and pleasant over delving deeper into the work. Sela-Smith (2002) describes 'the inherent potentials for profound transformation within heuristic method as well as… resistance to any self-search that I initiate' (p. 58), pointing out that any resistance needs to be confronted and worked through before full discovery may happen. My experience of feeling stuck at this point was palpable; I knew I needed to move but was unable to face my own resistance and resentment toward the research. Both the external pressures of balancing employment, family, and study, as well as the internal pressure of handling precious cultural treasures with integrity, left me frozen with fear and shame related to anticipated persecution by Samoan elders and academics who I imagined would dismiss my work. At times it felt as though these internal persecutory superego objects would take over, even though I knew I needed to keep writing.

In January 2016 several experiences in supervision propelled me into a different mental and emotional space. Rose and Loewenthal (2006) highlight the importance of having further support in order to work through potential blind spots, arguing that research is a component of psychotherapy practice, where in a supervisory relationship supervision occurs 'with the intention of gaining a new perspective; gaining new knowledge on the relationship, knowledge that has the potential for informing future practice' (p. 138). In making sense of my distress, I gained empathy for my shame and fear, which helped to shift me. The urgent sensation to evade conflict was highlighted as a great theme in the research, and I felt a shift away from the urge to interact with the tension, but found curiosity and learning from it.

Step seven: Incubation

Douglass and Moustakas (1985) suggest that if tacit knowledge and intuition are not acknowledged, the potential for discovery and comprehension is reduced. In this phase, the opposite or reverse of the immersion phase, it is necessary to take a break from the subject in order to allow new meaning to emerge. This is akin to what post-Kleinians refer to as 'reverie'. This stage of research required a reprieve from conscious efforts of understanding in order to allow the emergence of unconscious knowledge. A period where the overt search for information (looking in books, articles, and internet research) ceased for a period. During this time, journaling and relaxation through quiet meditation and mindfulness practices aided me to do this.

However, the time and spaciousness required to carry out the stages of heuristic research can be unrealistic in the face of day-to-day pressures of work, community, and family life. What transpired were short periods of reverie, usually after a few days of rest and relaxation. I then noticed vivid dreams, new perspectives about the research in light conversations with others, or associations to the work when I watched a television programme or listened to a song. A different kind of experience appeared to allow new information and ideas to emerge. It almost felt as though information formed itself and found me, rather than me going out hunting for it.

Step eight: Creative synthesis

Finally, in order to make sense of the phenomenological data, personal reflections, and the literature, the findings needed to be organised. In creating a large mind map, I drew out significant themes in the work, and began to draw a relationship between the words and themes. The terms 'relationship', 'connection', 'internal', and 'external' stood out as common aspects of the readings and I used these terms alongside my own meanings to draw results and conclusions.

In making sense of the different parts of data gathered, there needed to be a process to make sense of it all. The term 'realization' is used by Douglass and Moustakas (1985) to refer to the whole, assembled from pieces of data. The process of sifting, sorting, looking, and listening for meanings within meanings elicit qualities inherent within the data. Synthesis of these data creates a new reality as meanings are discerned from the data. In bringing a cultural lens to heuristic research, this meant the consideration of the way Samoan concepts provided meaning to the data. Culturally specific words, and object relations theoretical terms and themes, were analysed to gain the essence of the research question, and thus the research was recognised as gaining momentum, a life of its own.

Moustakas explains that knowledge gained during investigation may be expressed in the form of a 'narrative, story, poem, work of art, metaphor, analogy, or tale' (Moustakas, 1990, p. 52). My dissertation includes dreams, poems, and journal entries. As described in my introduction, there are three threads in this research: psychoanalytic theory (more specifically Melanie Klein's concept of internal objects), Samoan indigenous knowledge, and my knowledge and process. In a way, this research illustrates the way these threads can be woven together; sometimes one thread is 'thicker' than the other, at other times the weave comes apart, and occasionally, it makes a beautiful unique design.

A Pasifika experience of the heuristic method

As mentioned, the original plan for the research was to understand the data using the heuristic method. This meant using an innate cultural experience and continual self-searching. Part of this self-search required journaling and here a dream is recalled, which illuminates the way the heuristic method brought forward information made sense of through cultural experience.

> Dream: I'm holding my own infant baby and there are slugs everywhere, on my head, on the bed – gross! I'm trying to find a quiet room to soothe and feed my baby who is restless at a busy family function – I notice I have a jerking way of trying to move the baby around but I don't mean to be rough, I know I can be softer!
>
> (K. Mamea, journal entry, 22nd April 2016)

I had many thoughts about being a better 'mother' to my dissertation; I recognised many distractions, and fought to believe I have the skills or knowledge to do a good job. Mostly, I have struggled to soften to this process, to become confident in my strength, and tender with myself. In my dream I was not afraid of the unwanted slugs, but I knew I had to face them, touch them, to get them off me. Besides, I had a bigger goal in mind: to protect the baby. Perhaps the threat to fostering the growth and progression of this project has been my own trepidation of not being a 'good-enough mother' (Winnicott, 1953). Winnicott, a student of Klein, perceived the role of the good-enough mother to be a complete adaptation to her infant's needs at first, lessening this adaptation over time in order for the infant to grow in her ability to deal with mother's failure.

Much has been written about the process of constructing multiple identities in order to understand self from a Samoan perspective (Anae, 1998, 2003; Lupe, 2009; Mackley-Crump, 2015; Macpherson, 2001; Mila, 2008), all of whom express to some degree a painful need for flexibility and a move away from a rigid prescription to being Samoan. The vā, which focuses on the space between self and others from an insider viewpoint (Tuagalu, 2008), describes the space between self and multiple others, in order for the vā to impute cultural values of *fa'aaloalo* (respect) and *alofa* (love) (Tamasese, as cited in Suali'i-Sauni, 2011), conveyed through a sense of intimacy, sacredness, and spirituality (Tuagalu, 2008). The vā allows a sense of fluidity between self and other, making space for the inclusion of multiple 'selves'; indeed, a 'social space' in reference to relationships (Iosefo, 2016; Peteru & Percival, 2010; Wendt, 1999).

For me, the heuristic method and the cultural vā allowed a variability required for this transitional process. Perhaps the dream was about my insecurities; a comment on my ability to adapt to the demands (of resilience) in doing the research and integrating what I learnt. The slugs are my feelings of not being culturally fluent enough to write about a Samoan sense of self, nor competent enough in psychotherapy. In this field, I am learning how this means revealing my vulnerability, just enough to reveal my world to others. The cultural values involved in growing a part of myself (the flexibility to create multiple identities) fuelled my confidence and strength, and my (gross) fears of failing could stifle this growth. Therefore, it is possible my dream described my fears around creating another 'self', a psychotherapist.

Other methodologies

Samoan psychotherapist Karen Lupe (2007) states that the danger of ignoring the existence of two separate psyches/concepts/theories is the risk of subtly repeating a colonising process of 'whitening': 'The failure to appreciate the psychological differences of another culture leaves them as the alien other, in essence unknown and hence targets for shadow projection' (p. 130). That is, the undesirable aspects of one's culture become attributed to another culture as originating from the 'receiver' culture. In the avoidance of underestimating the legitimacy of the Samoan psyche, I felt as though I did not want to pit Western theories or methodologies against or to compare them to Indigenous/Pasifika concepts or methodologies of research.

Pacific methodologies such as the talanoa methodology may have been useful. Arguably (from within a Western worldview), the talanoa methodology can be seen as being grounded in phenomenology (Cammock et al., 2021; Vaioleti, 2006). However, talanoa is argued as being more of a method rather than a methodology (Tunufa'i, 2016). Described by Farrelly and Nabobo-Baba (2014) as 'Talking about nothing in particular, chat, or gossip and it is within the cultural milieu of Talanoa that knowledge and emotions are shared' (p. 1), a prime feature of talanoa is the empathy that is communicated as an emotional, intersubjective, embodied process between researcher and participant. In my case, this was between the researcher and the texts, discussions with other Pacific researchers, supervisors, classmates, and considering the relationship with the stories. Talanoa resonates with a psychotherapeutic way of relating, in that the intersubjective nature is a collaborative, interactive, and dynamic process which values all elements of communication: 'Even silence is far from empty… it requires a deep, interpersonal relationship and emotional sharing between all parties involved' (Farrelly & Nabobo-Baba, 2014, p. 3). It seems that, as a mix of intersubjective and Pacific ways of relating, talanoa would also have been an appropriate methodology to examine the relationship (even if not between a researcher and a participant per se).

Perhaps a methodology which understands Samoan ways of relating and is designed to build information through incorporating the linguistic skills mentioned earlier would render different results. Although the heuristic methodology was valuable, it must be acknowledged that the data may have been different if the talanoa method had been used. The perspective that the original did not require talanoa as there were no participants or co-participants evolved through the research. Nonetheless, it is interesting to note that viewing the research as a conversation between psyches may have elicited different personal processes.

Additionally, Sela-Smith (2002) describes how resistance to any heuristic self-search enquiry needs to be overcome before total discovery can exist (see Chapter 3). One of the reasons heuristic enquiry felt difficult at times was my refusal to acknowledge resistance. In recollecting experiences as a client in therapy, the intimacy of connecting to one person felt overwhelming and initially intrusive, compared with the process of navigating group membership and relationship. As noted earlier, the community (village, family) surrounding a Samoan sense of self were not direct participants in the research and, on reflection, perhaps could have been considered in this method/ology as such, being direct influences on the data. From a heuristic talanoa perspective, the impact of a communal sense of self could be considered in the overt acknowledgement of group members as co-participants.

Conclusion

Using a heuristic process of experience-led data collection, a sense of self was examined. This involved conversations with other people and journaling to highlight my own internal responses to the research. Key words were drawn from themes identified in these data and, after close examination of these words, a short rest period would follow. A more relaxed state elicited reflection, and mind mapping helped to organise the earlier identified themes. What occurred was a focus on key Samoan words and concepts, adding to the argument that a Samoan sense of self was emerging in the data, which interacted with my own experience of being Samoan. As a result, my sense of identity shifted, and was both adapted and affirmed using this process, which was a deeply personal, enriching, and educative experience, affirming both Moustakas's (1990) and Sela-Smith's (2002) view of heuristic research being transformative.

The heuristic method/ology allowed the inclusion of a third subjectivity as a central component to understanding the connection between theories and, indeed, the connection between psychotherapy training and Samoan cultural experiences. However, it is important to acknowledge or consider that the use of an approach informed by Samoan methodology may have yielded different results, which would likely have been and/or led to a more accurate reflection of the Samoan sense of self. Even though this research began with a heuristic process, the first author's lived experience and identity as a Samoan woman completing psychotherapy training inevitably and expectedly informed and guided the research journey.

Note

1 Née Mamea.

References

Anae, M. (1998). *Fofoa-i-vao-'ese: The identity journeys of NZ-born Samoans* [Doctoral thesis, University of Auckland]. A2 – University of Auckland Digital Doctoral Theses. https://hdl.handle.net/2292/66

Anae, M. (2003). O a'u/I: my identity journey. In P. Fairbairn-Dunlop & G. Sisifo Makisi (Eds.), *Making our place: Growing up PI in New Zealand* (pp. 89–101). Dunmore.

Auckland University of Technology Ethical Committee (AUTEC). (2016). *Exceptions to activities requiring AUTEC approval (6).* www.aut.ac.nz/research/researchethics/autec-guidelines-and-procedures/exceptions-to-activities-requiring-autec-approval-6

Cammock, R., Conn, C., & Nayar, S. (2021). Strengthening Pacific voices through Talanoa participatory action research. *AlterNative: An International Journal of Indigenous Peoples, 17*(1), 120–129. https://doi.org/10.1177/1177180121996321

Douglass, B., & Moustakas, C. (1985). Heuristic inquiry: The internal search to know. *Journal of Humanistic Psychology, 25*(3), 39–55. https://doi.org/10.1177/0022167885253004

Farrelly, T., & Nabobo-Baba, U. (2014). Talanoa as empathic apprenticeship. *Asia Pacific Viewpoint, 55*(3), 319–330. https://doi.org/10.1111/apv.12060

Gabbard, C. (2014). Sina and Nafanua: Mother goddess enacting primordial spirituality in Samoa. In T. M. Suaalii-Sauni, M. A. Wendt, V. Mo'a, N. Fuamatu, U. L. V'ai, R. Whaitiri, & S. L. Filipo (Eds.), *Whispers and vanities: Samoan indigenous knowledge and religion* (pp. 243–253). Huia.

Goes, J., & Simon, M. K. (2017). *Dissertation and scholarly research: Recipes for success. 2018 edition. A practical guide to start and complete your dissertation, thesis, or formal research project.* Dissertation Recipes LLC.

Hinshelwood, R. D. (1991). *A dictionary of Kleinian thought.* Free Association Books.

Hinshelwood, R. D. (2012). Kleinian theory. *The International Journal of Psychoanalysis, 93*(3), 741–743. https://doi.org/10.1111/j.1745-8315.2012.00567.x

Ioane, J. (2023). *You've just got to think about your family and what type of person you want to be: Listening to young Pasifika people in the youth justice system and their families. Research and recommendations.* Health Research Council of NZ and Massey University School of Psychology. http://hdl.handle.net/10179/18370

Ioane, J., & Tudor, K. (2017). The fa'asamoa, person-centered theory and cross-cultural practice. *Person-Centered & Experiential Psychotherapies, 16*(4), 287–302. https://doi.org/10.1080/14779757.2017.1361467

Iosefo, F. (2016). Third spaces: sites of resistance in higher education? *Higher Education Research & Development, 35*(1), 189–192. https://doi.org/10.1080/07294360.2016.1133273

Klein, M. (1975). *Envy and gratitude and other works 1946–1963* (M. M. R. Khan, Ed.). Free Press.

Lupe, K. (2007). An ocean with many shores: Indigenous consciousness and the thinking heart. In P. Culbertson, M. Nelson-Agee, & C. 'Ofa-Makasiale (Eds.), *Penina uliuli: Contemporary challenges in mental health for Pacific peoples* (pp. 122–135). University of Hawai'i Press.

Lupe, K. (2009). Standing at the threshold. In T. Suaalii-Sauni, I. Tuagalu, T. N. Kirifi-Alai, & N. Fuamatu (Eds.), *Su'esu'e Manogi. In search of fragrance* (pp. 248–264). The Centre for Sāmoan Studies, National University of Sāmoa.

Mackley-Crump, J. (2015). *The Pacific festivals of Aotearoa New Zealand: Negotiating place and identity in a new homeland.* University of Hawai'i Press.

Macpherson, C. (2001). One trunk sends out many branches: Pacific cultures and cultural identities. In C. Macpherson, P. Spoonley, & M. Anae (Eds.), *Tangata o te moana nui: The evolving identities of Pacific peoples in Aotearoa/New Zealand* (pp. 66–80). Dunmore Press.

Mageo, J. M. (1989). Aga, amio and loto: Perspectives on the structure of the self in Samoa. *Oceania, 59*(3), 181–199. https://doi.org/10.1002/j.1834-4461.1989.tb02321

Mamea, K. (2016). *Does Melanie Klein's concept of internal objects relate to Samoan writings on internal structures of the self? A phenomenologically-oriented heuristic enquiry* [Masters dissertation, Auckland University of Technology]. Tuwhera Research Repository. https://hdl.handle.net/10292/10098

Mila, K. (2008). *A well written body.* Huia Press.

Mo'a, V. (2015, July). *Fa'asinomaga (identity) and vā (relational space)* [Paper presentation]. 2015 Australian Association of Bioethics and Health Law Conference, Wellington, New Zealand.

Moustakas, C. (1990). *Heuristic research: Design, methodology, and applications.* Sage.

Ozertugrul, E. (2017). Heuristic self-search inquiry into one experience of obsessive-compulsive disorder. *Journal of Humanistic Psychology, 57*(3), 215–236. https://doi.org/10.1177/0022167815594966

Peteru, M. C., & Percival, T. (2010). *O 'Āiga o le 'anofale o afio'aga ma le fatu o le aganu'u: Samoan pathways to the prevention of sexual violence* [Research report]. Ministry of Pacific Island Affairs and Pacific Health, School of Population Health, University of Auckland.
Polanyi, M. (1969). *Knowing and being* (M. Green, Ed.). University of Chicago Press.
Rose, T., & Loewenthal, D. (2006). Heuristic research. In D. Loewenthal & D. Winter (Eds.), *What is psychotherapeutic research?* (pp. 133–143). Karnac Books.
Segal, H. (1988). *Introduction to the work of Melanie Klein*. Karnac.
Sela-Smith, S. (2002). Heuristic research: A review and critique of Moustakas's method. *Journal of Humanistic Psychology*, *42*(3), 53–88. https://doi.org/10.1177/0022167802423004
Suali'i-Sauni, T. (2011). 'It's in your bones!': Samoan custom and discourses of certainty. *New Zealand Yearbook of New Zealand Jurisprudence*, *13–14*, 70–88. www.nzlii.org/nz/journals/NZYbkNZJur/2011/10.html
Tamasese, K., Peteru, C., Waldegrave, C., & Bush, A. (2005). Ole taeao afua, the new morning: A qualitative investigation into Samoan perspectives on mental health and culturally appropriate services. *Australian & New Zealand Journal of Psychiatry*, *39*(4), 300–309. https://doi.org/10.1080/000486700782
Tuagalu, I. (2008). Heuristics of the vā. *AlterNative*, *4*(1), 107–126.
Tunufa'i, L. (2016). Pacific research: Rethinking the Talanoa 'methodology'. *New Zealand Sociology*, *31*(7), 227–239. https://search.informit.org/doi/10.3316/informit.561428501206421
Vaioleti, T. M. (2006). Talanoa research methodology: A developing position on Pacific research. *Waikato Journal of Education*, *12*(1). https://doi.org/10.15663/wje.v12i1.296
Wendt, A. (1999). Tatauing the post-colonial body. In V. Hereniko & R. Wilson (Eds.), *Inside out: Literature, politics, and identity in the new pacific* (pp. 399–412). Rowman & Littlefield.
Wendt-Young, L. (2011). *Telesā: The covenant keeper*. CreateSpace Independent Publishing Platform.
Winnicott, D. W. (1953). Transitional objects and transitional phenomena. *International Journal of Psycho-Analysis*, *34*, 89–97.

PART III

Method and methodology

8

THE HEURISM OF HELP-SEEKING

Disclosing and concealing obsessive-compulsive disorder

Chris Lorigan

Introduction

The focus of this chapter is my experience of using a heuristic method and methodology for my Master of Psychotherapy dissertation (Lorigan, 2018). In short, the study examined what it was like to disclose and conceal my diagnosis of obsessive-compulsive disorder (OCD). Although the dissertation is in the public domain, this chapter involves my disclosure to a new audience, and as I was writing it, I was aware of the intrinsic challenge in that. More people would know. More people could judge. The shame, fear, and risk of stigma emerged. I felt apprehensive but, more than that, I felt exposed.

Re-encountering the material engendered a kind of mini heuristic self-search inquiry (HSSI), a process I discuss below, regarding what I was experiencing. It was hard because I was re-living a deep, personal piece of work and slicing it up to fit a smaller format. I was also looking for a cohesive theme that would hold the chapter together as a distinct piece of writing separate from the dissertation itself, which ran to 30,000 words and represented nine months' work – and a lifetime of suffering.

While I certainly felt excited and proud to be invited to contribute to this volume, I noticed that I didn't remain excited about the opportunity to have my words published. As I worked with the material, with Keith as the editor and a research assistant, Angie Strachan, looking over it, I felt vulnerable and vaguely uncomfortable. It was as if I had been tasked with reducing the wholeness and completeness of an emotionally raw piece of writing and shrinking it, caging it, limiting it. I felt as if I were therefore limiting or reducing myself, and I wondered what that meant. Was I reducing 'my Self' in doing this? Is my identity tied up with being an OCD sufferer? I then noticed how the prospect of having academic work published slowly began to outweigh the discomfort of exposure, and I wondered what that meant.

As I worked on the chapter, I decided to simply wait for that cohesive, perhaps singular, theme to emerge and not to force it. I eventually noticed how much I connected on a deep, emotional level with the help-seeking elements of the study, with what it might be that prevents us (people with OCD) from reaching out. When I wrote the dissertation, I was a master's student who had been seeing a small number of clients in the university clinic as part of my training.

DOI: 10.4324/9781003685944-12

As I am writing this chapter almost seven years later, and having spent those years working as a psychotherapist in full-time private practice, seeing around 25 clients a week, half of whom have OCD, my perspective has changed. I have changed and so what jumped out at me now, for this, is informed by that.

I am connected to a lot of people who suffer in a very similar way to the way I have suffered, and I experience considerable empathy for them every day. I am thankful that they have sought help. My own story includes delays in help-seeking as seeking help meant I would have to tell someone, which in itself was distressing. My heuristic process was deeply immersive and took me into parts of myself I did not know were there. Yet these parts were exactly what I was looking for, as a result of which I have started to comprehend the barriers I experience in seeking support.

Studying my own OCD

As mentioned above, the focus of this chapter is my experience of using a heuristic method and methodology for my Master of Psychotherapy dissertation (Lorigan, 2018) in which I examined what it has been like to disclose and conceal my diagnosis of OCD. As I progressed through the initial literature review, delays in help-seeking among those living with OCD emerged as a salient feature, and I became aware that exploring disclosure and concealment might shed light on the question of why people, including myself, might be reluctant to seek the support they need and deserve. Stigma and shame became a considerable part of the picture, which certainly felt true for me as I explored my own experience. I also became aware, as I progressed, of what it is like to undertake heuristic research; what it is like to become closer to oneself; and what it is like to dwell in the internal world of subjectivity. But first, I would start by examining what other researchers have found in order to both frame and focus my work.

I found in the literature a correlation between sufferers' lack of disclosure and delays in help-seeking (Belloch et al., 2009; McCarty et al., 2017; Picco et al., 2018; Poyraz et al., 2015; Robinson et al., 2017), a phenomenon that has received limited attention (Belloch et al., 2009). I also discovered that there is very little literature of close relevance – that is, very little from the OCD sufferer's perspective – about what it is like to conceal or disclose their diagnosis.

I have lived with OCD for 36 years, since I was 14. My experience has been characterised by intense, torturous distress. For me, the disorder seems highly aberrant in the context of 'normal' human experience, and consequently I have mostly ensured it remains a secret. Hidden. Thus, I have mostly suffered in silence and loneliness.

OCD is characterised by the presence of obsessions – defined by the American Psychiatric Association (APA) in its *Diagnostic and Statistical Manual of Mental Disorders* (*DSM*-5) as 'recurrent and persistent thoughts, urges or images that are experienced as intrusive and unwanted… and cause marked distress or anxiety' – and compulsions – defined as 'repetitive behaviours or mental [compulsions] that an individual feels driven to perform in response to an obsession… [and which] aim to "reduce distress"' (APA, 2013, pp. 235–236). The *Psychodynamic Diagnostic Manual* defines OCD similarly: '"Obsessions" are recurrent thoughts, impulses, or images that impinge upon the affected person's mental functioning; "compulsions" are actions, mental activities, and repetitive behaviours that the patient experiences as "compulsory" and that significantly affect his or her functioning' (Lingiardi & McWilliams, 2017, p. 171).

Severe anxiety has, at various extended periods in my life, accompanied my thoughts, feelings, physical body, and behaviours, often constantly and oppressively, although this has lessened considerably in recent years as a result of therapy. Like all OCD sufferers, I have had the experience of getting locked and lost in an endless downward spiralling loop of anxiety, questioning, doubting, terror, checking, relief, uncertainty, panic, desperation, checking, relief, despair, dread, suddenly knowing, relief, questioning, anxiety, and more checking.

For some reason I wanted people to understand this, and at the same time I did not want anyone to know. I therefore wanted to examine what it was that allowed me to speak and what it was that kept me silent; what I thought and felt when I told others and what I thought and felt when I did not or could not.

In the early stages of the study, I considered what I wanted to say about OCD, to whom, and for what purpose. I was engaging in a heuristic inquiry that would involve all aspects of my experience and, therefore, the study itself would inherently mean revealing my OCD, which felt crucial and yet immensely challenging. Primarily, my focus was the experience of disclosure and concealment of the OCD diagnosis itself; I did not explore the experience of revealing or concealing its specific themes, obsessions, and compulsions.

What I found during my initial systematic literature review was that OCD sufferers seem to delay help-seeking because of perceived discrimination, stigma, and judgement associated with their diagnosis and experience (Belloch et al., 2009; McCarty et al., 2017; Picco et al., 2018; Poyraz et al., 2015; Robinson et al., 2017). In fact, Belloch et al. (2009) point out that just 34–40% of OCD sufferers 'have ever received mental health treatment' (p. 257) and that there is an average delay in treatment seeking of 7.6 years. The same authors contend that these delays have received limited attention. I believe my lived experience perspective helps provide insights into what it is like for people like me to face the dilemma of disclosure, and an understanding of this might offer clinicians a window on how to engage with these clients if they do seek help. As Greene (2009) argues, 'the crucial question is what underlies the decision processes and creates conditions for likely disclosure' (p. 227). I sought to explore this underlying domain.

The heuristic process

Heuristic research is a 'process of internal search through which one discovers the nature and meaning of experience' (Moustakas, 1990, p. 9). An issue, problem, challenge, or theme is focused on with a full inner, introspective, reflective awareness so that the researcher can 'come in touch with new regions of [him or her] self' (Moustakas, 1990, p. 9). For me, this aligns with the concept that psychotherapy seeks growth toward deeper self-knowledge and self-acceptance (McWilliams, 2004).

In my dissertation, I used a variation on the heuristic methodology described by Moustakas (1990), aligning myself more closely with Sela-Smith's (2002) HSSI, as discussed below. As Etherington (2004) contends, my 'self' became my 'major tool'; I used 'intuition, tacit knowing and felt sense' (p. 17) to illuminate the 'person at the heart of the work' (p. 25). Experientially – and phenomenologically – I sought to uncover 'that which is, as it is' (Douglass & Moustakas, 1985, p. 40).

The heuristic method, as Moustakas (1990) conceptualises it, comprises seven core concepts. These are the mechanisms of engagement with the self and the research question, the inextricably linked and non-linear processes underpinning each stage of the inquiry. The following outline is a brief example of how I understood and engaged with each of these:

- Identification with the focus of inquiry – I explored and 'became one' with the question (Moustakas, 1990, p. 15).

- Self-dialogue – I engaged back and forth internally, again and again in an open way, with the phenomenon and my experience of it as it developed.
- Tacit knowing – an implicit, untapped source of meaning, unique perceptions, feelings, intuitions, beliefs, and judgments. I allowed myself to feel, to mindfully and non-judgementally notice what I was feeling.
- Intuition – knowing that I know, which forms a bridge between implicit and explicit knowing via indwelling.
- Indwelling – which Moustakas (1990) describes as gazing 'unwaveringly' inward (p. 24), remaining with the experience without requiring it to take distinct shape, allowing intuition to flourish. I thus practised a kind of constant awareness of what I was experiencing cognitively, emotionally, and physically. I surrendered to an emergent process with as few expectations as possible.
- Focusing – precise engagement with the experience: mindfully noticing what is thematically emerging internally in relation to the research phenomena. I had to ensure that this precision did not become in itself obsessive or perfectionistic in an OCD sense. I wanted to allow and accept what I was experiencing.
- Internal frame of reference – acknowledges the subjective and personal nature of the inquiry. I was aware throughout the process of how this was my unique experience, and I allowed myself to accept what I found without pinning it to external assumptions, judgements, and expectations. I was also aware that this would not be directly generalisable on a socio-cultural level.

These concepts underpin the heuristic method or process, and emerge during any or all of the following six phases of heuristic research (Moustakas, 1990):

- Initial engagement – in which I found and grappled with the topic, the question, and the research frame; and in which I was driven to find something previously unknown.
- Immersion – in which I fully lived (and journaled) the experience of truly wondering about and feeling what it is like to disclose or conceal my OCD.
- Incubation – in which I took the time to allow my tacit and unconscious knowing to emerge, for my intuition to develop.
- Illumination – in which I found new and unexpected insights, themes, and qualities.
- Explication – which involved re-immersion in the data as I sought to understand, clarify, and delineate the core or dominant themes within the research phenomena.
- Creative synthesis – in which I expressed the transformational nature of the research experience.

These phases are non-linear, building on each other and occasionally looping back – for example, I found that illumination and explication occurred throughout the research process.

Selecting heuristic research

Heurism stood out as the most appropriate fit for my research for three key reasons. Firstly, my topic was a deeply personal one that seemed to call for what Moustakas (1990) describes as a 'steady inward gaze' (p. 13) before I could come to new understandings of myself. Secondly, the process would help me, as a psychotherapist, to better understand my contribution to and role in the therapeutic relationship (McWilliams, 2004; Shedler, 2010; Stolorow et al., 1987), which is widely believed to be the most crucial element of the healing endeavour of psychotherapy (Haugh & Paul, 2008; Kahn, 2001; McWilliams, 2004). Thirdly, I hoped the study would contribute to the field of psychotherapy by giving clinicians and researchers a rich, colourful insight into what it is like for a person to be immersed in the distress of an OCD concealment/disclosure dilemma, an insight that could also aid the development of empathy and a strong therapeutic relationship. I also consider that this phenomenon might have some relevance to the concealment and disclosure of mental illness more generally.

Moustakas (1990) names several influences on his development of heuristic research, of which two in particular – Michael Polanyi and Sidney Jourard – felt highly relevant as I engaged with my topic and with heuristic methodology.

Polanyi's (1966) articulation of the tacit dimension of human knowing suggests that we can turn our attention inward to find what we are perhaps intuiting – what we know without knowing we know it. The implications of this seemed to be relevant to my study: I experienced something when I could not disclose OCD, but I did not quite know what it was. I considered, though, that I might know tacitly, and that a heuristic inquiry could help me comprehend it. Further, Polanyi (1966) suggests that 'indwelling… is the proper means of knowing man and the humanities… the mind of a person can be understood only by reliving its workings' (p. 16). Indwelling became one of Moustakas's (1990) phases of heuristic research and the key means of self-exploration. For me, this is closely related to the psychoanalytic notion of the human unconscious, first introduced to the field of psychotherapy by Freud (1896/1966) and remaining one of its foundational concepts. This refers to material that lies deep within us, material we might access as we explore our inner experience. Moustakas (1990) believes that ignoring this dimension means 'we restrict the potential for new awareness and understanding… the depth of meanings that are inherent in every significant human experience' (p. 22).

As Jourard (1971) suggests, knowing oneself more deeply – the finding of parts previously unknown to us – is important for good health: if we know ourselves as fully as we can, we can achieve growth. To take this point one step further, heuristic research, like any self-reflection, can allow us to heal through the development of self-knowledge. Polanyi (1966) argues that it is not just the mind that can be understood in this way, but that tacit knowing, discovered through subjective indwelling, is the root of *all* knowledge. Jourard's (1971) writing has helped inform my understanding of heuristic methodology, but also of psychotherapeutic practice itself. If, as I mention above, heurism could help me to 'better understand my contribution to and role in the therapeutic relationship', then knowing myself on a deep level and coming into contact with tacit dimensions feels both personally and professionally important. On the professional front, Jourard (1971) considers a therapeutic alliance based on authenticity, congruence, trust, acceptance, and empathy is paramount, and that the dyadic effect – the idea that therapist disclosure encourages client disclosure – would be key to the facilitation of this. He contends that the client's disclosures are therapeutic because that person has probably not been able to know or express themselves authentically before. In doing so, and because of the therapeutic dyad, they experience aspects of themselves previously unknown to them. If, therefore, I were to understand myself better as a result of the heuristic endeavour, I might be able to reveal aspects of myself authentically and, thereby, to facilitate a safe and healing therapeutic relationship.

Subjectivity and the internal search

As Grant and Giddings (2002) argue, truth is subjective, which suggests to me that one might, through exploration and explication, be able to move beyond abstractions toward a felt sense of the essence of a phenomenon, which is precisely what I was attempting. Subjectivity is foundational to Husserlian phenomenology, which focuses on 'the meaning things have in our experience, notably the significance of objects, events, tools, the flow of time, the self, and others, as these things arise and are experienced in our "life-world"' (Smith, 2013, para. 6). Thus, phenomenology privileges the individual and the 'concern for the coherence and ultimate basis of experience' (Dostal, 2000, p. 53). As Dostal (2000) argues, 'a leading impulse of Husserl's early work is to turn away from the construction of abstract theories to the concrete description of the "things themselves"' (p. 53). For me this means that the first-person perspective is central to experience and perhaps the understanding of ourselves, others, and the world.

According to Grant and Giddings (2002), post-structuralists contend that our sense of ourselves as 'conscious, knowing, unified and rational' is illusory (Weedon, 1997, p. 21). So, while I made an attempt at explication during my research, this process cannot result in objective truth. It is *my* truth. There will be complexity and contradiction, which Grant and Giddings (2002) acknowledge stand in contrast to attempts at simplification or reconciliation, and all I could do was explore and wonder. I rested tentatively on new insights, which, for me, also describes the process of practising psychotherapy.

For Sela-Smith (2002), it is the subjective, internal search that is key: it leads to the tacit dimensions of one's inner world, and to feeling and knowing oneself. My original research and dissertation sought insight into my own experience with no expectation to make objective sense of it. As Sela-Smith (2002) points out, 'the feeling response, as experienced, is valid as it is' (p. 79), arguing that the – any HSSI – study needs to be a 'self-focus on feeling an experience' rather than 'thinking about and observing experience' (p. 82).

Douglass and Moustakas (1985) offer a clear delineation of heuristic research. However, a contradiction appeared, one that contributed to my favouring of Sela-Smith's HSSI. Douglass and Moustakas outline a clear methodology and method – as does Moustakas (1990) in his individual work – while at the same time suggesting a heuristic researcher be unbound by methodology. However, in Moustakas's (1990) heuristic research, there are defined phases which could reflect the very 'shackles of convention and tradition' (Douglass & Moustakas, 1985, p. 44) the authors are attempting to eschew. 'Freedom', 'flexibility', and 'openness' (p. 44) appear as core tenets of Douglass and Moustakas's (1985) heuristic endeavour, and I am not trying to say that these cannot co-exist within the six phases of heuristic research; what I am suggesting is that Sela-Smith (2002) offers an approach that is unshackled. As Sela-Smith (2002) argues regarding Moustakas's work: 'he creates a methodological structure for a process that he himself states must take place free from methodological structures if it is to be authentic' (p. 77). Sela-Smith's (2002) HSSI methodology is certainly less definitive; it is a surrender to feeling, a surrender to experience as it is – there is no 'controlling the process' (p. 83) and no method outlined. As I encountered myself in my concealment and disclosure of OCD, this felt potently liberating.

From the outset, I kept a journal outlining my somatic, emotional, and cognitive experiences regarding the disclosure and concealment of my OCD, no matter how insignificant it appeared at the time. This was a spontaneous, organic, and unsystematic process; I opened myself as fully as I could to these experiences. I wrote my responses to acts of concealment and disclosure both past and present, as well as to literature, film, music, art, clinical supervision, and academic literature. I also wrote anything that struck me as relevant during my daily life – anything that related to the anticipation of disclosure, actual disclosure, or to the experience of concealment. This was an intuitive process; it was uncensored as it made its way into the journal and was part of my heuristic surrendering and immersion.

Later, I strongly felt I needed space and solitude in order to deeply re-immerse myself in my journal data. I wanted as few distractions as possible so that I could feel and experience my entries. To facilitate this, I went away from home for a week, and the first thing that happened was that I had no idea what to do next. I wondered if this had something to do with the risk I was taking in disclosing my OCD in the act of writing; perhaps I was scared of the exposure. To make a start, I decided to split the work into the categories of concealment and disclosure before re-connecting with it to see what themes emerged.

This process encouraged many free-flowing written responses. As Moustakas (1990) suggests, I became one with my experience. I focused on the material during indwelling, letting my tacit knowing emerge via intuition. As Sela-Smith (2002) describes, this was a 'stepping into the unknown within feelings', a 'surrender into feeling-the-feelings' (p. 83). This provided moments of illumination. The feeling parts of me were not only sensate but expressed outwardly for me to explore again in writing. I tuned in to my thoughts, embodied responses, and emotional experience. What came next was a spontaneous series of words, without punctuation:

> awe loss pain envy fear power hurt hidden determination fight pity hero guts voice courage secret scared alone gone

I went back to these words and noticed my embodied responses more this time. I wrote more, as a theme of fear began to emerge:

> Leaping out of my body, my soul/guts/self needing to explode into the world. It was nervy and energised and it was moving upwards and it gritted its teeth and said no and why.
>
> It filled my abdomen and chest. It was colourless and shapeless and free. Yet it is tied down inside.

And later, some distinct themes were revealed, which I discuss below before offering some further reflections on the potential implications of heuristic research as it pertains to OCD.

Key themes

During the heuristic research process, I discovered new dimensions of the disclosure and concealment of my OCD beyond the abstract and the cognitive. These were phenomenological and visceral, emotional and, in some cases, quite profound for me to sit with. I briefly discuss these elements and experiences, and note the overarching themes of fear and being known that run through them.

Concealment and fear of reduction

I started feeling that the diagnostic label of OCD, when it was applied to me 30 years ago, helped me understand the 'crazy' and distressing thoughts I was having and their attendant repetitive behaviours. I had a thing, an 'illness', that was doing this. It was not that I was a freak. It had a name. And yet, perhaps because no one actually told me it was not my fault, it also started to define me to myself in a negative way: I became OCD, not Chris with OCD. This mostly occurred when it was at its worst, when I was consumed by OCD all day every day.

But, even when it was not consuming me to that extent, it was still an internal label that had become a core part of my identity. It was a label I needed to hide – and not, I have discovered, out of shame, a word that pervades the OCD literature (APA, 2013; Belloch et al., 2009; Harrington, 2014; Lingiardi & McWilliams, 2017; Robinson et al., 2017; Wheaton et al., 2016). It was, instead, out of *fear* that I would be reduced to this label by others as I was almost reducing myself. I would be lost, 'annihilated', simply because this one thing had come to dominate. Others would not take me seriously because how can they trust a 'crazy' person who has to keep checking everything and ruminates all the time? I found that this was how I had always experienced the prospect of OCD disclosure and why I had hidden it, despite limited concrete evidence.

Concealment and fear of negative judgement

The immersion process resulted in a series of words and terms that began to flesh out my experience. It is significant that many of these feelings and thoughts came from the mere *anticipation* of how I would be judged rather than how I was *actually* judged.

I imagined that, upon disclosing my OCD to certain people – some of my male friends, for example – I would be judged as weird, a broken freak, a flawed failure, a loser unable to control his thoughts, behaviours, urges, and fears; that I was not manly or worthy of being liked; that I had no power or did not deserve any; that I was weak at my core; that I was, therefore, unacceptable and unlovable.

This risk cuts deeply. It recalls my past trauma of rejection and loneliness, which I wanted to avoid. It made me feel that I could not fit into the world as a man with agency if other men saw me as weak for suffering from OCD. As if suffering is weakness and failure that ends in rejection.

I started to think that this was why I had been hiding. I felt deeply the sense of my own weakness and I wanted to hide it. I did not want to be profoundly lonely again.

Concealment and safety

The obvious corollary of concealing out of fear is concealing to stay safe. So what does safety mean? What might it look like? Was I really avoiding unworthiness or did I carry it within me? By not disclosing, I was perhaps attempting to stay okay in others' perceptions regardless of how I perceived myself. I was hiding the way I perceived myself (as unlovable and unworthy) because I believed it might be the only way others would see me; I wondered: how can they see me in any other way if I believe I am unworthy?

So, self-protection was key to the concealment. And it made sense as, to my mind, people can be judgemental, stigma exists, and people do not understand mental illness in general and OCD in particular. This has, in large part, to do with the perennially hidden nature of the disorder.

Concealment and self-judgement

When I looked back through my journal and my responses to the material, I noticed the lurking presence of self-judgement; I had not previously – consciously – known that this was such a salient part of my experience. This suggested that the difficulty in disclosing OCD lay with an internal pathogenic belief, as defined by Weiss (1993), that I was unworthy and therefore did not want others to know.

I then discovered that part of me wanted to disclose because I wished to be known for all of who I am, that I did not want to hide, despite how hard it was to reveal OCD and risk reduction, negative judgement, and rejection. I also found that part of me wanted people to know how much I have suffered; this was surprising because it seemed to contradict the feeling I have that people would think I was weak and flawed and unworthy if they knew of my suffering.

Disclosure and being known: Relief and wholeness

Part of my dissertation involved a presentation of the work to staff and students at Auckland University of Technology. This was a way of demonstrating what I was doing and how I was progressing; it provided an opportunity to hone my topic and get feedback before continuing with the study. I found this a challenging experience to contemplate, as it would involve disclosure. In this case, though, I had no choice, which is not the usual situation.

I used the presentation as heuristic research material and, while I was preparing it, I found that I wanted the audience to know how much intense suffering OCD caused me; that it is not trivial. I was living the heuristic process, discovering as I disclosed my OCD what it was like to be doing so.

What I found was that I was moderately anxious, afraid that I would get something wrong or not represent myself or the disorder 'correctly'. I was afraid of what people would think of me. Negative judgement and rejection loomed. I felt embarrassed and vulnerable, ready to be reduced; I felt nervous, I felt my leg trembling; I felt exposed, open to judgement, a freak.

But this feeling was soon replaced by one of joy: I was in a room of people I generally saw as 'safe' – psychotherapists and psychotherapy students – and I received an overwhelmingly warm, supportive, and caring response. I was hugged by several people. One of the lecturers said he was 'blown away' and another said she would 'trust me more' if I were her therapist and she knew this about me. I felt very accepted. I felt known. I felt valid and worthy and I was moved almost to tears as I wrote in my journal.

I also felt relief, something I have experienced in the context of OCD very few times and never so viscerally: I felt like a whole person. The fears were gone in that room in that moment and for a large part of the day, and I was free despite or perhaps because of my vulnerability.

This became one of my most rewarding findings: through disclosure, I could actually experience feeling known, which resulted in a wonderful sense of relief. Thus, one answer to my research question might be: My experience of disclosing my OCD is one of feeling acceptable as I am.

Further reflections: Heurism and healing

During the research, I came into very close relationship with my topic and myself-within-the-topic during my research process. The heuristic method I used seemed to have captured the complexity of the 'answers', the complexity of my experience, which helped me understand the barriers to my own help-seeking. Jourard (1971) aligns knowledge of our 'real selves' (p. viii) with good health: if we know ourselves as fully as we can, we can achieve growth.

Some of my themes came as no great shock, although I had not previously comprehended consciously the extent to which they impacted my life. Fear of negative judgement, for example, was not a surprising discovery; however, I was surprised by the extent to which it motivated my concealment and the way it was linked to the fear of being reduced to 'OCD person' and that this could, in turn, lead to rejection. I was also surprised about the experiences or core beliefs that underpinned these fears: feeling deeply or inherently unworthy and unlovable. The fact that there was also a negative self-judgement was a new discovery, and one that attests to the depth of suffering that can attend the OCD experience.

I believe that these findings reflect some of the elements and goals of psychodynamic psychotherapy: to understand one's pathogenic beliefs (Weiss, 1993), to obtain self-knowledge (McWilliams, 2004), and to uncover one's hidden feelings and point of maximum pain (Hinshelwood, 1991; Malan, 1995). The sense of judging myself as unworthy could warrant further heuristic inquiry, but here it points to the notion that my exploration into concealment and disclosure offers me new understanding in my own journey as an OCD sufferer. In this sense, then, I feel that this process has, to quote Shedler (2010), fostered my 'inner resources and capacities [and has helped me toward] a richer, freer, and more fulfilling' life (p. 107).

This is my experience and cannot be generalised – our experiences are unique and I am writing from the perspective of a middle-aged, middle class, heterosexual, Pākehā New Zealand male; yet I find myself wishing, as I did at the start of this study, for my findings to provide a measure of hope to and in other sufferers because there are so few expressions of the experience in the literature.

Heuristic research can be healing. I found and began to understand new parts of myself through this process; my fears found new expression, and I discovered a wholeness of being through disclosure. This has been immeasurably enlightening and rewarding. Concealment of OCD means I have at times delayed seeking help and treatment, largely due to the fears I have discovered. As Robinson et al. (2017) suggest, 'fear of stigma [can be] a barrier to seeking help' (p. 207). For me, this stigma is fear of reduction, negative judgement, and rejection, an experience that could provide practitioners with a broader understanding of OCD.

My research adds a rare human voice and colour to the body of knowledge pertaining to OCD, as well as to the difficulties many people have in coming forward to seek help. I hope that mental health theorists and practitioners find new insights here, and that the disorder can be treated in a way that honours its depth and complexity of experience. I also hope that by sharing my experience, other researchers may be encouraged to consider a heuristic method/methodology that might generate important insights. I would be interested, for example, in research from socio-cultural perspectives other than my own, and I would like to see research that examines disclosure and concealment experiences related to specific OCD themes, obsessions, and compulsions; I wonder if certain themes are easier to disclose. I am also interested in the subjective experiences of OCD sufferers as they deeply reflect, through heuristic immersion, on their early life, and whether or not light can be shed on the aetiology and development of the disorder through childhood experience.

I hope that by broadening our knowledge of OCD through research of this kind we might discover new approaches to treatment. I also hope that these insights might contribute to a reduction in shame and stigma and an increase in help-seeking behaviour.

References

American Psychiatric Association. (2013). *Diagnostic and statistical manual of mental disorders* (5th ed.). American Psychiatric Association.

Belloch, A., del Valle, G., Morillo, C., Carrió, C., & Cabedo, E. (2009). To seek advice or not to seek advice about the problem: The help-seeking dilemma for obsessive-compulsive disorder. *Social Psychiatry and Psychiatric Epidemiology*, *44*(4), 257–264. https://doi.org/10.1007/s00127-008-0423-0

Dostal, R. J. (2000). Subjectivism, philosophical reflection and the Husserlian phenomenological account of time. In O. K. Wiegand, T. M. Seebohm, R. J. Dostal, L. Embree, J. J. Kockelmans, & J. N. Mohanty (Eds.), *Phenomenology on Kant, German idealism, hermeneutics and logic: Philosophical essays in honor of Thomas M. Seebohm* (Vol. 39, pp. 53–65). Springer Science & Business Media.

Douglass, B. G., & Moustakas, C. E. (1985). Heuristic inquiry: The internal search to know. *Journal of Humanistic Psychology*, *25*(3), 39–55. https://doi.org/10.1177/0022167885253004

Etherington, K. (2004). *Becoming a reflexive researcher: Using our selves in research.* Jessica Kingsley Publishers.

Freud, S. (1966). *The complete psychological works of Sigmund Freud, Volume I* (J. Strachey, Ed.). The Hogarth Press and The Institute of Psychoanalysis. (Original work published 1896)

Grant, B., & Giddings, L. (2002). Making sense of methodologies: A paradigm framework for the novice researcher. *Contemporary Nurse*, *13*(1), 10–28. https://doi.org/10.5172/conu.13.1.10

Greene, K. (2009). An integrated model of health disclosure decision-making. In T. Afifi & W. Afifi (Eds.), *Uncertainty and information regulation in interpersonal contexts: Theories and applications* (pp. 226–253). Routledge.

Harrington, K. P. (2014). *Emerging from the wreckage: The exploration of mental health, stigma, and my experiences of living with obsessive-compulsive 'disorder'* [Master's thesis, Wilfrid Laurier University]. Theses and Dissertations (Comprehensive). https://scholars.wlu.ca/etd/1669

Haugh, S., & Paul, S. (2008). *The therapeutic relationship: Perspectives and themes*. PCCS Books.

Hinshelwood, R. (1991). Psychodynamic formulation in assessment for psychotherapy. *British Journal of Psychotherapy*, *8*(2), 166–174. https://doi.org/10.1111/j.1752-0118.1991.tb01173.x

Jourard, S. (1971). *The transparent self.* Litton Educational Publishing.

Kahn, M. (2001). *Between therapist and client: The new relationship*. Henry Holt and Company.

Lingiardi, V., & McWilliams, N. (Eds.). (2017). *Psychodynamic diagnostic manual: PDM-2* (2nd ed.). The Guilford Press.

Lorigan, C. (2018). *To speak or not to speak: The experience of disclosing and concealing my obsessive-compulsive disorder – A heuristic enquiry* [Master's dissertation, Auckland University of Technology]. Tuwhera Open Access Theses & Dissertations. https://hdl.handle.net/10292/12490

Malan, D. (1995). *Individual psychotherapy and the science of psychodynamics*. Butterworths.

McCarty, R. J., Guzick, A. G., Swan, L. K., & McNamara, J. P. (2017). Stigma and recognition of different types of symptoms in OCD. *Journal of Obsessive-Compulsive and Related Disorders*, *12*, 64–70. https://doi.org/10.1016/j.jocrd.2016.12.006

McWilliams, N. (2004). *Psychoanalytic psychotherapy: A practitioner's guide*. The Guilford Press.

Moustakas, C. E. (1990). *Heuristic research: Design, methodology, and applications*. Sage Publications.

Picco, L., Abdin, E., Pang, S., Vaingankar, J. A., Jeyagurunathan, A., Chong, S. A., & Subramaniam, M. (2018). Association between recognition and help-seeking preferences and stigma towards people with mental illness. *Epidemiology and Psychiatric Sciences*, *27*(1), 84–93. https://doi.org/10.1017/S2045796016000998

Polanyi, M. (1966). *The tacit dimension*. Peter Smith.

Poyraz, C. A., Turan, Ş., Sağlam, N. G. U., Batun, G. Ç., Yassa, A., & Duran, A. (2015). Factors associated with the duration of untreated illness among patients with obsessive compulsive disorder. *Comprehensive Psychiatry*, *58*, 88–93. https://doi.org/10.1016/j.comppsych.2014.12.019

Robinson, K. J., Rose, D., & Salkovskis, P. M. (2017). Seeking help for obsessive compulsive disorder (OCD): A qualitative study of the enablers and barriers conducted by a researcher with personal experience of OCD. *Psychology and Psychotherapy: Theory, Research and Practice*, *90*(2), 193–211. https://doi.org/10.1111/papt.12090

Sela-Smith, S. (2002). Heuristic research: A review and critique of Moustakas's method. *Journal of Humanistic Psychology*, *42*(3), 53–88. https://doi.org/10.1177/00267802042003004

Shedler, J. (2010). The efficacy of psychodynamic psychotherapy. *American Psychologist, 65*(2), 98–109. https://doi.org/10.1037/a0018378

Smith, D. W. (2013). Phenomenology. In *Stanford encyclopedia of philosophy* (Winter 2013 Edition). http://plato.stanford.edu/archives/win2013/entries/phenomenology

Stolorow, R. D., Brandchaft, B., & Atwood, G. E. (1987). *Psychoanalytic treatment: An intersubjective approach*. The Analytic Press.

Weedon, C. (1997). *Feminist practice and poststructuralist theory*. Basil Blackwell.

Weiss, J. (1993). *How psychotherapy works: Process and technique*. Guilford Press.

Wheaton, M. G., Sternberg, L., McFarlane, K., & Sarda, A. (2016). Self-concealment in obsessive-compulsive disorder: Associations with symptom dimensions, help seeking attitudes, and treatment expectancy. *Journal of Obsessive-Compulsive and Related Disorders, 11*, 43–48. https://doi.org/10.1016/j.jocrd.2016.08.002

9

THE BURDEN OF CHRONIC PAIN ON HEURISTIC METHODOLOGY AND METHOD

Tzach Maya-Chipman and Keith Tudor

The first part of the chapter discusses the methodology employed in the original study and how the first author (the first-person voice in the chapter) utilised some of its concepts in relation to his experience of chronic pain throughout the period of the study (2022–2024). The second part of the chapter applies the same approach to Moustakas's phases of heuristic study. As the first author employed various modes of heuristic expression in undertaking his study, including writing poetry, keeping a diary, drawing, painting, and sourcing images, the chapter integrates these – and their purpose with regard to this kind of heuristic enquiry – into the text and discussion.

Introduction

This chapter both illustrates and challenges aspects of heuristics based on research undertaken by the first author, supervised by the second author. The original heuristic enquiry was a heuristic self-search inquiry (HSSI), based on Sela-Smith's (2002) work, into the first author's experience of chronic pain, and formed the dissertation element of the degree of Master of Psychotherapy at Auckland University of Technology (Maya-Chipman, 2024). The chapter focuses on the impact of the first author's experience of chronic pain with regard to both a number of heuristic processes (the methodology), and the phases (or method) of heuristic enquiry.

The first part of the chapter discusses the methodology employed in the original study and how the first author (the first-person voice in the chapter) utilised some of its concepts in relation to his experience of chronic pain throughout the period of the study (2021–2024). The second part of the chapter applies the same approach to Moustakas's (1990) phases of heuristic study. As the first author employed various modes of heuristic expression in undertaking his study, including writing poetry, keeping a diary, drawing, painting, and sourcing images, the chapter integrates these – and their purpose with regard to this kind of heuristic enquiry – into the text and discussion.

DOI: 10.4324/9781003685944-13

Methodology

> I would advise every sick person to evolve a style or develop a voice for his or her illness.
>
> (Broyard, 1992, p. 61)

My desire to elucidate the complex phenomenon of the experience of chronic pain led me to choose a qualitative methodology. I was not drawn toward a quantitative approach since my personal and professional worldview opposes any generalisation of human experience that risks diluting the subjective as lived experience, and, therefore, viewing it as unimportant.

Learning about heuristic methodology enabled me to investigate the meaning of chronic pain experience using myself as the subject of enquiry. Although I considered other research methods such as hermeneutics, I concluded that heuristics were the most effective way to address my research question regarding the nature and significance of my chronic pain. Heuristic research provided me with a way of engaging with and exploring my experience. Above all, and perhaps most importantly, the philosophical ideas underlying heuristic research align very well with my values and beliefs, including my views as a psychotherapist.

My chosen methodology for this research was Sela-Smith's (2002) HSSI, which is based on Moustakas's (1990) heuristic methodology and method. As an exploratory qualitative investigation and personal approach to research, heuristic inquiry (or, here, enquiry), refers to a process of internal search in a journey by which 'one discovers the nature and [underlying] meaning of experience' (Moustakas, 1990, p. 9). Moreover, integrating various forms of artistic expression within HSSI helped me as the researcher to focus on my subjectivity and to develop emergent, creative findings throughout the research process.

According to Sela-Smith (2002), a heuristic approach can be used in 'research endeavour[s] where the inquiry is on the cutting edge of new territory being explored' (p. 58), which is how I am situating myself with regard to my subjective experience of chronic pain. As Moustakas (1990) clarifies, there is a fundamental necessity in this type of research for the phenomenon being investigated to arise within the researcher's 'personal encounter with the phenomenon' (p. 14), which, in turn, enables the experience to become transformative. The subjective experience of pain speaks to this approach as I seek to come closer to the origins of my chronic pain experience.

Drawing on the work of Michael Polanyi (1966/2009) and originating from Douglass and Moustakas (1985), Moustakas (1990) developed heuristic inquiry as a research methodology, which he defined as

> a search for discovery of meaning and essence in significant human experience. It requires a subjective process of reflecting, exploring, sifting, and elucidating the nature of the phenomenon under investigation. Its ultimate purpose is to cast light on a focused problem, question or theme.
>
> (p. 40)

As a method of researching the subjective, heuristic research is informed by constructivism, humanistic psychology, and phenomenology (Douglass & Moustakas, 1985; Moustakas, 1990). In constructivist epistemology, meaning and truth are generated by engagement with the world; consequently, the truth is not absolute but, rather, constructed, resulting in a fluid worldview open to and made accessible by multiple meanings based on diverse relational contexts (Crotty, 1998).

The constructivist view proposes that subjects and objects produce meaning together, which, amongst other things, acknowledged the researcher's involvement in the research. Indeed, this perspective emphasises the centrality of the researcher's experience and viewpoint, aiming for them to become explicit (Crotty, 1998). A distinguishing feature of heuristic research is its explicit integration of the experience of researcher as well as the phenomena of the research. A constructivist viewpoint recognises how we create meaning mainly by tacit knowledge, a central concept in the process (or methodology) of heuristic enquiry (Douglass & Moustakas, 1985; Moustakas, 1990; Polanyi, 1958/2015). Constructivism aims to make the implicit explicit and comprehend how we construct context-related meaning (Crotty, 1998). Heuristics are also grounded in phenomenology, with the idea that experience is structured by meanings that need to be discovered (Grbich, 1999).

This perspective lends itself well to a psychotherapy study suitable for researching 'authentic accounts of human experience' (Hiles, 2002, p. 1). Hiles (2002) links the process of 'knowing through participation' to psychotherapy as an 'authentic participatory practice' (p. 1). As a psychotherapist investigating a subjective experience of chronic pain, a phenomenon which is also encountered in clinical practice, Hiles's (2002) statement strengthens my sense of alignment between the research question, the chosen methodology, and both personal and clinical experiences of pain.

Heuristic enquiry also strikes a chord with how I practice psychotherapy. Indeed, Rose and Loewenthal (2006) promote heuristics as 'a relational research method that facilitates exploration of the lived experience of psychotherapy' (p. 133). Heuristic research and psychotherapy are both relational endeavours that require participants to engage in self-reflection, reflexivity, and subjective awareness, and require a refined capacity to explore one's interior landscape. Stevens (2006) also highlights the organic position of heuristic enquiry in the therapeutic process, asserting that 'heuristic research explicitly operates at third-order awareness – awareness of awareness – creating a cognitive discourse that makes the subjective experience of doing therapy accessible research through self-reflection' (p. 173).

The heuristic method includes engagement with uncertainty, doubt, incompletion, and questioning as necessary ingredients that ignite the possibility for continuous discovery and illumination of the research question. As a result, I entered this journey with an appreciation of the eureka process rather than focusing on the findings. As Heidegger (1962/2010) expresses at the end of *Being and Time*, 'whether this is the only way or even the right one at all, can be decided *after* one has gone along it' (p. 487, our emphasis).

In my endeavour to explore the primordial process of chronic pain experiences, I committed myself to emotional engagement and openness. Heidegger (1962/2010) articulates this position when he writes that 'knowing oneself is grounded in being with' (p. 161) and about the primordial existential connection between knowing oneself and others which is fundamental to our existence, adding that 'in concernful solicitude, the other is proximally disclosed' (p. 161), a view that was also (and a year earlier) expressed by Rogers (1961/1996) in his assertion that the most personal is also the most general. Moreover, a primary argument for applying a heuristic approach in researching chronic pain is that the most personal and anecdotal are essential to this psychotherapeutic study. This argument is supported by Carel (2016) who asserts that personal suffering and personal growth cannot be abstracted from the context of an individual life in which illness is experienced.

Heuristics acknowledges the scientist's internal processes as the most valid and valuable avenue to novel scientific discovery. It accentuates the scientist/researcher's profound commitment to the search for understanding their personal experience. Polanyi (1958/2015) refers to the destructiveness of so-called scientific detachment of the researcher from their personal experience when he writes:

> I start by rejecting the ideal of scientific detachment. In the exact sciences, this false ideal is harmless, for it is disregarded there by scientists. However, we shall see that it exercises a destructive influence in biology, psychology and sociology and falsifies our whole outlook far beyond the domain of science.
>
> (p. vii)

A crucial tenet of heuristic research recognises that the researcher's biases are inevitable in all studies and thus do enter the study. So, rather than trying to avoid or control against bias, the heuristic researcher acknowledges and embraces it. Indeed, I hold the position that there is added value in examining a problem of great personal significance – both to the researcher as a matter of personal experience, and for its general significance (Rogers, 1961/1996). Such benefits include increased enthusiasm, dedication, innovative thinking, and insight – and represent a different, qualitative paradigm of knowledge and research. While, like other chapters in this volume, I refer to the methodology of heuristic research in terms of some key concepts, the focus and contribution of this particular chapter is on the impact of my chronic pain on those very concepts.

Identification with the focus of enquiry

This involves immersing oneself entirely within the study question, seeking to promote internal understanding of the phenomenon through unstructured, self-directed exploration. As Moustakas (1990) describes it, the researcher merges with the study question, experiencing it first-hand in order to gain insight into it. The concept of identifying with the focus of enquiry encouraged me to delve deeply into the enquiry and to investigate its various components in order to gain an in-depth awareness of my experience (Sultan, 2019).

The research enquiry I undertook in the context of studying for a master's degree in psychotherapy put me in the context of my painful experiences and motivated me to seek healing, a journey that is my life's work. Everything I do – and did in the course of the enquiry on which this chapter is based – serves to understand my chronic pain better; everything else fades into insignificance. The degree to which I could – and did – relate to the enquiry indicated the importance to me of finding a way out of illness.

Self-dialogue

Self-dialogue is an invitation to engage in a conversation with the phenomenon, beginning with one's thoughts and feelings. This allows the researcher to inquire into their own experience with the phenomenon, which can lead to new insights (Moustakas, 1990). For me, it was the internal dialogue when on the journey which helped me to find the direction in which to head: the steady stream of thought or discourse that informs my next step.

My self-dialogue collaborated with my inner compass, drawing emerging insights from the landscape of the tacit dimension (see below). Therefore, essential to this process was my ability to be open, trusting, and receptive to all parts of my experience while in pain, and to be rigorously congruent in both my self-dialogue and self-disclosure.

Indwelling

Moustakas (1990) defines indwelling as 'the heuristic process of turning inwards to seek a deeper, more extended comprehension of the nature or meaning of a quality or theme of human experience' (p. 24). As a means of grasping its constituent qualities and its wholeness, he states that 'it involves a willingness to gaze with unwavering attention and concentration into some facets of human experience' (p. 24).

As I entered the process of indwelling in my research, I felt like a diver descending into deep, unknown waters. It began with a sense of curiosity, a longing to discover something new and profound. I arrived closer to what I refer to as 'the terrain of pain', allowing data and understanding to flow like waves, enveloping me completely. My indwelling experience was not just a mental exercise but also a physical one, an experience that I found challenging, demanding, and literally painful. I pushed myself to explore new perspectives and challenging ideas, sometimes struggling, and sometimes gliding effortlessly, whereby each descent towards the abyss took me further down and closer to the ocean terrain, though there were times when the terrain appeared further down and out of reach.

Tacit knowledge

The concept of tacit knowledge is essential to the heuristic process. Drawing on the work of Michael Polanyi (1966/2009), Moustakas (1990) asserts that 'underlying all other concepts in heuristic research, at the base of all heuristic discovery, is the power of revelation in tacit knowing' (p. 20). The main idea with tacit knowledge is that 'we can know more than we can tell' (Polanyi, 1966/2009, p. 4). Moustakas (1990) refers to tacit knowledge as the deep structure encompassing distinctive perceptions, emotions, intuitions, beliefs, and judgments lodged in a person's internal frame of reference that defines how we interpret experience. Since the underpinning of all knowledge is either tacit knowledge or grounded in tacit knowledge (Polanyi, 1966/2009), and alongside the idea that the earliest foundation of tacit knowledge is disconnected from the verbal-thinking self, we consider that tacit knowledge is accessed through thought linked to the intuitive, somatic-focused experience of wholes, rather than logical reasoning which compartmentalises experience (see Tudor & Worrall, 2006). Thus, such knowledge finds its way out, at least for me, through artistic forms in poetic writing and drawing. As Sela-Smith (2002) puts it, 'it is not the thinking-observing self but rather the *I-who-feels* who is experiencing the feeling that provides access to the aspects of the tacit dimension of nonverbal thought' (p. 62). In my understanding, tacit knowing is an extension of my identity that does not require conscious thought. Sternberg and Horvath (1999) describe it as 'knowing *how*' rather than 'knowing *that*'. This knowledge is not something I could or can understand or express(ed) concretely; instead, it is a deeply embedded quality of who I am that has been honed and shaped by experience. It is a silent expertise just below the surface and ready to be called upon in times of need. It points me in new ways in search of new meaning-making prospects for my experience. My tacit knowledge is whole and thus cannot be segmented into pieces. I either embrace it as such or not at all.

In order to access this knowing and knowledge, I used various modes of enquiry, including poetic inquiry (Faulkner, 2017), not least as the sounds and rhythms of poetry travel beyond the boundary of the conscious mind to ignite and nourish the imagination.

Intuition

Moustakas (1990) describes intuition as the link between implicit and explicit knowledge, and emphasises the importance of intuition when he states that 'every act of achieving integration, unity, or wholeness of anything, requires intuition' (p. 23). During the course of their study, the researcher is encouraged to pay attention to their emerging inner knowledge which reveals itself throughout the research journey. Many authors, such as Shirley and Langan-Fox (1996), contrast intuition with logic and reason as unique problem-solving strategies. According to Nisbett and Wilson (1977), people are sometimes unaware that an intuitive process occurs until an answer enters their awareness. In response to that, Vaughan (1979) describes intuition as 'knowing without being able to explain how we know' (p. 46). In addition, Shirley and Langan-Fox (1996) concur that intuition is also defined by unwavering trust in intuitive feelings and sensations.

As I noted in the diary I kept during my research enquiry,

> Intuition is my compass, pointing towards the true north of the self. The voice that whispers in my mind and heart guides me through the twists and turns of the research labyrinth. Like a skilled sailor who relies on the stars and tide to navigate through great oceans, I, too, need to trust my intuition to navigate the wilderness in search of the root cause of my illness. It is a rare moment when intuition takes centre stage and shines a light on my path, illuminating the way forward.
>
> (T. Maya-Chipman, Personal diary notes, 24th September 2019)

As a heuristic researcher, I followed my intuition, which often led me to new avenues of enquiry; to discover valuable resources; to modify my approach; and to develop new perspectives in order to pursue meaningful insights.

Focusing

Gendlin (1978/1981) crafted deliberate experiential methods for employing centring, attentiveness, and introspection in the therapeutic practice known as *focusing*, which, as Cornell and McGavin (2002) describe it, 'is a simple matter of holding open, non-judging attention to something which is directly experienced but not yet in words' (p. i). At one level, focusing is simple but, at another level, it is difficult, and like the experience of pain, it is both intricate and full of paradox: 'It is direct and indirect, subtle, and concrete, active, and receptive' (Cornell & McGavin, 2002, p. i).

For me, focusing was a process that allowed me the autonomy to choose my inner trail and to adjust my course as needed; and to tap into the meaning stored in my body, whether I was consciously aware of that meaning or not. In the study of pain, focusing enabled me to both 'plug in' and connect with my bodily experience and to look at pain from within the inner structure of my being. It formed structure and illuminated the path towards understanding experience that, as it turned out, was chaotic, paradoxical, and confusing. For my writing to be truly transformative, a process Sela-Smith (2002) identifies as central to HSSI, I needed to focus inward on the experience of pain, and so my journal entries comprise my experiences, theoretical ideas, and musings on living with pain.

However, while focusing is an inward-looking process based on a one-person psychology (Stark, 1999), this needs to be balanced with a more outward-looking, two-person process such as mirroring. According to Eisner (1995), the use of visual images offers an 'all-at-onceness' (p. 1) that discloses what would be challenging to comprehend in diachronic forms using language and statistics alone. Using visual imagery is not a privilege or an add-on to scholarship but is, in many instances and research, essential. In my experience, pain and illness require visual mirroring in order to give them both depth and width (see Tudor, 2014/2017), which points to knowing that pain is embedded in the world. In my experience, giving an invisible feeling of pain and illness a symbolic visual expression allowed it to break through what is already known about the experience – and got me to think outside of my theoretical comfort zone.

Internal frame of reference

Understanding the traits, nature, and significance of the study depended on the internal frame of reference of the experiencing person (Moustakas, 1990). Thus, the researcher's own background, worldview(s), perspective, values, beliefs, position(s), past experiences, and knowledge are considered important in shaping and orienting the researcher with regard to and towards the phenomenon under investigation, for instance, my position about subjective experience and knowledge (above). I understand this as functioning in the undercurrents of my psyche which also formulates the researcher's bias towards the research question.

Having considered the impact of pain on some of the processes (methodology) of heuristic research, we now consider how it impacted the practice or method of the research.

Method

As noted, in this research, I followed the HSSI approach developed by Sela-Smith (2001, 2002), which was both influenced by the heuristic methodology of Moustakas (1990) and highly critical of it. Sela-Smith's (2001, 2002) methodology is oriented on researching the self, centred on the '*I-who-feels*', wherein tacit knowledge emerges from connecting to one's feelings and embodied experience. In my original research (Maya-Chipman, 2024), I drew on my own experiences of chronic pain, delving into it in order to find different answers instead of relating to the pain by analysing it intellectually as a cognitive endeavour. This process led to a creative synthesis akin to that described by Moustakas (1990) (see below).

For the most part, I followed the six phases identified by Moustakas (1990), which supported the exploratory, introspective, creative, and experiential nature of this particular research as an elastic membrane around the time of the enquiry.

Initial engagement

Within each researcher exists a topic, theme, problem, or question that represents a critical interest and area of research. According to Moustakas (1990), the task of the initial engagement is 'to discover an intense interest, a passionate concern that calls out to the researcher, one that holds essential social meanings and personal, compelling implications' (p. 27). HSSI calls for a deep engagement with the research question by entering the focus of interest, weaving in the researcher's inner and outer landscapes with the research question, and living through it (Sela-Smith, 2001). Sela-Smith (2001) also writes about how HSSI is generally motivated by a crisis to which one must attend. For me, this was my inner voice calling for the need to resolve my pain, and I found that HSSI offered a secure-based container for me as the researcher to delve into my personal life narrative and to navigate a journey towards healing. By utilising an 'inside-out' process of self-discovery, I wove in reflective elements from poetry, literature, images, drawings, personal journaling (diary), and creative writing (Matousek, 2017) as methods that fostered the illumination and explication of my chronic pain experience.

> I step into the wilderness,
> my eyes fixed on the horizon,
> eager to get on a quest for discovery.
> (Maya-Chipman, 2018)

Engagement with poetry highlights the flaws, struggles, and complexities of my experiences of pain rather than speaking about them. It created, at least for me, space for making, as Leggo (2006) puts it, 'the world in words' (p. 74) by offering 'textual spaces that invite and create ways of knowing and becoming in the world' (Leggo, 2008, p. 167).

This phase of initial engagement is also a time when the researcher may experience a need to go inward for answers and, as Rilke (1993/2023) puts it, to 'live the questions' (p. 15). Even if the researcher does not know what to do in response to this calling, they know that ignoring it would deny a core part of themselves (Sela-Smith, 2001). Here, the research question emerges through the call to the researcher. David Whyte (2020) articulates the necessity of asking meaningful questions as an 'entry point' to the realm of self-search when he wrote about questions:

> Questions
> that can make
> or unmake
> a life,
> questions
> that have patiently
> waited for you, questions
> that have no right
> to go away.
> (Whyte, 2020, p. 19)

For me, the chronic experience of constant pain and the health crisis which I experienced prior to conducting the research ignited my inner resource of knowledge into asking a meaningful question, one that 'can make or unmake a life', a question that unlocked my access to the intuitive, tacit, and inner voice of self-knowledge in a search for healing: what is the meaning and lived experience of my physical chronic pain?

Immersion

The immersion process comprises sustained and focused attention in which 'the researcher lives and breathes the question' (Tudor, 2018, p. 152). Having identified the topic of the research and the research question(s), the researcher 'fully lives the research while awake, asleep and dreaming' (West et al., 2001, p. 62). It is a journey of inner depths (Sherwood, 2019). For me, this process was facilitated through self-dialogue (and self-searching), indwelling, and being aware of my internal frame of reference about chronic pain.

Kenny (2012) writes that the immersion phase is an invitation to 'stay fully with the experience of the phenomenon in whatever form it takes' (p. 8). The indwelling quality aided this intentional process of gazing inward to grasp an aspect of my experience more deeply (Kenny, 2012). The essence of the immersion process is a near-obsessive preoccupation with the question in mind. It is, in the words of Pólya (2014), 'more accessible to anything that seems connected to the problem and less accessible to anything that seems unconnected' (p. 145). Getting immersed in the topic entails, according to Rogers (1965), 'soaking up experience like a sponge so that it is taken in in all its complexity' (p. 187).

During this stage, no conscious effort is made to compile, organise, or analyse the information the researcher is ingesting. Instead, the researcher is receptive to all information and takes it all in by tolerating, as Rogers (1965) puts it, 'ambiguity and contradiction, [and] a resistance to the need for closure' (p. 187). While immersed, the researcher becomes receptive to the process of indwelling and tacit knowledge in order to acquire data from the most unexpected sources and settings.

For me, journaling and poetry gave me the freedom to explore my own reactions, questions, and intuitions without worrying that they would have to conform to any defined theoretical frameworks. Creating my artwork and collecting images furthered this dialogue, and, from this stage, I arrived at the critical beginning of self-dialogue (Moustakas, 1990). Dewey (1933) led me to a deeper understanding of the value of journaling activity, specifically his view that journaling enables a metaphorical detoxification of pain by letting go, flushing out, and eliminating the burden.

Incubation

Moustakas (1990) refers to incubation as 'the process in which the researcher retreats from the intense, concentrated focus on the question' (p. 28). This self-imposed internal retreat aims 'to seek a deeper, more extended comprehension of the nature or meaning of a quality or theme of human experience' (Moustakas, 1990, p. 24). When the researcher steps away from the focus of the question, the expansion of knowledge unfolds on a deeper level of awareness. Moustakas (1990) states that 'incubation allows the inner workings of the tacit dimension and intuition to continue to clarify and extend understanding on all levels outside immediate awareness' (p. 29). However, although Moustakas describes this process as a voluntary act of power, a kind of self-asserting distinction between the phenomenon itself and the researcher themselves by, in effect, putting cognition aside for a while, it seems like this process holds a degree of privilege in heuristic research on the basis of the assumption that a personal question about one's experience can hold a degree of separation from it.

Here, I offer a critique of Moustakas in asserting that it is impossible to separate from certain experiences, such as chronic pain, since this experience is, to some degree, ever-present. Thus, the researcher is always making meaning through the experience and lens of pain, even to the point of realising (as I did) that pain is a method of its own accord. In pain, incubation is a privilege as the severe chronic pain sufferer has no self-control over their experience and is subject to the totalitarian force of pain.

Too much pain causes cognitive and somatic shutdown. On the other hand, no pain attracts resistance and a breakdown of the ever-present pain bond, rejecting any desire to engage with the question by embracing the positive feeling of pain-free moments. In this place of 'no escape', I had to learn to tune in and recognise degrees of pain intensities that allowed tacit knowledge, intuition, and unconscious processes to reveal themselves. By embracing the varying degrees of pain intensity, I was able to tap into a deeper understanding of myself and my experiences. This process of tuning in to and recognising different levels of pain allowed me to access hidden insights and wisdom that would otherwise have remained unconscious. Through this exploration, I began to appreciate the complex relationship between pain and self-discovery which, ultimately, led me towards healing and growth.

Illumination

When the researcher is receptive to intuition and implicit knowing, the illumination process happens organically. An illumination is the conscious awareness of qualities and the clustering of qualities into themes associated with the question (Moustakas, 1990). According to Moustakas (1990), illumination brings unconscious content into conscious awareness. New aspects and viewpoints arise while one is unintentionally processing (other) material. When the researcher stays curious and attentive, new dimensions of experience or understanding of themes emerge, and what might have been cryptic meanings are clarified. According to Sela-Smith (2002), illumination permits previously dissociated components of oneself to be integrated when there is a break from dissociation to awareness of wholes and clusters of wholes that create themes inherent to an issue. For me, the illumination phase was both distressing and exhilarating.

However, although illumination is conceptualised as the fourth phase of the heuristic method, the eureka moment of new realisations is, more commonly, experienced and woven spontaneously in all phases of heuristic enquiry (Tudor, 2022, 2023), and in a process independent of conscious awareness (Sela-Smith, 2002). My own eureka moments in my original research enquiry accorded with Sela-Smith's comment that illumination 'may take place in a single moment or it may take place in waves of awareness over time' (p. 67). I found that writing poetry both grounded my being and fostered such illuminations of my pain experience, which were constantly re-envisioned and re-interpreted. In my diary notes, I sought to capture these understanding shifts as they occurred while keeping open to their ongoing progress. Even though the discoveries were unpleasant, the assimilation of the eureka moments transformed the terrible experiences from nothing to something, and from meaningless to meaningful.

Explication

The explication phase aims to explore what has emerged in conscious awareness to comprehend its multiple meanings (Moustakas, 1990). During this period, my previously internalised consciousness expanded into the exterior world by shifting implicit awareness into explicit form, leading to what Moustakas (1990) describes as a new perspective in the researcher.

A more comprehensive picture of the phenomenon emerges as new viewpoints, explanations, and patterns are discovered (Djuraskovic & Arthur, 2010). According to Moustakas (1990), this cannot transpire if the primary data source is based on the experience of others. Nevertheless, what starts as a personal process often leads to a striving for the generalised and/or universal facets of the experience. For example, at this point in the research, I sought and resonated with the experiences of pain described by other writers, which validated the genuineness of my research.

As a tool for communication and articulation of pain and illness, poetic writing emphasises in its singular manner ambiguity, awe, and the complex relationship between words and the lived body (McEntyre, 2012) or between words and embodiment. For myself, through poetic enquiry, I learnt to listen differently to words in a way that liberated me from the fixed notion of what was already known to me in its predictable forms, sequences, and patterns.

Creative synthesis

In heuristic research, once the researcher has mastered the materials that illuminate and explicate the question, they are challenged to craft a creative synthesis of the findings (Moustakas, 1990). According to the heuristic method, results are presented as an individual depiction and/or an exemplary portrait in a creative synthesis so that 'both the phenomenon and the individual persons emerge in a vital and unified way' (Moustakas, 1990, p. 52). At this point, usually the stage of writing up the research, the main task is to evaluate all the acquired data in novel ways. Douglass and Moustakas (1985) clarify the essence of creative synthesis when they state that, at this point, 'the researcher is challenged to generate a new reality, a new monolithic significance that embodies the essence of the heuristic truth' (p. 52). The purpose of the heuristic researcher in generating this synthesis is to capture the key meanings that arise from the lived experience (and/or phenomena) and to convey the essence of that experience to others who may or may not have had that in order for them to grasp it at an even greater depth (Clark, 1987). Further, Moustakas (1990) suggests that the data presentation should 'be told in such a way that in itself enables self-transformation' (p. 13); and Sela-Smith (2002) suggests that, when a story is constructed with its embedded transformation, it has 'the power to transform anyone who surrenders to it' (p. 64), including the reader.

Creative synthesis can be expressed in various ways (Moustakas, 1990). It is not a summary or a recapitulation of the research, and it is more than a simple description of what occurred in the enquiry; it is, according to Djuraskovic and Arthur (2010), 'the complete depiction of human experience in all its wholeness' (p. 1579). For me, the arrival at this profound personal understanding of chronic pain occurred by engaging with Moustakas's (1990) distinctive yet interconnected concepts (as described in the first part of this chapter) that are central to the process of heuristic enquiry.

References

Broyard, A. (1992). *Intoxicated by my illness: And other writings on life and death*. Fawcett.

Carel, H. (2016). *Illness: The cry of the flesh*. Routledge.

Clark, J. B. (1987). *Duet: The experience of the psychologically androgynous male*. The Union for Experimenting Colleges and Universities.

Cornell, A. W., & McGavin, B. (2002). *The focusing student's and companion's manual*. Focusing Resources.
Crotty, M. (1998). *The foundations of social research: Meaning and perspective in the research process*. Allen & Unwin.
Dewey, J. (1933). *How we think: A restatement of the relation of reflective thinking to the educative process*. Houghton Mifflin.
Djuraskovic, I., & Arthur, N. (2010). Heuristic inquiry: A personal journey of acculturation and identity reconstruction. *The Qualitative Report*, *15*(6), 1569–1593. https://doi.org/10.46743/2160-3715/2010.1361
Douglass, B. G., & Moustakas, C. (1985). Heuristic inquiry. *Journal of Humanistic Psychology*, *25*(3), 39–55. https://doi.org/10.1177/0022167885253004
Eisner, E. W. (1995). What artistically crafted research can help us understand about schools. *Educational Theory*, *45*(1), 1–6. https://doi.org/10.1111/j.1741-5446.1995.00001.x
Faulkner, S. (2017). Poetic inquiry: Poetry as/in/for social research. In P. Leavy (Ed.), *Handbook of arts-based research* (pp. 208–230). Guilford Publications.
Gendlin, E. T. (1981). *Focusing* (2nd ed.). Bantam. (Original work published 1978)
Grbich, C. (1999). *Qualitative research in health*. Allen & Unwin.
Heidegger, M. (2010). *Being and time*. SUNY Press. (Original work published 1962)
Hiles, B. (2002, October 15). *Narrative and heuristic approaches to transpersonal research and practice* [Paper presentation]. CCPE, London. http://psy.dmu.ac.uk/drhiles/N&Hpaper.htm
Kenny, G. (2012). An introduction to Moustakas's heuristic method. *Nurse Researcher*, *19*(3), 6–11. https://doi.org/10.7748/nr2012.04.19.3.6.c9052
Leggo, C. (2006). End of the line: A poet's postmodern musings on writing. *English Teaching: Practice and Critique*, *5*(2), 69–92.
Leggo, C. (2008). Astonishing silence: Knowing in poetry. In G. J. Knowles & A. L. Cole (Eds.), *Handbook of the arts in qualitative research: Perspectives, methodologies, examples, and issues* (pp. 165–174). Sage.
Matousek, M. (2017). *Writing to awaken: A journey of truth, transformation, and self-discovery*. New Harbinger Publications.
Maya-Chipman, T. (2018). *Journey into the unknown* [Journal]. Unpublished manuscript.
Maya-Chipman, T. (2024). *Navigating the wilderness – A heuristic self-search inquiry into the lived experience of chronic pain* [Master's dissertation, Auckland University of Technology]. Tuwhera Open Access Theses & Dissertations. http://hdl.handle.net/10292/17183
McEntyre, M. C. (2012). *Patient poets: Illness from inside out*. University of California.
Moustakas, C. (1990). *Heuristic research: Design, methodology, and applications*. Sage Publications.
Nisbett, R. E., & Wilson, T. D. (1977). Telling more than we can know: Verbal reports on mental processes. *Psychological Review*, *84*(3), 231–259. https://doi.org/10.1037/0033-295X.84.3.231
Polanyi, M. (2009). *The tacit dimension*. University of Chicago Press. (Original work published 1966)
Polanyi, M. (2015). *Personal knowledge: Towards a post-critical philosophy*. University of Chicago Press. (Original work published 1958)
Pólya, G. (2014). *How to solve it: A new aspect of mathematical method*. Princeton University Press.
Rilke, R. M. (2023). *Letters to a young poet: The Norton centenary edition*. W. W. Norton & Company. (Original work published 1993)
Rogers, C. R. (1965). Some thoughts regarding the current philosophy of the behavioral sciences. *Journal of Humanistic Psychology*, *5*(2), 182–194. https://doi.org/10.1177/002216786500500207
Rogers, C. R. (1996). *On becoming a person: A therapist's view of psychotherapy*. Peter Smith Pub. (Original work published 1961)
Rose, T., & Loewenthal, D. (2006). Heuristic research. In D. Loewenthal & D. Winter (Eds.), *What is psychotherapeutic research?* (pp. 133–143). Karnac Books.
Sela-Smith, S. (2001). *Heuristic self-search inquiry: Clarification of Moustakas' heuristic research* [Doctoral dissertation, Saybrook Graduate School and Research Center]. ProQuest Dissertations & Theses.

Sela-Smith, S. (2002). Heuristic research: A review and critique of Moustakas's method. *Journal of Humanistic Psychology*, *42*(3), 53. https://doi.org/10.1177/0022167802128803116

Sherwood, V. (2019). *Haunting Minnie Dean: A heuristic inquiry into baby farming, psychological infanticide and closed stranger adoption* [Unpublished doctoral thesis]. Auckland University of Technology.

Shirley, D. A., & Langan-Fox, J. (1996). Intuition: A review of the literature. *Psychological Reports*, *79*(2), 563–584. https://doi.org/10.2466/pr0.1996.79.2.563

Stark, M. (1999). *Modes of therapeutic action: Enhancement of knowledge, provision of experience, and engagement in relationship*. Jason Aronson.

Sternberg, R. J., & Horvath, J. A. (1999). *Tacit knowledge in professional practice: Researcher and practitioner perspectives*. Psychology Press.

Stevens, C. (2006). A heuristic-dialogical model for reflective psychotherapy practice. In D. Loewenthal & D. A. Winter (Eds.), *What is psychotherapeutic research?* (pp. 171–181). Karnac Books.

Sultan, N. (2019). *Heuristic inquiry: Researching human experience holistically*. Sage Publications.

Tudor, K. (2017). The relational, the vertical, and the horizontal: A critique of 'relational depth' (2014). In K. Tudor, *Conscience and critic: The selected works of Keith Tudor* (pp. 191–201). Routledge. (Original work published 2014)

Tudor, K. (2018). The fight for health: An heuristic enquiry (2010). In K. Tudor, *Conscience and critic: The selected works of Keith Tudor* (pp. 143–168). Routledge.

Tudor, K. (2022). Supporting critical self-enquiry: Doing heuristic research. In S. Bager-Charleson & A. McBeath (Eds.), *Supporting research in counselling and psychotherapy* (pp. 57–79). Springer.

Tudor, K. (2023). Critical heuristics: From 'I who feels' to 'We who care – and act'. In K. Tudor & J. Wyatt, (Eds.), *Qualitative research approaches for psychotherapy: Reflexivity, methodology, and criticality* (pp. 115–132). Routledge.

Tudor, K., & Worrall, M. (2006). *Person-centred therapy: A clinical philosophy*. Routledge.

Vaughan, F. E. (1979). *Awakening intuition*. Anchor.

West, W., Milner, P., & Palmer, S. (2001). Critical subjectivity: Use of self in counselling research. In *The BACP counselling reader* (pp. 60–74). Sage & the British Association of Counselling and Psychotherapy.

Whyte, D. (2020). *David Whyte essentials*. Many Rivers Press.

10

ALLOWING TIME AND SPACE FOR HEURISTIC AND AESTHETIC ENQUIRY

A psychotherapy trainee's self-search

Sian Haydon and Keith Tudor

Introduction

As human beings we have all been engaging with aesthetics for our whole lives, with varying degrees of recognition and appreciation. A reminder is often required to rediscover that recognition and appreciation for what can be found through deep relationships with art, our surroundings, others, and our inner selves. To form these relationships, the noise of our daily lives must be quietened and a sort of permission must be granted to embark on a personal enquiry; a slower pace and an expanded sense of spaciousness is necessary. To some this comes easier than others. In psychotherapy, it can be argued that the same philosophy is needed. The therapist creates space for deep contemplation in a way that is different from daily life, hopefully forming this kind of capacity in their clients also. The reminder above was written in the book *Your Brain on Art* by Magsamen and Ross (2023); it both sets the scene for the concepts in this chapter and was the impetus for one of the author's burgeoning journey into an aesthetic way of being. As Magsamen and Ross (2023) put it: 'So much beauty and meaning is obscured by our preoccupations' (p. 128).

For my master's dissertation, I, Sian (the first author of and the first-person voice in this chapter) embarked on a heuristic self-search that followed my re-engagement with aesthetic enquiry, under the supervision of Keith (the second author) (Haydon, 2024). More than ten years prior, I had completed a bachelor's degree in design, and worked as a graphic designer, among various other creative tangents. Although there were some similarities – an awareness of subjectivity, self-expression, abstract thinking, and human centredness – studying psychotherapy was a step into a new world, a comparatively immaterial one. Towards the end of my studies, after keeping my 'old creative self' and 'new therapist self' in separate boxes for some time, it became apparent that artistry and creativity were waiting to be part of my new vocation. The way to achieve this had not been immediately clear to me: at times, an aesthetic way of thinking felt incompatible with psychodynamic psychotherapy. I set out to explore what this meant and how it might be important in the context of my country, Aotearoa New Zealand. I decided that re-engagement with aesthetic enquiry through a heuristic and arts-based approach to research and discovery was the means to do so.

DOI: 10.4324/9781003685944-14

In this chapter, we bring together Sian's interest in aesthetic enquiry, and Keith's interest in time, specifically kairos (Tudor, 2001, 2002, 2008), and space, specifically temenos (Embleton Tudor & Tudor, 1999; Tudor, 2001; Tudor & Embleton Tudor, 1999), to explore and explicate their relationship and significance for heuristic self-search research.

The beginning of a self-search

I am someone who has always had a whole-hearted appreciation for the visual and creative dimensions of life. As a child, when I had a vision for a new creation, I would excitedly pull all the parts together to create and share it: short stories written and illustrated on paper bound with staples; bedroom furniture heaved around the room for a new 'feel' to the space; dance routines crafted to the song of the moment, incorporating playground structures and whoever I could find to submit to my directorial demands. I was a sort of fledgling creative producer. Although I didn't have the words for it then, my pursuit was of the full-bodied excitement and saliency of the arts: finding colours, textures, and movements that 'spoke to me'. I have come to know this as an aesthetic experience.

Only once the term 'aesthetic shivers' arrived in my ears one day via a podcast episode (Grant, 2023) did I officially commit to researching the topic. Fizzing with a surge of knowing and excitement, this was my first fully conscious experience of how the body and soul viscerally responds (or shivers) when a part of itself is recognised, although I knew I had already experienced this many times before in the presence of art, music, performance, design, and architecture.

With my supervisor's sage guidance, a broad and experiential question led the self-search: '*How might re-engaging with aesthetic enquiry impact upon a trainee psychotherapist?*' Moustakas's (1990) research method considers initial engagement as the first phase in heuristic research. Using the term 're-engagement' in my question was pertinent as it became clear that the true initial engagement had been as a child, but that I had changed and times had changed since then, the effects of which would be uncovered, or discovered, by heuristic research.

Aesthetics and the self

Aesthetic enquiry is a concept conceived of by Greene (1977) in the context of art education, a finding of meaning through a 'wide-awakeness'. This involves artistic creation and a reflective acknowledgement of what it is birthed from – with regard to psychosocial and cultural factors (see also Chapter 9 in this volume). It is a broad encounter with the aesthetic world: being attentive to both the beauty and cruelty of life.

The etymology of the word 'aesthetics' is from the German *ästhetisch*, 'pertaining to taste or discernment', borrowed from the Greek *aisthētikós*, 'of sense perception, sensitive, perceptive' (Merriam-Webster, n.d.). The use of aesthetics as a modern science or enquiry was conceived as such in the 18th century (Common Era) as *sensible knowledge*. Aesthetics can be undervalued in the Western world, viewed merely as a 'decorative aspect of life' (Sarasso et al., 2022b, p. 723), and its importance as a process of knowledge acquisition overlooked. The essence of this original 'thought of the senses', as Griffero (2017, p. viii) puts it, is considered to have been lost to hard science. Countering this view, Berleant (2015) proposes the term 'aesthetic sensibility' (p. 2). This represents the original Greek root of aesthetics, and acknowledges this as an intrinsic human sensibility, starting with early handcrafted tools, glyphs in caves, and decorative pieces, and now, arguably, has expanded to include everyday experiences in urban and industrial as well as rural settings.

An alternative school of thought has grown from the Kantian concept of 'disinterested pleasure' (Kant, 1790/1987, p. 52). The disinterested stance allows the viewer simply to admire art without the desire for anything more, making way for appreciation, or openness and creativity (Sarasso et al., 2022a). Although feelings of openness and creativity can certainly be achieved through being with art, compared to my own experiences, this stance feels detached. Beholding art seems to be frequently spoken about in this slightly removed way. Rather than keep my distance, I explored the topic through my aesthetic sensibility á la Greene (1977) and Berleant (2015).

A sense of the literature

A sense of the literature was formed in the spirit of heuristic research (i.e., that subjectivity is meaningful and intuition is followed). It was a 'literature view', which started with the discovery of Natalie Rogers' (2000) concept of the artist-therapist. Tudor (2022, 2023) proposes a literature 'view', rather than a formal traditional or systematic 'review', to bring this part of research and the process of research into alignment with the freedom to roam that Douglass and Moustakas (1985) promote. Aesthetic enquiry prescribes a necessarily wide gaze for the enquirer, therefore, the term 'literature view' is all the more fitting. As such, I was guided through the references cited in contemporary papers on aesthetic enquiry and psychotherapy, and I engaged with poems, songs, art, and artist biographies, some of which are woven throughout this chapter.

Speaking of the embodied nature of heuristic enquiry, Sultan (2019) reminds us that human beings are more than simply eyes, ears, and noses. Physiologically, our nervous system is using these bodily organs to link sensory information with our internal representations (Gallese, 2019; Magsamen & Ross, 2023). Drawing a line between this and Greene's philosophy, we may understand how meaningful personal discovery by 'knowing, understanding, and feeling about the world' (Greene, 2001, p. 5) can occur through dialogue between an artist and their creation. Dewey (1934), Ryan (2014), Berleant (2015), Gaines (2016), and Griffero (2017), among others, have written about this from a Western perspective. An even greater level of interconnectedness between aspects of the living and non-living world is emphasised in te ao Māori, the indigenous world view in Aotearoa New Zealand. Recent research in neuroaesthetics (Magsamen & Ross, 2023) appears to bridge the gap between Western science and indigenous philosophies previously hampered by hard science. In my own research (Haydon, 2024), aesthetic enquiry seemed to blur the invisible boundaries to allow me to reside within this gap.

Within the realm of psychotherapy, aesthetics appears to be largely embedded in the distinct disciplines of art therapy, Gestalt therapy, person-centred expressive arts (N. Rogers, 2011), and the more recent development of arts psychotherapies. A selection of articles, introduced by Geller (2018), stood out from these disciplines and highlighted aesthetics in psychoanalytic or psychodynamic psychotherapy. Within the tradition of humanistic psychology and after recognising that artists witnessed healing in the creative process, Natalie Rogers (2000) established expressive arts therapy, a therapeutic modality of its own. Some of these people became artist-therapists, a term that resonated with me, though, naturally, I had some trepidation that the appellation 'artist-therapist' was a fraudulent claim. Even with the title 'therapist' or 'psychotherapist', I already experienced the dreaded – and, for a trainee, almost unavoidable – imposter syndrome. Furthermore, with regard to art, the conflict I experienced is also reflected in the traditional psychotherapy literature. Making art was pathologised and considered an avoidance of reality (Freud, 1920/2009), or, conversely, a magical act of creation (Jung, 1966), or an aspect of creativity and a path to growth and wholeness (C. Rogers, 1967). There is a breadth of contemporary literature supporting the importance of the creative process for learning and psychological health, but this does not appear to reduce the systemic challenges practitioners face in the helping and teaching professions to inject more art and creativity into their facilitation or practice (Gaines, 2016). Students before me at Auckland University of Technology had researched their own artistic pursuits (Christophers, 2019; McCall, 2021), providing me with the reassurance needed to start discovering some answers for myself.

Methodology: An imaginative, experiential co-creation

> The prerequisites for growth: the openness to experience events and the willingness to be changed by them.
>
> (Mau, 1998, section 1)

In order to explore aesthetics, it is essential to experience it through both *being* with it (an internal exploration) and by *doing* things with it (an external creation). A methodology based on Moustakas's (1990) heuristic research and Sela-Smith's (2002) 'self-search', alongside an aesthetic approach is described below. It is a personal framework of sorts and, as with any heuristic search, is not strict or invariant, and, as such, not intended to be followed uncritically.

Anyone attempting to articulate their heuristic philosophy is undertaking a project of self-exploration all of their own. Heuristic research is not a prescribed methodology, rather it offers a conceptual framework or attitude with which to approach research (Douglass & Moustakas, 1985). As Tudor (2023) states, this requires the researcher to engage fully from the start in order to provide their own methodology. This style of research is qualitative, personal, constructivist (social or otherwise), and phenomenological. It is also experiential, emancipatory, imaginative, and creative (Sultan, 2019). It is an exploratory process particularly suited to exploring change over time and depth of experience. If a researcher is seeking to undergo a personal enquiry (as was the case with me), a self-search (Sela-Smith, 2002) is a qualitative approach that is highly suited to such in-depth exploration.

Humanistic theorists such as C. Rogers (1967), Maslow (1971), and Gendlin (1978) place high value on experiencing as a path to self-awareness, and Moustakas (1990) does the same. Sultan (2019) describes Gendlin's philosophy of 'experience happens when a person and the world encounter one another' (p. 42) as central to heuristic research. Aesthetic enquiry follows a similar course. Co-constructed knowledge between oneself and the world is fundamental to this type of enquiry. The methodology discussed in this section is underpinned by both heuristic and aesthetic enquiry as humanistic, sensory, and embodied.

Considerations of context and time

A self-search enquiry positions the researcher also as the sole participant providing data. My dissertation included subjective data from my own experience as a Pākehā woman training as a psychotherapist (Haydon, 2024). This chapter is the same. This subjectivity can be criticised as anecdotal, and/or or unable to provide definitive answers (Lyons, 2007). Focus on the individual experience may be considered Eurocentric (Sultan, 2019), or an overvaluation of autonomy over homonomy, which Tudor (2023) points out can be true of both heuristic research and psychotherapy. However, as C. Rogers (1967) writes, 'what is most personal is most general' (p. 26). Questions that are not readily researched via other methods can have particular social significance. For example, Aotearoa New Zealand is a country with diverse perspectives on wellbeing and aesthetic importance that are unique to its bicultural context (Gain, 2022; Tudor et al., 2013) and not widely explored. In addition, using an aesthetic lens can illuminate inchoate layers of knowledge.

Moustakas (1990) considered that heuristic research is a process that cannot or should not be constrained by clock time; experiential time, rather than clock time, allows the researcher to move with intuition, following lines of enquiry through a sense of what holds meaning for them (as described in the literature view). However, in my case, following clock time could not be avoided as it was required to complete a dissertation within eight months (see Cousins et al., 2025, and Chapter 4 in this volume).

The six phase method: Fostering an aesthetic sensibility

Moustakas's (1990) method involves the following phases: initial engagement, immersion, incubation, illumination, explication, and creative synthesis. More recently, both Sultan (2019) and Tudor (2023) each comment that the phases do not unfold neatly, but, rather, overlap while the researcher moves backwards and forwards as if in a dance. The overall purpose of Moustakas's (1990) method remains true, that is, searching for 'qualities, conditions, and relationships that underlie a fundamental question' (p. 11) by 'moving from whole to part to whole again' (p. 16). Both Moustakas's and Sela-Smith's methods are inclusive of artistic practices as a means to gain data, to supplement depictions of experience, and as a vehicle to transform the researcher's tacit knowledge into explicit knowledge. Moustakas (1990) refers to artworks, diagrams, and poetry, while Sela-Smith (2001) beholds and reflects upon photographs as part of her own self-search. Furthermore, the final phase is a creative synthesis which may be crafted via various forms of creative expression, for example, through written language, visual art, dance, and movement. Below, I emphasise the ways in which aesthetic engagement was brought to the foreground in each phase of my dissertation.

Initial engagement

This phase involved a 'setting of the scene' in order to reacquaint myself and evolve my everyday relationship with aesthetics. Acknowledgement of prior engagements with the research topic can open up an entry point for a new relationship. For example, my key prior engagements with my topic were as a child, and, 15 years ago, as a university student. The initial re-engagement for the original research (Haydon, 2024) on which this chapter is based was as a postgraduate psychotherapy student.

I began an intuitive, nondescript process of reading, seeing, and creating, then re-seeing and re-creating what I had just made: a kind of call and response to my inner artist, and a way to get back into the process of deep engagement with my own art. At this early stage, I had a dream about being the passenger in a van that reversed its way through a pile of hard-shell suitcases. The suitcases were attractive pastel colours but were crushed by the wheels of the reversing van. I felt powerless to stop the van despite foreseeing the mess that would ensue. Contents of the candy-coloured suitcases were somehow soggy and wet.

This dream uncovered a fearful anticipation of my self-search breaking open, and perhaps ruining my existing relationship to aesthetics – or what I thought it was in any case (no pun intended). Interpreting this dream was a way of establishing my internal experience of the initial engagement phase.

Immersion

Moustakas (1990) considers this phase to be one of truly living the research question. Being alert to the potentialities in conversations, places, nature, and literature; our everyday experiences. In order to immerse in everyday experiences, I practised Greene's (2001) wide-awakeness; as a result, my topic seemed to be everywhere. I gazed at my interior surroundings and breathed in the suburban landscape where I lived. I wrote poems, one about a vase that looked 'as if its bright yellow dots could dress up its sadness' (S. Haydon, diary entry, 19th April 2024), and realised that I'd been buying a lot of yellow lately. Poetry seemed to come naturally before visual art making, perhaps not surprising as psychotherapy studies focus on expression via language. I visited art galleries, heard messages in the lyrics of songs, and meditated on imagery in the relaxation room at our university clinic. Importantly, I regularly used an art diary. This time was beautifully littered with synchronicities. I began selecting items from my wardrobe that had symbolic meaning to me – which others often noticed when I wore them. As Berleant (2015) would say, I was building my own aesthetic sensibility, one small act at a time. In doing so, one can begin to remove those preoccupations obscuring beauty and meaning to which Magsamen and Ross (2023) refer, and begin to notice oneself as part of a continuum of self and environment, both creator and perceiver.

Incubation

A design lecturer once shared the advice that, when designing a logo from scratch, one should not 'jump on the spot', meaning that, to make small obsessive adjustments in pursuit of perfection can stop you from moving forward; conversely, stepping away from something in order to gain perspective can offer a leap in a new, maybe much-needed, direction. This advice is, I believe, rather necessary for those of us who are artistically minded and prone to making things obsessively, even when the clock is against them or the idea isn't progressing. An unplanned incubation occurred after the discovery of my old school reports. I had to reckon with my longing for a different experience at school – a more engaged, artistic one. This intuitive shift to incubation was an instrumental way to process shame and grief and to open up potential for greater discovery.

Illumination

Moments or periods of illumination are a culmination of everything that has come before; and I agree with Tudor (2023) that these 'eureka' moments cannot be planned, rather that they occur as a series of moments throughout the exploration. Early in the research process I wrote down two sections from designer Bruce Mau's *An Incomplete Manifesto for Growth* (1998), a manifesto that I had admired as a design student. The first one is a call to embrace change in order to grow, and here is the second: 'coffee breaks, cab rides, green rooms. Real growth often happens outside of where we intend it to, in the interstitial spaces – what Dr Seuss calls "the waiting place"' (Mau, 1998, section 39). The interstitial spaces offer mini-incubations, and *these* are often the moments in which illumination happens. Many a time, illuminations occurred when I had stepped away from my computer to walk the dog, in the in-between of leaving and returning home.

Like aesthetic shivers, illuminations are embodied and feel other worldly. One evening I watched a music documentary which showed people walking into a church. Above the threshold was a banner which said 'Signs Wonders Miracles'. My attention was piqued. I felt that engaging in aesthetic enquiry was like a religious or spiritual experience, as though moving through a threshold into a new space, a space that doesn't feel like a slave to clock time. Something about it felt like magic, and that I wasn't alone.

Explication

Moustakas (1990) saw the purpose of the explication phase as fully examining 'what has awakened in consciousness' (p. 31) through illuminations during immersion and incubation. It is a more cognitively creative phase than that of the misty musings of illuminations. Language becomes fully formed around previously unconscious notions and the loose strings connecting concepts are reigned in more tightly and pertinently. Through use of a digital (and aesthetically pleasing) notebook app in which notes could be coded with a full colour background, I organised diary entries, artwork, and poetry into a hashtag system to begin to identify themes. I also made drawings of my process over time (Figure 10.1). Key terms were plotted against main themes in a cluster to demonstrate core qualities and connected components (Moustakas, 1990). I found two heuristic practices, focusing and indwelling, especially useful in allowing themes, qualities, and components brought forth during earlier stages of the research to be fully elucidated.

Creative synthesis

The final synthesis of heuristic research weaves together the researcher's experience as a whole in any creative means that best convey an essence of what the researcher has come to know about their topic (Sela-Smith, 2002; Sultan, 2019). In essence, my research discoveries related to time and tension: a sense of pressure against deadlines, having to 'put a lid on' creative exploration and make something final to fulfil requirements and to be graded. However, instead of being dictated to by clock time, unwittingly, I protested it in my creative synthesis. It was entitled 'Work-in-Progress', in which I chose to pull together a large collage of each of the pieces of art I had created and the words and phrases that had stood out to me throughout the research (Figure 10.2). It was a collage of what I had absorbed throughout the self-search.

Tools for creation and discovery

Moustakas (1990) offers a number of concepts which can be used as practices or tools one can draw on to gain knowledge about an area of enquiry, two of which I referred to in the explication section. Many naturally occur throughout the research process but, within a project being conducted in a limited timeframe, of all of these tools, I found focusing and tacit knowing

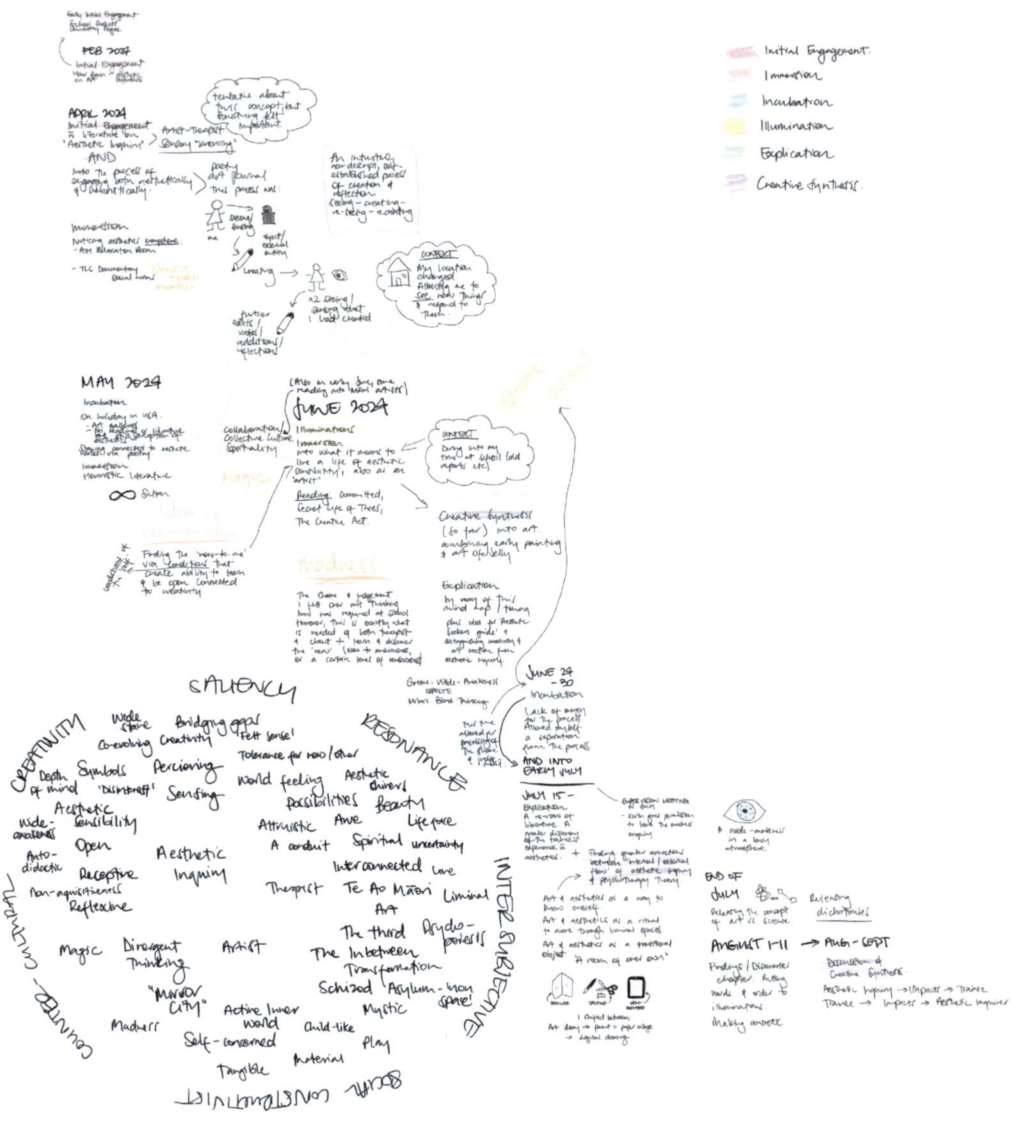

FIGURE 10.1 Heuristic process and key words map.

of particular aid in an aesthetic-based exploration, along with a third, that of self-dialogue, from Sela-Smith (2002).

- *Focusing* is based on Gendlin's (1978) slow and intentional process of inward attention in order to understand or gain awareness of a 'felt sense' or the essence of a problem, concern, or situation. The active process of artistic creation can be effectively counterbalanced by focusing; the expression of creation is complemented by an inward reflection.
- *Tacit knowing* is described as the sense of something's wholeness from its individual parts (Moustakas, 1990). This sense is often unknown or preconscious. In focusing inward to

FIGURE 10.2 A work-in-progress.

investigate feelings and intuitions, the researcher allows knowledge to emerge (Moustakas, 1990; Sultan, 2019). For me, this was encapsulated – and embodied – in the idea of aesthetic shivers, a knowing of the body.

- *Self-dialogue* is a naturally occurring tool for checking accuracy and truth while exploring what the researcher is communicating in their own work. In this case, art was used more intentionally (see, for instance, Ozertugrul, 2017). Such enquiry is also a way to check and judge research validity (Moustakas [1990] introduces Bridgman's [1950] thoughts on subjective validation to attest to this manner of checking, judging, and validating a researcher's own depiction). Conversations with the self through internal dialogue and conversations with art are part of this process, a process I describe further in the next section.

The discoveries of an aesthetic enquiry: Creations and meditations

Greene (2001) speaks of seeing the world with a wide-awakeness, being attentive to both the beauty and cruelty of life. A self-enquiry involves surrender, engaging deeply with emerging ideas, themes, illuminations, and feelings. In my experience it is a chance to discover a sense of something. In my dissertation (Haydon, 2024), I uncovered themes related to time and space. Due to the nature of this type of enquiry, much of my writing during this time was poetic, fragments of sentences and meditations, rather than a purely narrative style that might move along quicker. This style appears to aid a self-searcher to reach a certain essence, to capture a moment in time, to move through layers of thought and felt sense.

Personal art, self-dialogues, and immersive aesthetic experiences also fed the discoveries. These pieces of art were not planned pieces or intended for exhibit outside this research; mostly, they were emergent and made with whichever tools or materials were in front of me at the time. In other words (I suppose I'm offering a disclaimer), they weren't intended to be 'good'.

Below, I summarise a selection of themes from my dissertation and have grouped them into three categories – a sense of self, a sense of space, and a sense of time – and present them here, along with a discussion of the thoughts of others who sit in the artist-therapist or general aesthetics space.

A sense of self

There is a tendency to think of aesthetic aspects of our world as simply decorative, as objects. Some may perceive this topic as materialistic. Despite describing to you, the reader, the fledgling creative producer at the start of this chapter, I faced my own self judgement: shouldn't the answers of self-discovery be inside oneself, not outside, or at least found in the relational field between people? But I found the answer was, of course, that engaging with aesthetics is relational. Artist and therapist Pivnick (2018) writes: 'Perhaps what is most human about artfulness is the fact that it is not an *object* but a *relationship*' (p. 222). For me, this was true. At the start of my research, the first drawing I made was a humble one with marker pens and a notepad. Afterwards, there was a long dialogue between the art and myself ('myself' was both the artist and the beholder). This became my standard practice. Almost inevitably, during these conversations, it became unclear whose role was which, as both the art and the artist-beholder shifted between asking questions and answering them. A dual process emerged, and clearly defined roles disappeared. Turning object to subject allowed for infinite relational potential, just as a human-to-human interaction allows for infinite potential.

I attended a group art therapy class where I was asked to create art that 'represented my relationship to art' (Figure 10.3). Although I felt that this piece was incohesive and even ugly due to the tension in colour and mix of materials, from it I learned about my experience of tension between organic desire, structure, and magic: the artist confronted by convention. There were many times in my past where I felt I needed to supress artistic enthusiasm to conform, particularly at school.

At school there was often no time to excitedly explore the potential that was waiting; instead, demonstrating achievement was the objective. Through a self-search though, there was time to reflect upon materials, marks, and symbols, and to discover and reaffirm aspects of my self and the wider world. With less need for labels like 'the artist' or 'the beholder', one can see themselves instead as a human being who is a 'subject to' the aesthetic environment (Griffero, 2017).

A sense of space

Being 'subject to' the environment, it may be that we take on the role of a channel. Rubin (2023) considers his role as a music producer and student of the creative process to be that of a conduit. He throws out any sense of artist as 'almighty creator', instead viewing them (the artist) as a

FIGURE 10.3 My relationship to art.

subject who is in collaboration with the universe. In light of a newly developed sensitivity and appreciation for aesthetic atmosphere, my own version of this was to create something close to meditation in writing and art making. Hence the ad-hoc, in-the-moment nature of its creation. It was a co-creation. Figure 10.4 is a representation of what it was like to feel like a conduit, followed by a personal reflection/interpretation of the work from my research diary.

> A painted eye is sitting in the middle of recycled paper, paper full of remnants of the natural world – a visual representation of 'atmosphere', the 'material' Rick Rubin speaks of. From this atmosphere the eye finds meaning, shown through icons and symbols. Dichotomies of existence that co-exist but appear on opposite sides of a mediating, central pupil (intact love and broken love, ground and sky, infinity and death, open and shut), dichotomies that exist 'out there' and 'in here'.
>
> (S. Haydon, diary entry, 29th July 2024)

As a trainee, I often felt I didn't have solid ground to stand on while moving between university lectures, placements, different clinic rooms, and supervisors. Environments and expectations were constantly changing, all while I was attempting to establish my unique voice and style (Gabbard & Ogden, 2009) or 'analytic attitude' (Lemma, 2015). As Lemma (2015) puts it, this attitude is rather intangible and adds to the complexity of the factors mentioned above, for

FIGURE 10.4 Sight.

further discussion of which see Haydon (2024). Most important in this process was use of an art diary and a ritual of using it to bring form to some of these intangible, inchoate experiences which acted as a way to time stamp the learning process.

The work in my art diary reflected a new sensitivity and appreciation for the sense of atmosphere in the places and spaces that I occupied. Even the most ethereal and hazy; the psychotherapy room throughout sessions with clients, or the feeling of limbo that accompanied being a student. The art accentuated moments in-between the usual markers of time, and honoured moments when work was in progress.

A sense of time

Artist-therapist Milner developed her own engagement with art and literature and subsequently published her personal 'meta-diaries'. In them, Milner (1934/2024) writes about her desire 'to sink down beneath the level of chattering thoughts and simply feel what it meant to be alive' (p. 176).

I knew what she meant. I tended to feel as if I was in a race towards the finish line, running to find more; but, one day, I found that a word emerged in my mind. It was, simply, 'less'. Aesthetic enquiry felt like a slow, reflexive state of being that was in high contrast to the fast-paced, active, and achievement-driven life outside it. The art therapy meetings I attended allowed for a slower state of being. I wrote in my diary about a feeling of unfamiliar spaciousness and calmness due to the invitation of both time and lack of outcome requirements. At one of these meetings,

FIGURE 10.5 Compassion.

I created an art piece (Figure 10.5) that embodied the comfort and compassion of slowness through its circular form, soft materials, and curved undulating lines.

An aesthetic sensibility: Permission required

In its simplest form, creative expression might be thought of as a consumerist endeavour; the designed products people purchase and display in their homes or pick out for their outfits each day. Here, the process is forgotten. The process of 'making, doing, teaching, critiquing and becoming whole' (Magsamen & Ross, 2023, p. 214). This process can open up synchronicities that emerge through a state of open dialogue with the aesthetic world. This can be facilitated by reading, hearing, writing, reading, touching, and painting as a cycle of meaning-making, and allowing what emerged to resonate and connect. To do this, however, takes time. As I have mentioned, time is what I came to see as my central preoccupation, both throughout the dissertation and throughout my years of learning and discovering. Time is what I was craving. Wanting more of it. To achieve more with it. Trying to stop it. In a way, I wanted to be in-between time and had achieved it at times in my self-search.

Since artistic, aesthetic, or deep enquiry felt counter to the perceived norms in education systems (Costes-Onishi et al., 2020; Gaines, 2016), at the end of my research I appreciated that there was an element of 'permission giving' required to approach learning in this more personal, creative way. To begin, I more readily described myself as a creative producer rather than an artist. 'Producer' sits comfortably within a society where speed, productivity, and consumption are highly valued. An artist might deliberately sit outside of these values. They may intentionally sit in those interstitial spaces for a while – Dr Seuss's 'waiting place' – rather than run to complete a task. The interstitial spaces are liminal spaces, the shift into which is often accompanied by a ritual that marks a change in place or state (Turner, 1969). I am thinking back now to the 'Signs Wonders Miracles' banner at the threshold of the church. Rituals not only mark a change but give permission to shift into a slower and more reflective state. I argue that heuristic and aesthetic enquiry can aid this shift to occur when we wish to learn, to find our authenticity, and become curious and creative.

Slowing down in learning

Rosa (2019) proposes that 'If acceleration is the problem, then resonance may well be the solution' (p. 1). Art and aesthetics can offer resonance (Magsamen & Ross, 2023; Wexler, 2018). An aesthetic enquiry, as a way to form resonance, is a worthy solution. When evaluated against standardised testing in education, Greene's (1977) philosophy can be seen as more holistic, engaged, and able to produce higher levels of rigour (Gaines, 2016). This brings me back to Berleant's (2015) and Griffero's (2017) point that this is a steadfast and long-demonstrated human sensibility and path to knowledge.

The conditions for finding resonance are not always built into the environments we operate our lives within, despite reports that a slower process such as aesthetic enquiry can lead to active engagement, collaboration, capacity for ongoing learning, involvement in social issues, and personal fulfilment for students (Costes-Onishi et al., 2020; Dewey, 1934; Gaines, 2016; Greene, 2001).

Neuroaesthetics research recognises the aesthetic-mindedness of indigenous cultures, and attempts to sit between the gap that exists between traditional science and the holistic beliefs that are essential to, for example, an indigenous Māori world view (Magsamen & Ross, 2023). Ways of learning that include aesthetic enquiry could be particularly important in a country such as Aotearoa New Zealand, which is bicultural and generally culturally diverse (Gain, 2022). Learning is also central to psychotherapy – both from the perspective of the trainee therapist learning about themselves, and from the perspective of the client and therapist learning together as part of the clinical work.

Throughout a self-search, dancing back and forth between the phases is comparable to shifting into different gears. Time feels different in these gears. Artistic creation as a way of communicating to *know and understand* might be one 'gear'. Another 'gear', akin to *being and becoming*, includes an aesthetic sensibility and conduit-ness. The two complement each other.

Slowing down in psychotherapy

The idea of two gears, I argue, enhances the relevancy of this methodology as an approach to psychotherapeutic research. In psychotherapy practice these two mindsets also coexist and enrich one another. Ogden (2019) names them *epistemological* (knowing) and *ontological* (being) psychotherapy.

Much like contemplating brushstrokes on canvas or stepping into an art gallery can offer a sense of stillness, the therapy room – if it evokes a meditative atmosphere – promises a reprieve from outside noise. In fact, Loewald (1975) considers that the patient and the analyst become 'both artist and medium for each other' (p. 297), which I find particularly apt.

Innovative art psychotherapy programmes conducted in art galleries and museums found that those environments – which are inherently contemplative and educational – supported creativity, expanded therapeutic work, and addressed power imbalances (Watson et al., 2021). Therapists said they had to work much harder to create this atmosphere in clinical environments in which rooms are often not fit for purpose, and/or the context was restrictive. In the current climate – which is rather fast-paced – preserving the sacred nature of our therapeutic spaces is important, yet challenging. In this context, we hope that this chapter encourages some further thought for how, when we find ourselves caught up in the speed, productivity, and consumption of life, we might make an intentional shift into a new relationship with time (see Tudor, 2002, 2008), through artistic pursuits and/or changing the environment.

Conclusion

Writing a conclusion is, yet again, a reminder that time does run out. Nevertheless, through heuristic research, through forging a deep connection with art and through fostering our inherent aesthetic sensibility, we can relish what we discover in-between the start and end of our own enquiry. There is that old adage – trust the process. During my years as a design student I can't tell you how many times we spoke about 'the process'. The process can sometimes be so intangible and invisible that it is uncomfortable. This type of enquiry has potential to increase one's capacity to be an active participant in work-in-progress. Beyond the labels of artist or therapist, once I gave myself permission to spend time in the world with a wider gaze, I simply embraced my aesthetic sensibility as a way of being. Now the task is to keep this sensibility alive and free.

References

Berleant, A. (2015). Aesthetic sensibility. *Ambiances*. https://doi.org/10.4000/ambiances.526

Bridgman, P. (1950). *Reflections of a physicist*. Philosophical Library.

Christophers, J. (2019). *Dance into the unknown: A heuristic enquiry* [Master's dissertation, Auckland University of Technology]. Tuwhera Open Access Theses & Dissertations. https://hdl.handle.net/10292/12523

Costes-Onishi, P., Baildon, M., & Aghazadeh, S. (2020). Moving enquiry-based learning forward: A meta-synthesis on enquiry-based classroom practices for pedagogical innovation and school improvement in the humanities and arts. *Asia Pacific Journal of Education*, *40*(4), 552–575. https://doi.org/10.1080/02188791.2020.1838883

Cousins, G., Humphris, A., Kingi, A., Oram, L., & Tudor, K. (2025). Heuristic research in a time-limited context. In W. Ings & K. Tudor (Eds.), *Heuristic enquiries: Research across disciplines and professions* (pp. 162–180). Routledge.

Dewey, J. (1934). *Art as experience*. Minton.

Douglass, B., & Moustakas, C. (1985). Heuristic enquiry: The internal search to know. *Journal of Humanistic Psychology*, *25*(3), 39–55. https://doi.org/10.1177/0022167885253004

Embleton Tudor, L., & Tudor, K. (1999). The history of Temenos. *Self & Society*, *27*(2), 28–31. https://doi.org/10.1080/03060497.1999.11085934

Freud, S. (2009). Twenty-third lecture: The development of the symptoms. In S. Freud (Ed.), *A general introduction to psychoanalysis* (pp. 358–377). The Floating Press. (Original work published 1920)

Gabbard, G. O., & Ogden, T. H. (2009). On becoming a psychoanalyst. *The International Journal of Psychoanalysis, 90*(2), 311–327. https://doi.org/10.1111/j.1745-8315.2009.00130.x

Gain, P. (2022). Aesthetic enquiry for bicultural arts education in Aotearoa New Zealand. *Teachers and Curriculum, 22*(1), 27–33. https://doi.org/10.15663/tandc.v22i1.395

Gaines, A. M. (2016). Ambassadors of aesthetic experience: The healing legacy of Maxine Greene. *Teaching Artist Journal, 14*(1), 24–29. https://doi.org/10.1080/15411796.2016.1147801

Gallese, V. (2019). Embodied simulation: Its bearing on aesthetic experience and the dialogue between neuroscience and the humanities. *Gestalt Theory, 41*(2), 113–127. https://doi.org/10.2478/gth-2019-0013

Geller, J. (2018). Introduction: The transformative powers of aesthetic experiences in psychotherapy. *Journal of Clinical Psychology, 74*(2), 200–207. http://doi.org/10.1002/jclp.22582

Gendlin, E. (1978). *Focusing*. Everest House.

Grant, A. (Host). (2023, December 12). Your brain on art with Ivy Ross and Susan Magsamen. [Audio podcast episode]. In *Work Life with Adam Grant*. Ted Audio Collective. https://podcasts.apple.com/us/podcast/your-brain-on-art-with-ivy-ross-and-susan-magsamen/id1346314086?i=1000638235681

Greene, M. (1977). Toward wide-awakeness: An argument for the arts and humanities in education. *Teachers College Record, 79*(1), 119–125. https://doi.org/10.1177/016146817707900105

Greene, M. (2001). *Variations on a blue guitar: The Lincoln Center Institute lectures on aesthetic education*. Teachers College Press.

Griffero, T. (2017). *Quasi-things: The paradigm of atmospheres*. State University of New York Press.

Haydon, S. (2024). *Work-in-progress: A trainee psychotherapist's experience with aesthetic inquiry* [Master's dissertation, Auckland University of Technology]. Tuwhera Open Access Research Outputs. http://hdl.handle.net/10292/20043

Jung, C. G. (1966). *The spirit in man, art, and literature: C.G. Jung* (R. F. C. Hull, Trans.). Routledge.

Kant, I. (1987). *Critique of judgment* (W. S. Pluhar, Trans.). Cambridge University Press. (Original work published 1790)

Lemma, A. (2015). *Introduction to the practice of psychoanalytic psychotherapy*. John Wiley & Sons.

Loewald, H. W. (1975). Psychoanalysis as art and the fantasy character of the psychoanalytic situation. *Journal of the American Psychoanalytic Association, 23*(2), 277–299. https://doi.org/10.1177/000306517502300201

Lyons, E. (2007). Doing qualitative research: Initial questions. In E. Lyons & A. Coyle (Eds.), *Analysing qualitative data in psychology* (pp. 3–8). Sage. https://doi.org/10.4135/9781446207536.d6

Magsamen, S., & Ross, I. (2023). *Your brain on art: How the arts transform us*. Random House.

Maslow, A. H. (1971). *The farther reaches of human nature*. Arkana/Penguin Books.

Mau, B. (1998). *An incomplete manifesto for growth*. Bruce Mau Studio. https://brucemaustudio.com/projects/an-incomplete-manifesto-for-growth

McCall, J. (2021). *The art of mourning – Exploring the impact of artistic creation upon the psychotherapist* [Master's dissertation, Auckland University of Technology]. Tuwhera Open Access Theses & Dissertations. https://hdl.handle.net/10292/14395

Merriam-Webster. (n.d.). Aesthetic. In *Merriam-Webster Dictionary*. www.merriam-webster.com/dictionary/aesthetic

Milner, M. (2024). *A life of one's own*. Taylor & Francis Group. (Original work published 1934)

Moustakas, C. (1990). *Heuristic research: Design, methodology, and applications*. Sage Publications.

Ogden, T. H. (2019). Ontological psychoanalysis or 'what do you want to do when you grow up?' *The Psychoanalytic Quarterly, 88*(4), 661–648. http://doi.org/10.1080/00332828.2019.1656928

Ozertugrul, E. (2017). Heuristic self-search inquiry into one experience of obsessive–compulsive disorder. *Journal of Humanistic Psychology, 57*(3), 215–236. https://doi.org/10.1177/0022167815592503

Pivnick, B. A. (2018). Behind the lines: Toward an aesthetic framework for psychoanalytic psychotherapy. *Journal of Clinical Psychology, 74*(2), 218–232. https://doi.org/10.1002/jclp.22578

Rogers, C. (1967). *On becoming a person: A therapist's view of psychotherapy*. Houghton Mifflin.

Rogers, N. (2000). *The creative connection: Expressive arts as healing*. PCCS Books.

Rogers, N. (2011). *The creative connection for groups: Person-centered expressive arts for healing and social change*. Science and Behavior Books.

Rosa, H. (2019). *Resonance: A sociology of our relationship to the world*. Polity Press.

Rubin, R. (2023). *The creative act: A way of being*. Penguin Press.

Ryan, M. (2014). Reflexivity and aesthetic enquiry: Building dialogues between the arts and literacy. *English Teaching: Practice and Critique*, *13*(2), 5–18.

Sarasso, P., Francesetti, G., Roubal, J., Gecele, M., Ronga, I., Neppi-Modona, M., & Sacco, K. (2022a). Beauty and uncertainty as transformative factors: A free energy principle account of aesthetic diagnosis and intervention in gestalt psychotherapy. *Frontiers in Human Neuroscience*, *16*, Article 906188. http://doi.org/10.3389/fnhum.2022.906188

Sarasso, P., Neppi-Modona, M., Sacco, K., & Ronga, I. (2022b). 'Stopping for knowledge': The sense of beauty in the perception-action cycle. *Neuroscience & Biobehavioral Reviews*, *118*, 723–738. https://doi.org/10.1016/j.neubiorev.2020.09.004

Sela-Smith, S. (2001). *Heuristic self-search inquiry: Clarification of Moustakas' heuristic research* [Doctoral dissertation, Saybrook Graduate School and Research Center]. ProQuest Dissertations & Theses.

Sela-Smith, S. (2002). Heuristic research: A review and critique of Moustakas's method. *Journal of Humanistic Psychology*, *42*(3), 53–88. https://doi.org/10.1177/0022167802423004

Sultan, N. (2019). *Heuristic enquiry: Researching human experience holistically*. Sage. https://doi.org/10.4135/9781071802632

Tudor, K. (2001). Change, time, place and community. In P. Lapworth, C. Sills, & S. Fish (Eds.), *Integration in counselling and psychotherapy* (pp. 142–151). Sage.

Tudor, K. (2002). Introduction. In K. Tudor (Ed.), *Transactional approaches to brief therapy or what do you say between saying hello and goodbye?* (pp. 1–18). Sage.

Tudor, K. (2008). Introduction. In K. Tudor (Ed.), *Brief person-centred therapies* (pp. 1–12). Sage.

Tudor, K. (2022). Supporting critical self-enquiry: Doing heuristic research. In S. Bager-Charleson & A. McBeath (Eds.), *Supporting research in counselling and psychotherapy* (pp. 57–79). Springer.

Tudor, K. (2023). Critical heuristics in psychotherapy research. In K. Tudor & J. Wyatt (Eds.), *Qualitative research approaches for psychotherapy: Reflexivity, methodology, and criticality* (pp. 115–132). Routledge.

Tudor, K. (Ed.), Cockburn, G., Daniels, J., Goulding, J., Hubbard, P., Larsen, S., Levien, B., Milton, C., Morgaine, J., Palmer, H., Solomon, M., & Stuthridge, J. (2013). Reflexive theory: Critical reflections on Western psychotherapy. *Ata: Journal of Psychotherapy Aotearoa New Zealand*, *17*(1), 27–54. https://doi.org/10.9791/ajpanz.2013.03

Tudor, K., & Embleton Tudor, L. (1999). The philosophy of Temenos. *Self & Society*, *27*(2), 32–37. https://doi.org/10.1080/03060497.1999.11085934

Turner, V. (1969). *The ritual process: Structure and anti-structure*. Aldine Publishing.

Watson, E., Coles, A., & Jury, H. (2021). 'A space that worked for them': Museum-based art psychotherapy, power dynamics, social inclusion and autonomy. *International Journal of Art Therapy*, *26*(4), 137–146. https://doi.org/10.1080/17454832.2020.1866046

Wexler, J. (2018). Therapeutic action and aesthetic experience: Resonance and reorganization. *Journal of Clinical Psychology*, *74*(2), 208–212. https://doi.org/10.1002/jclp.22575

11

A HEURISTIC SELF-SEARCH ENQUIRY INTO ABRUPT ENDINGS

An unwavering search for what feels true

Dana Chue and Keith Tudor

Introduction

This chapter presents the first author's experience of using the heuristic self-search enquiry research method to explore her experience of abrupt endings within her psychotherapy training (and thus the 'I', 'me', and 'my' in this chapter), supervised by the second author. Sela-Smith (2002) highlights the fact that heuristic self-search inquiry (HSSI) calls for a personal surrendering to understand one's experience of a phenomenon, and also recognises the subsequent force of resistance to this. In the process of surrender, the timing of new discoveries cannot be quantitatively measured by linear time (chronos) but, rather, qualitative measures of the right time (i.e., kairos). In response to such personal searching, the experience of self-doubt was prominent as a form of resistance to the surrender.

This chapter emphasises that the concepts of kairos and self-doubt are important aspects of self-search enquiry that the heuristic researcher must acknowledge and understand. It presents the results of my engagement with the subject of abrupt endings and the application of heuristic research for examining my experiences of such endings within my psychotherapy training. It firstly discusses heuristic methodology and the application of its key concepts, as identified by Moustakas (1990) and Sela-Smith (2002). It then describes the phases of my heuristic enquiry, and journey of searching for what feels true.

Heuristic methodology

Qualitative heuristic research was developed by Clark Moustakas (1990), an American humanistic psychologist, from his personal experience of investigating the phenomenon of loneliness. Heuristics refers to the 'process of internal search through which one discovers the nature and meaning of experience' (Moustakas, 1990, p. 9). It provides a framework to investigate and understand human experience. The focus of the heuristic methodology is to foster the researcher's lived experience of a phenomenon, by drawing on their life events, relationships, thoughts, and feelings (Moustakas, 1990). Through this rigorous searching and re-searching

DOI: 10.4324/9781003685944-15

within, and engagement with the raw material of one's own experience, heuristic research seeks to illuminate the heart and soul of one's lived experience (Hiles, 2001; Moustakas, 1990).

The tree of knowledge – Philosophical foundations

At the heart of all research there is a quest to generate conversation, a striving towards a better understanding of our human encounters (Greene, 1994, as cited in Grant & Giddings, 2002). Considerations of ontology and epistemology form the foundation of research, as they define views about the nature of reality (what exists) and the relationship of the researcher to that reality (how we know what exists), respectively (Grant & Giddings, 2002). Differing ontologies and epistemologies, therefore, determine research paradigms and methodologies. Whilst the positivist research paradigm assumes and seeks the (or an) objective truth of phenomena, the interpretivist research paradigm, which assumes multiple realities, therefore seeks understandings and meanings of individual human experience (Grant & Giddings, 2002; Ryan et al., 2007). The interpretivist paradigm was developed within the social sciences in response to the reductionist positivist paradigm, and focuses on what it means to be human.

Phenomenological research, which sits within the interpretivist paradigm, contends that the subjective self is the closest connection to the phenomenon itself, and aims to use stories to reveal understanding and meaning through human experiences (Grant & Giddings, 2002; Smythe, 2012). Phenomenology attempts to remain experience-near, to get back to the phenomenon itself, and to capture its essence without a prescribed viewpoint. Within phenomenological research, the heuristic research methodology emphasises the explicit involvement of the researcher, in which the focus of the research is on the researcher's lived experience (Hiles, 2012).

Heuristic research holds the view that the deepest, most profound source(s) of meaning and knowledge lie(s) within us and our being – in our feelings, senses, perceptions, and beliefs (Moustakas, 1990). Heuristics truly honours the knowing and knowledge within the individual, phenomena that cannot be obtained outside the individual's frame of experience (Hiles, 2012; Moustakas, 1990). The research requires a personal encounter with a phenomenon, in which the heuristic methodology provides a framework to access the researcher's inner knowledge of the encounter (Hiles, 2012; Moustakas, 1990). This facilitates the inner exploration of the researcher's experience of the phenomenon, to map its terrain, in the hopes of discovering and illuminating the nuances of its landscape (Moustakas, 1990; Rose & Loewenthal, 2006; Sela-Smith, 2002).

From her own heuristic research, Sela-Smith (2002) contends that there is a natural resistance to remaining experience-near. She highlights what she considers to be Moustakas's own resistance to experience, by his emphasis on including other participants in order to validate his self-experience. Sela-Smith distinguishes between the researcher's internal experience and their observed experience, identifying that such resistance can result in a shift to focusing and relying on the observed experience. As a result, she proposed the HSSI, a heuristic methodology that acknowledges this resistance and emphasises the researcher's focus on their experiencing-self.

Background to my research

As I reflect on why I chose heuristics as my methodology, I feel stirred. I find myself in awe as I realise I am experiencing synchronicity. Synchronicity refers to the psychic experience of meaningful coincidences occurring over time (Jung, 1987). These unique events appear to have no connection and are independent of space and time, yet they have a spiritual feeling of what was meant to be.

I feel this synchronicity in my chest, a 'coming together' within me that is both peaceful and heart-blowing (similar to mind-blowing). I am connecting to the full force of my being and the personal history behind and in this research. It is the culmination of my life experiences that have led me to this place: to researching my experience of abrupt endings, within my psychotherapy training, and to heuristics. Two significant moments within this web of synchronicity stand out: when I chose psychotherapy, and when I chose heuristics. Both meaningfully explain who I am as a being, and, thus, define my ontology.

I had known for more than a decade that I wanted to become a therapist, but it took me a while to discern what kind of therapist or healer. From various experiences, I realised that I wanted to become one that was not the expert and who was personally involved in the therapeutic relationship. I feared this was unacceptable in society, illegal even, until I sat in Te Tuinga (the whānau meeting room on the North Shore campus of Auckland University of Technology). Here, I experienced being held by the Psychotherapy Department and felt the permission to feel, both alone and together. I couldn't believe that I found what I was looking for: what I thought didn't and couldn't exist. It was in this moment that I felt a sentimental sense of finding home, finding where I belong.

I chose heuristic research when I learnt about it two years previously. It was mentioned in class that the heuristic research question is one of a personal nature, one that might have been present for years before the research process even formally began. I felt an immediate connection to this, an awakening within me. I had one such question, one I had been grappling with for nearly a decade – I just didn't know what the question was, and I didn't even realise that I was asking. It was as if my question was speaking to me, telling me that it had been there all along. I knew in that moment that I had to choose heuristics, or, perhaps, it would be more fitting to say that heuristics chose me.

It's the only way for me

Endings are never easy. The experience of ending(s) connects me with mixed and confusing emotions and an intense visceral response, to which the addition of abruptness ramps this up a hundredfold. The phenomenon of abrupt endings has gripped me throughout my life. I have spent the last decade struggling to understand its grip, attempting to make sense of what it means to me and what I can do with it. Although I have found much wisdom and even some peace in dealing with abrupt endings rationally, the grip is still pulsating in me: What is my experience of abrupt endings? I realise I have been looking everywhere else and to everyone else for answers, except within myself.

Although the realm of human experience is closest to us, it is also the most resistant to our grasp of understanding it (Hiles, 2001). In my search for understanding the experience of abrupt endings in the context of the original study (Chue, 2021), I definitely felt this sense of trying to grasp sand in my hands, but the tighter I grasped the quicker it slipped out of reach. Personally, I believe the nature of the experience of abrupt endings demands an interpretivist perspective, particularly a heuristic endeavour, as it provides a framework for me to enter the sand, as it were, and feel into its granularity as well as the landscape it forms (Hiles, 2001; Moustakas, 1990).

The heuristic methodology also fits particularly well with research in psychotherapy, with significant parallels between both the heuristic researcher's and the psychotherapist's endeavours

(Beck, 1979; Hiles, 2012; Kenny, 2012; O'Hara, 1986; Rose & Loewenthal, 2006). Both are unique for the involvement of the researcher/therapist in the process, in which the researcher/therapist is the main instrument and their individuality is prized (Kenny, 2012; McWilliams, 2004). The the self in the researcher's intuition and in the therapist's countertransference is used to gather and make sense of the data received (Kenny, 2012; McWilliams, 2004). Both endeavours also value the process of deepening understanding, in which the focus is on the journey of the research/therapy, rather than arriving at a specific destination of truth or outcome (Kenny, 2012; McWilliams, 2004). Knowing becomes a process that is shaped along the journey which allows for an engagement with the 'I who does not know' and it compels a commitment to searching for what feels true (Kenny, 2012; McWilliams, 2004).

The researcher/therapist's personal involvement and deepening understanding nurtures self-understanding, and this creates the self-transformative element that is essential to both the heuristic and the psychotherapeutic process (McWilliams, 2004; Moustakas, 1990). Through processes of reflection and discovery, there is greater awareness, and the researcher/therapist's discernment is sharpened (Hiles, 2012; McWilliams, 2004): a necessary tool when embarking on a personal journey of what feels true.

The heuristic methodology and method recognises the personal and unquantifiable nature of the therapist's practice and countertransference process within the therapeutic relationship (Rose & Loewenthal, 2006). Therefore, using heuristic methodology for research in psychotherapy is, arguably, highly relevant, as the framework allows for the integration of the researcher's experience and knowledge, ultimately generating research that is practice- and experience-led (Kenny, 2012; Rose & Loewenthal, 2006).

Smythe (2012) suggests that the synergistic harmony between person–methodology–topic creates methodological congruence. My experience of synchronicity reflects this synergistic harmony: a coming together of the strands of my personal history and question, my journey in psychotherapy, and now (then) my heuristic journey. For me, these various strands form my ontology, and there really is no other way for me to research what is calling out from within that is yearning to be understood (Sela-Smith, 2002).

An explorer's toolkit – Heuristic concepts

In deepening my understanding and experience of the heuristic process, I was inspired by Sela-Smith's (2002) analogy of the final frontier, which invited me to delve into the interiority of my experience. I pictured myself as an explorer, venturing into an unknown terrain, with the task of mapping out its landscape: every contour, colour, shade, facet, angle, and crack. I felt excited and scared, eyes big with wonder and heart beating with life. I was venturing where I had never been before, and I knew I was the only one who could go there. My sense of expedition is illustrated in Figure 11.1. Moustakas's (1990) heuristic methodology was my aeroplane, my vehicle to transport me to this unknown terrain. The seven heuristic concepts (which I elaborate and illustrate in this section) are my tools and skills, including my map, my compass, and my shadow sidekick.

Identifying with the focus of enquiry – The treasure

The focus of the enquiry is the research question itself. In heuristic research, this question begins with me; it is borne out of my history and life experiences (Sultan, 2019). This concept invites

FIGURE 11.1 *An explorer's expedition* (Illustration by Corey Khalil).

me to immerse myself in the question and explore its different facets, with the aim of thoroughly knowing my relationship to the enquiry (Sultan, 2019). In this process, the researcher becomes one with the research question, living the question to get inside it and to achieve a personal understanding of it (Hiles, 2001; Moustakas, 1990). For me, this represents the concept of 'treasure' while on a quest. The question holds my personal treasure, my own pot of gold that no one else desires the way I do. I live the quest to find this treasure: it consumes me, changing the focus of my life and the way I live, everything I do is in relation to grasping it and nothing else matters. It becomes my purpose and focus.

Tacit knowing – The terrain

Polanyi's (1983) insight into tacit knowledge forms the foundation of heuristic enquiry (Moustakas, 1990). Tacit knowledge refers to information that is known deeply, often without the individual's conscious awareness of how this knowledge has been obtained. Polanyi's statement 'we can know more than we can tell' (p. 4), sums up the bizarre experience of 'I know I know, but I don't know how I know it, and I can't explain it'. Tacit knowing refers to this implicit personal knowledge, and it forms the basis of all explicit knowing (Polanyi, 1969, as cited in Sela-Smith, 2002). It belongs to the tacit dimension, the realm of the unknown known, in which knowledge can never fully be grasped and made conscious (Moustakas, 1990; Sultan, 2019). The tacit dimension is the internal place where feeling, experience, and meaning converge, creating the terrain of one's inner world (Sela-Smith, 2002).

This is the interior terrain I was sent to venture: the rock formations, caves, stalactites, and stalagmites. They are built out of each moment I experienced, adding layer upon layer, to form the whole. This is the foundation of my 'physical' inner world, the source of my being and meaning-making. It is an ever-present terrain that is ineffable. Tacit knowing was my soul in my heuristic journey, a spiritual realm of infinite wisdom that was impossible for me to access consciously. Instead, I needed to create an environment conducive to accessing this realm. Usually this involved music. Connecting to my tacit dimension was a surreal experience; it was both comforting and unnerving to know that it existed. I sometimes felt sceptical of this realm and its knowledge; however, when the revelations came through, it was undeniable. I recognised the material as mine, yet completely new to me.

Intuition – The compass, my sidekick

Intuition is the bridge that connects explicit knowledge (observable, describable) and tacit knowledge (unspecifiable); it supports the researcher to tune into the tacit dimension by drawing on clues, patterns, or meanings that lead to enhanced knowledge (Moustakas, 1990). For me, this is my internal compass that mysteriously senses and perceives my 'North', drawing me closer to my treasure. This is the experience of my question speaking to me. When I connected to this, I had an image of my intuition personified. She is a little shadow being. Alive and playful, she is reaching out to me, pulling me towards particular experiences or thoughts, desperate to tell me what is really going on. I liken her to the inner Child within, except she is not me at every age. She is the me who has experienced everything I have experienced, but on another dimension: the tacit dimension. She is my sidekick on this journey.

Intuition was my heart in my heuristic journey, my gut instinct or hunch that I could follow. There were many times when I got lost in my self-search, and I felt so confused and overwhelmed with all the information that was mine. I eventually learnt that what I needed was to connect back to my heart, and once there, my intuition would eagerly lead the way. I simply needed to surrender, listen, and trust.

Indwelling – Traversing the terrain

Indwelling is the conscious process of turning inward with an unwavering concentration to seek a deeper understanding of the phenomenon (Hiles, 2001; Moustakas, 1990). It requires that the researcher deliberately dwells in the experience, using a combination of tacit knowing, explicit knowing, and intuition to explore the phenomenon in its entirety (Sultan, 2019). There is a persistence and patience in continually returning to the experience, in the hopes of unearthing its essence.

For me, indwelling represented traversing the terrain first-hand. I had to stay with the experience of an abrupt ending, and map out the terrain. It was the voice that declared 'I'm going in!'. Full of intensity and wonder, I was feeling the terrain against my hands and knees as I crawled across every rock and into every nook and cranny.

When an abrupt ending happened, I would explicitly dwell in the experience. Taking my heart and mind back to the scene of the crime to collect my evidence, I noted everything in my journal. Although this was a painful process, I realised I naturally had the persistence because this enquiry was linked to my purpose. In fact, I also often instinctively did this without being aware: it felt like an unconscious obsession. In this way, I consider that the grip that abrupt endings had over me supported me with the indwelling process.

Focusing – A midnight campfire

Focusing is a concept and process developed by Gendlin (1978), and refers to an inner attention, a staying with the phenomenon in a relaxed and receptive state. It requires a pause, an internal space clear of any tangling elements, to allow perceptions to be clarified and insights that are out of consciousness to come to the fore (Moustakas, 1990; Sultan, 2019).

Focusing represents a time away from the busy doing of the quest. It is the act of setting up a campfire for the night. A space is cleared to connect in a more dream-like way, and there, amidst the storytelling and discussions of the day's events, lies the essence of what is true and what really matters in this quest. It is a time to rest, to let go of the intensity of actively pursuing the experience; instead I am allowing the key aspects of the experience to come to me.

I have always been a creature of the night. Taking refuge in the dead stillness, I do my best work in that existential calm. Across my research, I recognised my 2:00 am process, in which I would wake up with key illuminations, clear felt-senses, and even plans for my research all laid out. It was all dream-like and unconscious, but those elusive yet illuminative moments felt like swimming: feeling every molecule of the water around me, I could feel my way through my process so clearly. This was my experience of focusing, in which the night was my space of clearing, connecting me to the tacit realm.

Self-dialogue – Connecting to myself

Self-dialogue is the call to begin with oneself by entering into dialogue with the phenomenon. This facilitates self-enquiry, allowing the phenomenon to interact and speak directly to the researcher's experience, and to discover deeper understanding (Moustakas, 1990). This reflects the mumblings of problem-solving while on a quest, the wondering out loud which way to go, the constant train of thought or conversation that led me to my next move. It is also the interactions with my shadow sidekick, engaging with her experience of the tacit dimension.

Through all my experiences of endings, I never did fully share how I felt with anyone. I have always been in my own self-dialogue: it is a place of comfort and familiarity. Music played a big part in this. In the riffs and crescendos, I could feel out my emotions, and in the lyrics, I could understand something of my own experience. Music helped me find my voice when I could no longer navigate alone in my self-dialogue. Throughout my research, I relied on speaking to myself as well as on music to support my connection with myself, to navigate my journey.

Internal frame of reference – The map

The heuristic endeavour has to be placed within the context of the researcher's internal frame of reference (Hiles, 2001; Moustakas, 1990). This represents the map I am creating of the unknown terrain of abrupt endings, a map for others to see, know, and understand. It is I who is creating this map, I who decides what is included or excluded and what it will look like. It is through my eyes and perceptions that the map is created, and by looking at it, the perceiver will know something of my frame of experience. I will rely on this map to guide me, returning again and again to it, to get to my treasure (Sultan, 2019).

The internal frame of reference was my 'mind map' throughout my heuristic journey. It often entailed the mental task of re-orientating myself within a map that was already there, yet constantly changing. On a larger scale, I was constantly figuring out what the boundaries of my map were, while also referring to it as a guide, and updating the map as I went along. On the smallest scale, I engaged with this concept in every word I typed. Each word reflecting who I am and where this journey has taken me, revealing my frame of experience.

One example of this orientation, disorientation, and need for re-orientation was in relation to the literature.

> **Vignette #1 Finding my voice in a cave of echoes**
> Initially, I was confident, arrogant even, that the literature on abrupt endings was lacking and that no one else had done this research. I doubted it could provide me with much, yet I needed to map it out. As I immersed myself in the literature, I was overwhelmed by its enormity. I was swept away by all the content; lost with each voice and what they said; stuck and unable to find my way through. It felt as though I was in an immense, dark cave – with each book, chapter, and article forming the historical rock. I knew I stood within a gap, but where? How could I map this out to place where I stood, when there was so much I could not see and could not feel? My confidence waned and my voice suddenly felt little amongst the echoes of the past.
>
> When I began writing, I was caught up with all these other voices, tangled in the technical know-how of terminations in therapy. I did not want to include this but, academically, I felt I needed to. I could feel my shadow sidekick in a ball of tension as I tried to force something out of me that was not mine. I finally asked my supervisor for support and felt relieved when I was told to simply follow my intuition and tacit knowing with the literature. Upon reflection, I realise I had lost track of my internal frame of reference, I had strayed from my map and got lost in the world of terminations.
>
> The heuristic research method calls for my personal experience of the literature, in which I am following my intuition as a 'way of being informed, a way of knowing' (Moustakas, 1990, p. 10) to further elucidate my experience of abrupt endings. Thus, the intention was not to provide an exhaustive review, but rather my view of the literature that resonates most within me (K. Tudor, personal communication, November 24, 2020). In this way, I found my voice again. I was calling out to the literature, feeling which of my echoes reverberated and resonated back to me, to firmly place where I stood against the backdrop of this historical cave.

Having illustrated heuristic methodology through its primary concepts, I now turn to the heuristic method, regarding which I drew on the phases identified by Moustakas (1990).

An explorer's journey – Heuristic phases

Moustakas's (1990) heuristic research method – the six phases of initial engagement, immersion, incubation, illumination, explication, and creative synthesis – guided my journey through the unknown terrain of my research.

Initial engagement

The initial engagement marked the start of my inner search. A search that calls out to my soul (Sela-Smith, 2002), that which is just beneath the surface, yet hauntingly out of reach. This phase, therefore, was the beginning, yet not the beginning. It required a process of encountering that which I already was and am – my history, experiences, and relationships – to elucidate my question of concern (Moustakas, 1990).

For me, abrupt endings related to those moments that stopped me in my tracks, forcing me to feel and contemplate the impact of the end. It is the unexpected phone call in the middle of the night, the client who never returns for another session, the news of a deadly outbreak, or a sudden death on an ordinary day; those moments that leave me hanging. Thus, I was already engaged with abrupt endings; and the research question was within me – and so I relied on self-dialogue, intuition, and tacit knowing to discern what the exact question was, which would become the focus of my enquiry (Moustakas, 1990; Sultan, 2019). This question holds personal meaning and power, and will likely translate to significant social and universal implications.

Immersion

Immersion is the active phase of engaging with HSSI. Personally, I was living the question and it became the air I breathed (Moustakas, 1990). Everything in my life was either about or connected to abrupt endings. It consumed my thoughts, feelings, and experiences, permeating my conscious, unconscious, and dream states (Moustakas, 1990; Sultan, 2019). My antenna became hypersensitive to the experience, and as I remained open to any information and where it may lead me, my knowledge and understanding of abrupt endings deepened (Moustakas, 1990).

Incubation

This phase marks an intentional retreat from the intense pursuit of the enquiry (Sultan, 2019). It requires a detachment from the research, that releases the researcher from immersion. During incubation, I was unconsciously digesting the information I had taken in to that point. I was allowing my intuition and tacit dimension to work in a way that was free from active striving (Moustakas, 1990). This gestation was a period of trust. I was surrendering and trusting my process so that my understanding would grow creatively and my tacit knowing would reveal itself to me (Moustakas, 1990).

In my heuristic journey, this was a forced incubation as I had to step away from my research to complete the final case study for my degree. It was difficult to retreat based on external demands, rather than choosing to do so as part of my organic journey. I believe this called for more surrender and trust, that although I was stepping away, my understanding was still developing – and it was.

Illumination

Illumination is the natural process of tacit knowing revealing itself. By remaining open to the free workings of the tacit dimension and intuition, my tacit knowledge emerged and became explicitly known (Moustakas, 1990, and above, pp. 159–160). Illumination may modify present understanding, integrate fragmented aspects, clarify themes, or provide insight into previously unknown aspects of my research (Moustakas, 1990). For me, illumination felt like a lightbulb moment. There was a deeper sense of clarity and understanding, a coming together of sorts, from that which was already present. Ultimately, this reveals an essential truth of the phenomenon

(Moustakas, 1990) which can happen at any stage (see Tudor, 2022, 2023, and pp. 169, 173, below), for example:

- Initial engagement
- Immersion
- Incubation
- Explication
- Creative synthesis

Explication

Explication is the process of laying it all out on the table, as it were, and analysing all the themes and discoveries that have been made conscious from the tacit dimension (Moustakas, 1990). The aim of this phase is to understand the intricacies of these findings and how these might connect to form a comprehensive depiction (Moustakas, 1990). For me, this was the process of sifting for gold, after I had mined my source. I relied on indwelling, focusing, and my internal frame of reference to identify the gems of my treasure (Moustakas, 1990). I underwent a process of refining this gold, and understanding its essential aspects, in preparation for presenting the treasure of my expedition to the world. Figure 11.2 illustrates this process of laying it all out. Collating and examining over 50 pages of reflections, I created this mind map of themes and discoveries, which elucidated the gems and essences of my research and formed a foundation for me to explicate my findings.

This is the original and only map I created. It is included to demonstrate the expansive process and is not intended for close reading. Two sections are magnified for closer reading (Figures 11.3 and 11.4).

Creative synthesis

Creative synthesis is the final phase in the research and is both a process and a product. Now that all the knowledge and experience had been acquired and refined throughout the research journey, it was time to create an all-encompassing synthesis (Moustakas, 1990). This required a space of solitude to reflect on my whole journey. In this phase, I continually relied on my intuition and exploration of the tacit dimension to guide the production of this synthesis (Moustakas, 1990). This creative synthesis was completely personally inspired, capturing the essence of my journey and my discoveries. In viewing my treasure, my journey comes to life and, hopefully, the audience – in this case, you the reader – can resonate with my experience, understanding more of the terrain I traversed and the fundamental components of the phenomenon (Sela-Smith, 2002).

Having demonstrated my understanding of both heuristic methodology and method, I now share my experience of resistance and surrender throughout my research journey, and how it fostered a deepening connection to the terrain.

My journey of resistance and surrender

The dissertation disconnection

During my initial engagement, I struggled to work on my dissertation. In fact, I was actively avoiding connecting to abrupt endings. I thought this was my procrastination, but then I noticed

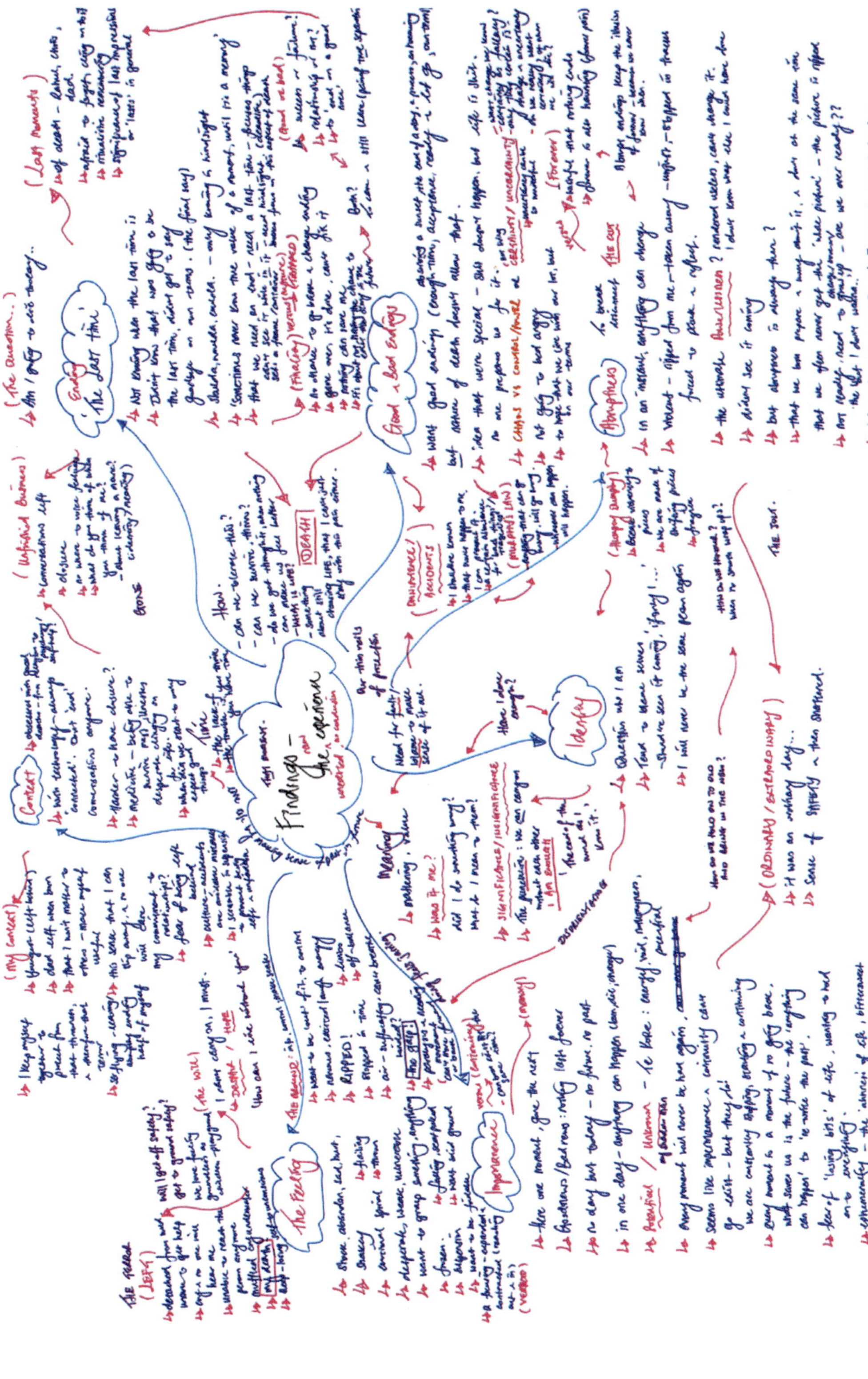

FIGURE 11.2 The treasure map.

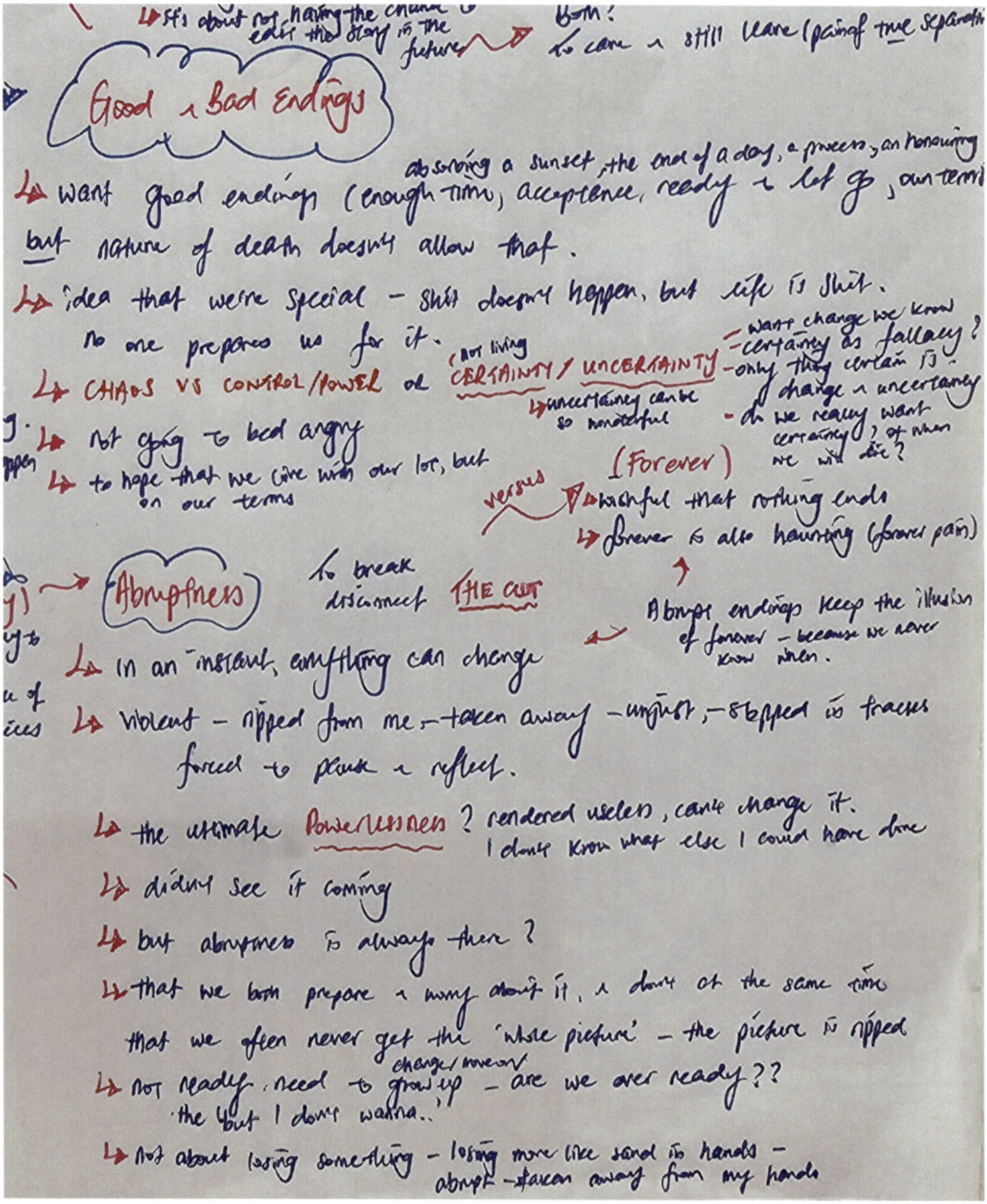

FIGURE 11.3 A section of the treasure map.

how fearful I was to begin my research. Having to take that first step, I was awakened to just how personal this was for me, and I felt my resistance to go there.

> I feel like it's stuck in my throat, this fear of many abrupt endings. I fear that if I say it and state it, it will materialize into reality. So, I am afraid to even think it, to connect to it, to acknowledge it.
>
> (D. Chue, journal entry, 23rd March 2020)

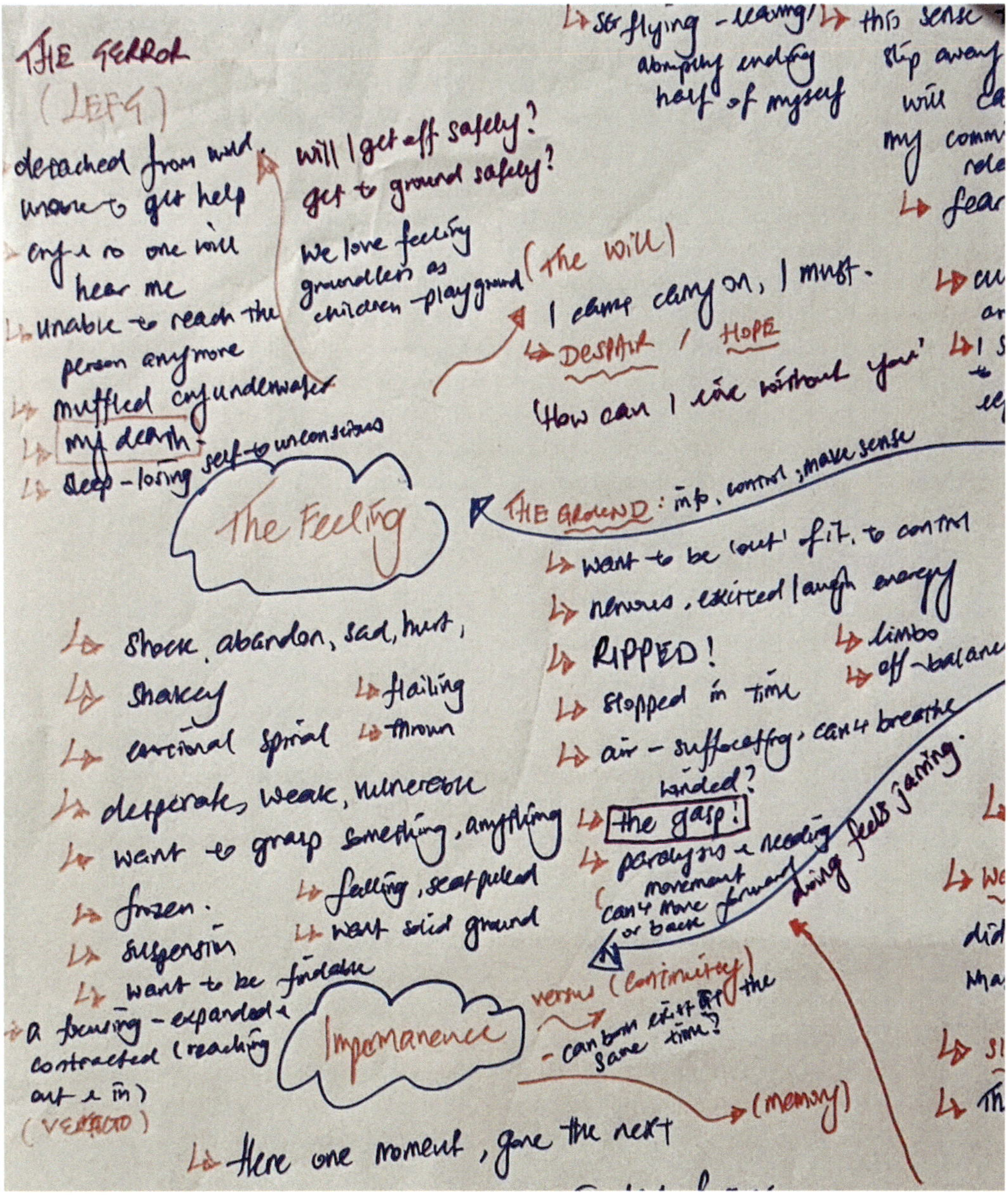

FIGURE 11.4 Another section of the treasure map.

The early months of my research coincided with the first half of 2020. True to the nature of abrupt endings, there was no easing into the experience. As it dawned on the world that COVID-19 was a global pandemic and governments abruptly closed borders and restricted travel and social gatherings, the magnitude of abrupt endings was dawning on me and I wanted to shut it out. I was confronted with the cutting reality of just how ever-present and inescapable abrupt endings were, and perhaps, as with the virus, I feared becoming uncontained. I feared losing myself in the heuristic process and the world losing itself in the face of the virus. My fears intertwined throughout this parallel process:

> I'm afraid of connecting to how I really feel, because I'm afraid I will be overwhelmed and that I can't contain it. I'm so scared. I almost feel like I could have a panic attack. I feel the existential fear in me, as my world shuts down. It feels like the end of the world as we know it.
>
> (D. Chue, journal entry, 25th March 2020 [The first day of Alert Level 4 'Lockdown' in Aotearoa New Zealand])

At the start of the pandemic and lockdown(s), it seemed unfathomable that no one knew what our lives would become over the next month or year. It also felt unfathomable not knowing where the research would lead me. Would we make it through this pandemic? Would I make it through this research? Who would we/I be at the end? There was so much unknown within me and all around me and, like Sela-Smith (2002), I was afraid to take the leap and fall into a 'forever darkness' (p. 57). My safe and known ways of organising my world were being threatened on all fronts. I feared experiencing what Winnicott (1974) termed 'fear of breakdown', in which engaging with the unknown meant an unravelling, a falling apart of 'my world as I knew it'. I doubted I could survive the unknown of my research during the unknown of this pandemic.

The personal connection

Although, at the time, it did not feel like it, I had started to immerse in my topic. I mostly trusted that I had the right research question. However, part of me also questioned if there was, in fact, more for me to find, as I had thought about death and endings for years.

One April evening, I was on my daily lockdown walk, listening to a podcast. It mentioned that psychotherapy was about going into those difficult places, into that lifetime terror, the very thing we design our lives to avoid. The sun was beginning to set earlier, and it was dark and stormy. I felt scared and I was immediately transported back to a memory of a stormy day when I was little. I sensed that somehow this memory was related to abrupt endings, and to my lifetime terror, but how? In my journal, I wrote:

> I thought of the incident with the lift, being left and having the doors close on me. Is it 'being left', 'being alone' or 'being abandoned', that I fear?
>
> I thought of my fear of not being grounded, physically. My fear of flying and diving. Feeling detached from the world and unable to get any form of help. It's terrifying. The immensity and the feeling of being floaty, into the unknown… I'm not sure if any of this is linked. But somehow, with abrupt endings, I feel it touches on that young memory of being left and alone on that stormy day. My fear that I'll cry and no one will hear me, or even be there to hear me.
>
> (D. Chue, journal entry, 8th April 2020)

I realised that these core memories of mine all revolved around my fear of feeling physically groundless. It was a feeling I could only access through my body, the feeling of my heart dropping as I lost contact with the ground. I became tingly with fear and excitement, feeling I was on to something, but not yet knowing how the pieces all fit together.

Connecting to my lifetime terror felt like an engagement with the tacit dimension, an unknown known that I knew so well yet could not name. Ghent (1990) poetically conveys how I felt about my lifetime terror, when he highlights an aspect of dread as being 'so shrouded in history as to feel nameless and "existential"' (p. 127). I never quite understood the intensity of my terror, which felt existential and annihilating, in response to seemingly benign fears of heights and being alone. This realisation beckoned me to question if my connection to abrupt endings went deeper and further back in my history than I initially thought. This was scary to consider and yet it felt true. As Winnicott (1974) proposes, the fear of breakdown is, in fact, the fear of a breakdown already experienced but not yet integrated, thus rendering it to the realm of the unknown known.

Although it remained unclear what the original breakdown or terror was, this was a moment of illumination that jolted me. It became a torch within me, providing the fuel and power for my search, and lighting a clearer path for my findings to come. Like passing a signpost along a hike (walk), I felt reassured I was on the right track: there was more to find, so keep searching (I told myself). My self-search was now more than a personal question I wanted to answer; it was my lifetime terror that I needed to know and understand.

The emotional connection – Connecting to my 'I-who-feels' (Sela-Smith, 2002)

Throughout the early months of journaling, I felt unsure if I was on track. I did not know what to reflect on or how to reflect, and I often felt the process was futile. Almost every day I was having a different, incomplete reflection on abrupt endings. It was frustrating not knowing if something was an important lead to delve deeper into, and I was sceptical that this would all eventually amount to something.

A monthly heuristic seminar group was invaluable in developing my understanding of the heuristic process. I clearly remember my lecturer emphasising a vital point, that, as psychotherapists we were trained to analyse, and as such we were often attached to the thoughts that come after an experience (M. Solomon, personal communication, 5 May 2020). The heuristic challenge, therefore, was to keep bringing myself back to the experience itself, not to explain it away or be quick to attach meaning to it. This reflected Sela-Smith's (2002) call for researchers to surrender to the '*I-who-feels*' (p. 57) and immerse themselves in the realm of feeling, instead of connecting to the thinking-observing self. I am grateful this distinction was highlighted early in my heuristic process, because I realised I was observing and reflecting on the experience of abrupt endings, rather than feeling my experience.

When I first tried journaling from the I-who-feels, I struggled. Without the meaning I normally attached to it, it felt silly to journal the felt experience. In this struggle, I was directly grappling with the known and unknown. It was difficult not to approach my experiences from a knowing place, in which I could observe and make meaning, and to immediately know where I was going. I realised I needed to surrender and allow myself to engage with what Keats (1817) terms 'Negative Capability, that is, when a man is capable of being in uncertainties, mysteries, doubts, without any irritable reaching after fact and reason' (as quoted by Ou, 2011, p. 1). This was a necessary shift if I wanted to truly encounter the tacit dimension.

Surrendering to my I-who-feels

With each abrupt ending, I became more comfortable connecting to my I-who-feels. Slowly I opened myself to engaging with the unknown and feeling deeper into my experience. Interestingly, a key event that plunged me deeper into the tacit dimension and helped me value connecting to my I-who-feels was not an abrupt ending. One evening, I was feeling nauseous and dizzy; when I got up in the middle of the night I could barely walk.

> Everything is spinning around me, I am off balance, out of kilter. I am lying still yet my head is swirling and nothing is okay. Closing my eyes doesn't make it better either. I'm nauseous, stomach churning. I am trying desperately to stop spinning, trying to hold on to something, anything.
>
> (D. Chue, journal entry, 12th September 2020)

I suddenly clicked that I was experiencing vertigo, a sudden internal or external spinning sensation, in which it feels like the surroundings are moving when there is no movement (Ministry of Health, 2014).

> I realise it is not a physical 'holding on to' that I need, it is an internal one. I do not know which way is up, and there is no ground on which I can stand. It feels terrifying, not being able to control anything, not knowing my centre, my foundation from which I emanate. That same experience of having an abrupt ending, the inability to move, the focusing on one thing, yet being unable to focus on anything. I feel a sense of losing myself to the atmosphere around me, like I don't exist anymore. The world keeps spinning but I am standing still.
>
> (D. Chue, journal entry, 12th September 2020)

I was puzzled. It was a purely internal and physical experience, but I still felt the mental whirlwind of disorientation, the fear of being out of control, the inability to move and the sensation of not feeling the ground supporting me. This was all without an actual ending or being physically off the ground.

I was surprised, it activated the internal scramble and scream I experienced whenever I was physically up in the air, ever bracing for the fall. It helped me realise that my fears of being physically groundless were about an internal groundlessness, which abrupt endings threw me into. The bodily experience of vertigo helped me connect to my I-who-feels in such a physical way that it accessed a different facet of my experience of abrupt endings. I was beginning to trust the importance of my bodily response. Without the need to mentally process an event, and with no ability to stop the physical sensation of spinning, I had to stay with feeling from my I-who-feels, with how it felt in my body and the emotions it evoked.

Up until this experience, I thought I had surrendered to the heuristic process. However, as I felt the terror of not being in control of my physical body and my internal mind, I connected to a depth of vulnerability that truly forced me to surrender. I was powerless to escape, forced to engage in negative capability and be with the terror. Despite my initial discomfort and resistance, there was a sense of liberation when I surrendered. Ghent (1990) makes the distinction clear that surrender relates to a 'letting go', a 'letting down of defensive barriers' (p. 108), rather than defeat. For me, this meant it was not just about carefully abseiling into the abyss, but allowing a freefall into the abyss.

This experience of surrender opened up new experiences and provided me with a deeper understanding of my research, inevitably confirming that the feeling of groundlessness was the link between my fears, lifetime terror, and abrupt endings. I had finally arrived at the very landscape I was meant to explore.

Reflections

In the last part of this chapter, I offer some reflections on the process with regard to the research journey, as well as a number of limitations; and a conclusion.

Endings, death, and the heuristic process

From its inception, without realising, my self-search enquiry was, in fact, my attempt to lean as far in to death while still being able to retreat safely. Throughout my research on abrupt endings, I felt the dance with death, a dance of resistance and surrender: leaning in and retreating, plunging in and fighting.

Within my research, I tried to stay emotionally connected to my experience of abrupt endings and death; however, it was incredibly difficult to do this on my own. There was always a resistance, a desire to retreat to thinking and intellectualising, instead of feeling. To overcome this resistance, I needed a segue to feel emotionally open to endings and death. I relied on watching movies, reading books, poetry, and listening to music, anything that emotionally moved me, to support me in my process. Even then, as soon as I felt too emotionally exposed, I would immediately retreat to the safety of my lifeline. I could only go so far, for so long.

The heuristic methodology supported my personal challenge to face death, by providing a safe method to inch closer towards the unknown. As illustrated in Figure 11.5, the heuristic phases provided a framework for my lean in towards death. I had space to slowly engage, before immersing myself and stepping back to incubate, and then moving on to reflect and explicate. The heuristic concepts also provided tools to encourage my process of surrendering and engaging with the unknown, allowing me to connect as much as I could to feelings of powerlessness.

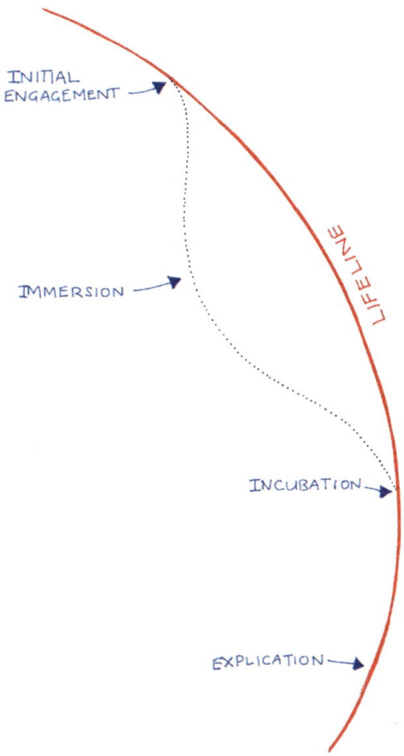

FIGURE 11.5 The lean towards death.

My journey through the phases

Overall, my journey differed greatly from Moustakas's (1990) heuristic method (see Figure 11.6). Most noticeably, I cycled through the phases multiple times and did not follow the original order of phases. I often jumped between phases because I was not ready to move on to the next phase outlined. For example, I sometimes needed to begin another process of initial engagement or to immerse myself again because I stepped away from the research for too long.

Limitations

The limitations of the heuristic methodology relate to the personal nature of the research. This occurs when the researcher's personal process conflicts with wider external requirements, and also when this process is too internal and narrow. The original heuristic method as outlined by Moustakas suggests that the phases occur chronologically and only once throughout the research process. However, following the phases specifically limits the researcher's organic process. In this sense, I agree with both Tudor (2010/2017) and Sultan (2019) that the heuristic process is not linear, and that creative freedom is necessary for the research to unfold naturally. This might mean connecting to the phases out of chronological order, for varying lengths of time and at varying intensities. I sometimes struggled to move from incubation through to illumination, and then explication. Sometimes I needed to re-immerse myself, to connect with my intuition and tacit dimension again, before moving to explication and, in this, I appreciated my supervisor's constant encouragement to be free in my process and to trust where it took me.

Also, as this research was conducted in fulfilment of a Master's degree, my heuristic process was limited by the time restraints set out by the university. These restraints created a battle

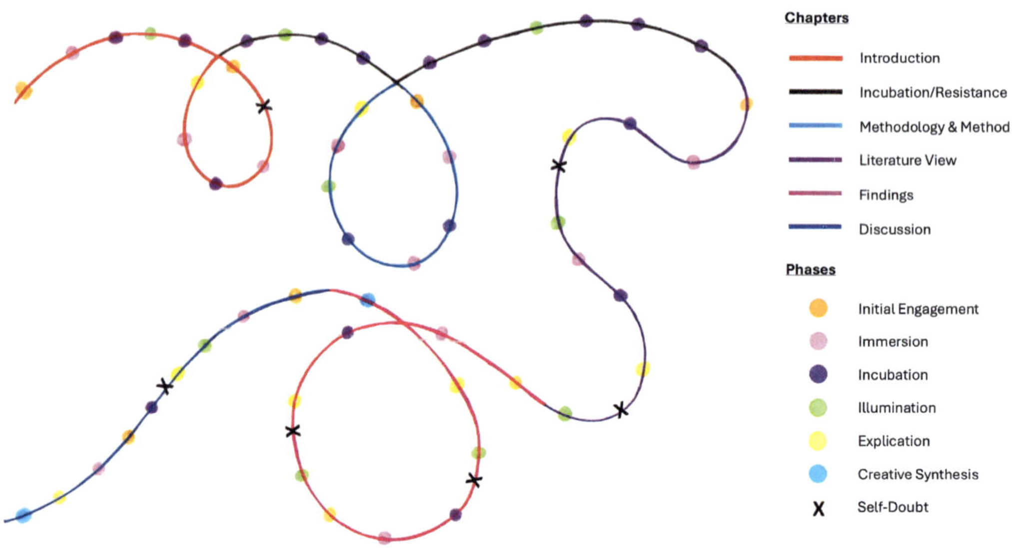

FIGURE 11.6 My journey through the heuristic phases.

Note. The coloured lines represent the chapters within the original dissertation (Chue, 2021), and the coloured dots represent the six heuristic phases. As I went further in my journey, I connected deeper to my process, as indicated by the plunges.

between following my internal time and rushing my process to meet deadlines. This reflects the immediate conflict between chronos and kairos, in which chronos refers to quantitative time measured by the clock, and kairos refers to qualitative time that is measured in moments, such as the right time (Smith, 1969). I experienced this conflict most acutely in relation to the illumination phase. I noticed a pattern (illustrated in Figure 11.4), in which I tried to move quickly from incubation to explication, in an attempt to stay on top of writing my chapters. I would then hit a wall and doubt myself, and it was only when I experienced illumination that I could continue my process again. I suggest that the concept of illumination is based on kairos, rather than chronos, and, therefore, is not a separate phase that can be timed after incubation. Rather, it is a process that sits alongside the heuristic enquiry, and reveals itself in spontaneous moments according to my personal time (K. Tudor, personal communication, 5 May 2020; see also Tudor, 2010/2017, 2023).

The personal nature of heuristic research can also be limiting by being too self-referential, and the researcher's own blind spots and resistances can get in the way of their research (Ings, 2011). Personally, I relied on openly sharing my process with my supervisor, clinical supervisor, therapist, and close friends in order to support me with my blind spots. Due to the emotional intensity of my enquiry, I often experienced resistance and was grateful that both lecturers who were supporting me in this research shared ways to identify and move through feelings of resistance. Although Sela-Smith's (2002) HSSI addresses resistance, it is yet to be widely acknowledged as a concept within the literature on heuristic research. For myself, in Figure 11.4, I have acknowledged periods of resistance in the incubation phase. We would suggest that resistance is acknowledged as a distinct process that is part of the heuristic journey, to allow it to be anticipated, recognised, and worked through (see Tudor & McCann, 2026 [Chapter 2 in this volume]).

Finally, I wonder about self-doubt as a specific type of resistance, and the ways in which this can limit the research. Throughout each chapter of my dissertation, I noticed I would always hit a moment of self-doubt. This was usually when I considered all the external pressures, such as time restraints or grading requirements. However, it was also when I felt the weight of researching my own experience, where I questioned if I could really do this on my own. In my illustration (Figure 11.6), I have labelled self-doubt separately with an x – thus x marks the spot of self-doubt. I realised my experiences of self-doubt would often be followed by moments of illumination, and I wonder if self-doubt might in fact be an essential aspect of the heuristic process that forces the researcher to examine if they are still connecting to themselves?

An unwavering search for what feels true

My journey with heuristic research was fraught with the tension between resistance and surrender, the known and the unknown. It was a cycle of fearing the breakdown and of holding myself together, breaking down and falling apart, then surrendering and coming together. In a continual process of getting lost and finding myself again, it was confusing and overwhelming, yet oddly familiar and soothing. I felt like a blind soul, relying on my feelings (intuition) and the sound of my voice (self-dialogue) to navigate, all along never really knowing where I was going, never quite able to make out the entire landscape before me. Each experience of an abrupt ending provided a thread for me to hold, and to follow wherever my feelings and reflections took me. Down one train of thought, up a mountain of feeling, through blind spots and known territory… sometimes I lost the thread, sometimes I hit a dead end, other times I went down the same thread again and again, or connected to other threads I had already followed.

In getting lost, I was confronted with unnerving feelings of terror, doubt, uncertainty, the free fall into the unknown, and thoughts of 'I'm not good enough', 'I can't do this', and 'I can't survive this'. Many times, it was anguishing: I couldn't stay with the unknown as it felt unbearable, and I couldn't tolerate being in a state of pieces and of re-organisation.

As I opened to a way of being that could slowly tolerate and engage with the unknown, I came to experience the power of surrender and thus, acknowledge my powerlessness and vulnerability in my research process. I learnt to trust a different process of tacit knowing to experience what feels true for me, a process in which resistance, self-doubt, and patience for the right time (kairos) are inevitable. This allowed me to encounter deeply meaningful experiences, in which I found a sense of wonder at the vast unknown, and strangely, the freedom to be myself.

At some point, there were more connections than loose threads in the web of my experience. It was wonderful to feel it all coming together and that I was getting closer to the thing itself. After continuously digging deeper, and deeper still, I could not quite believe I had reached my precious discoveries on this self-search journey.

During metamorphosis, the caterpillar creates a safe cocoon for the process of transformation. Breaking its own body down, the caterpillar digests itself, and with the same essence, morphs into a butterfly (Jabr, 2012).

In true heuristic fashion, this self-search enquiry has demanded all of me. In my journey inward, I have encountered myself in a way I have never experienced. Breaking myself down, I digested my history, experiences, terrors, and 'knowns'. As my illuminations and discoveries have emerged, so have I.

References

Beck, G. (1979). *Heuristic psychotherapy* [Unpublished paper]. Merrill-Palmer Institute.

Chue, D. (2021). *Falling into the abyss: A heuristic self-inquiry into a psychotherapist's experience of abrupt endings* [Master's dissertation, Auckland University of Technology]. Tuwhera Open Access Theses & Dissertations. https://hdl.handle.net/10292/14790

Gendlin, E. T. (1978). *Focusing*. Bantam Books.

Ghent, E. (1990). Masochism, submission, surrender – Masochism as a perversion of surrender. *Contemporary Psychoanalysis*, *26*(1), 108–136. https://doi.org/10.1080/00107530.1990.10746643

Grant, B. M., & Giddings, L. S. (2002). Making sense of methodologies: A paradigm framework for the novice researcher. *Contemporary Nurse*, *13*(1), 10–28. https://doi.org/10.5172/conu.13.1.10

Hiles, D. R. (2001, October). *Heuristic inquiry and transpersonal research* [Paper presentation]. Centre for Counselling and Psychotherapy Education Conference, London, UK. www.psy.dmu.ac.uk/drhiles/HIpaper.htm

Hiles, D. R. (2012). Heuristic inquiry. In L. M. Given (Ed.), *The Sage encyclopedia of qualitative research methods* (Vol. 2, pp. 390–392). https://doi.org/10.4135/9781412963909

Ings, W. (2011). Managing heuristics as a method of inquiry in autobiographical graphic design theses. *International Journal of Art and Design Education*, *30*(2), 226–241. https://doi.org/10.1111/j.1476-8070.2011.01699.x

Jabr, F. (2012). How does a caterpillar turn into a butterfly? *Scientific American*. www.scientificamerican.com/article/caterpillar-butterfly-metamorphosis-explainer

Jung, C. G. (1987). *Synchronicity: An acausal connecting principle*. Ark Paperbacks.

Kenny, G. (2012). An introduction to Moustakas's heuristic method. *Nurse Researcher*, *19*(3), 6–11. https://doi.org/10.7748/nr2012.04.19.3.6.c9052

McWilliams, N. (2004). *Psychoanalytic psychotherapy*. The Guilford Press.
Ministry of Health. (2014, April 15). *Vertigo*. www.health.govt.nz/your-health/conditions-and-treatments/diseases-and-illnesses/vertigo
Moustakas, C. E. (1990). *Heuristic research: Design, methodology, and applications*. Sage Publications.
O'Hara, M. (1986). Heuristic inquiry as psychotherapy: The client-centered approach. *Person Centered Review*, *1*(2), 172–183.
Ou, L. (2011). *Keats and negative capability*. Bloomsbury.
Polanyi, M. (1983). *The tacit dimension*. Peter Smith.
Rose, T., & Loewenthal, D. (2006). Heuristic research. In D. Loewenthal & D. Winter (Eds.), *What is psychotherapeutic research?* (pp. 133–143). Karnac Books.
Ryan, F., Coughlan, M., & Cronin, P. (2007). Step-by-step guide to critiquing research. Part 2: Qualitative research. *British Journal of Nursing*, *16*(12), 738–744. https://doi.org/10.12968/bjon.2007.16.12.23726
Sela-Smith, S. (2002). Heuristic research: A review and critique of Moustakas's method. *Journal of Humanistic Psychology*, *42*(3), 53–88. https://doi.org/10.1177/002216702128803116
Smith, J. E. (1969). Time, times, and the 'right time': Chronos and kairos. *The Monist*, *53*(1), 1–13. https://doi.org/10.5840/monist196953115
Smythe, L. (2012). Discerning which qualitative approach fits best. *New Zealand College of Midwives*, *46*, 5–12. www.midwife.org.nz/wp-content/uploads/2019/01/JNL-46-June-2012.pdf
Sultan, N. (2019). *Heuristic inquiry: Researching human experience holistically*. Sage Publications.
Tudor, K. (2017). The fight for health: An heuristic enquiry (2010). In K. Tudor, *Conscience and critic: The selected works of Keith Tudor* (pp. 143–168). Routledge. (Original work published 2010)
Tudor, K. (2022). Supporting critical self-enquiry: Doing heuristic research. In S. Bager-Charleson & A. McBeath (Eds.), *Supporting research in counselling and psychotherapy* (pp. 57–79). Springer.
Tudor, K. (2023). Critical heuristics: From 'I who feels' to 'We who care – and act'. In K. Tudor & J. Wyatt, (Eds.), *Qualitative research approaches for psychotherapy: Reflexivity, methodology, and criticality* (pp. 115–132). Routledge.
Tudor, K., & McCann, M. (2026). Explicating heuristic methodology through enquiry into unintentional racial microaggressions. In K. Tudor (Ed.), *Heuristic research in psychotherapy* (pp. xx–xx). Routledge.
Winnicott, D. W. (1974). Fear of breakdown. *International Review of Psycho-Analysis*, *1*, 103–107.

INDEX

Note: Pages in *italics* refer to figures, pages in **bold** refer to tables, and pages followed by 'n' refer to notes. Also, given the nature of the book, and the extent of citations to the work of Moustakas, Sela-Smith, and Tudor, this index does not include entries to their work.

For Product Safety Concerns and Information please contact our
EU representative GPSR@taylorandfrancis.com Taylor & Francis
Verlag GmbH, Kaufingerstraße 24, 80331 München, Germany